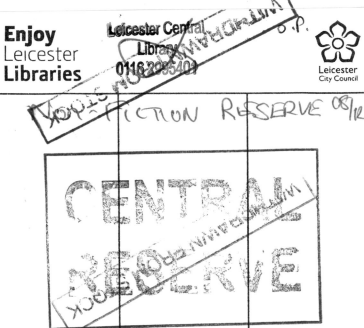
at the Policy
markets and
fellows in the
ation *Cultural*
*t: The Polemics*

st (one of the
nt of National

Policy Studies Institute (PSI) is one of Europe's leading independent research organisations undertaking studies of economic, industrial and social policy and the workings of political institutions.

PSI is a registered charity, run on a non-profit basis, and is not associated with any political party, pressure group or commercial interest.

PSI attaches great importance to covering a wide range of subject areas with its multidisciplinary approach. The Institute's researchers are organised in groups which currently cover the following programmes:

*Crime, Justice and Youth Studies – Employment – Ethnic Equality and Diversity – Family Finances – Information and Citizenship – Information and Cultural Studies – Social Care and Health Studies – Work, Benefits and Social Participation*

*Information about the work of PSI and a catalogue of publications can be obtained from:*
Publications Department, Policy Studies Institute, 100 Park Village East, London NW1 3SR

# Culture as Commodity?

## The economics of the arts and built heritage in the UK

Bernard Casey
Rachael Dunlop
Sara Selwood

The publishing imprint of the independent
POLICY STUDIES INSTITUTE
100 Park Village East, London NW1 3SR
Tel. 0171 468 0468   Fax. 0171 388 0914

© **Policy Studies Institute, 1996**

ISBN 0 85374 699 0
PSI Report 825

PSI publications are available from:
BEBC Distribution Ltd, P O Box 1496, Poole, Dorset BH12 3YD

Books will normally be dispatched within 24 hours. Cheques should be
made payable to BEBC Distribution Ltd.

Credit cards and telephone/fax orders may be placed on the following
freephone numbers:
FREEPHONE     0800 262260
FREEFAX          0800 262266

Booktrade representation (UK and Eire):
Broadcast Books, 24 De Montfort Road, London SW16 1LZ
Tel. 0181 677 5129

PSI subscriptions are available from PSI's subscription agent:
Carfax Publishing Company Ltd,
P O Box 25, Abingdon, Oxford OX14 3UE

Typeset by PCS Mapping & DTP

Printed in Great Britain by
Unwin Brothers Ltd
The Gresham Press
Old Woking, Surrey GU22 9LH
A Member of the Martins Printing
Group

# Contents

List of tables     vi
Abbreviations, symbols and conventions     xi
Acknowledgements     xv
Executive summary     xvii

## Part I Introduction and background

1 Introduction     1
2 Distributing funding to the cultural sector     13
3 Employment in the cultural sector     40
4 Audiences     58

## Part II Cultural activities

5 The performing arts     72
6 Combined arts and arts festivals     93
7 Museums, galleries and the visual arts     107
8 The media industries     128
9 The built heritage     140

## Part III Conclusions

10 Conclusions     161

Bibliography     171
Appendix: survey methodology     179

# List of tables

## 2 Distributing funding to the cultural sector in the UK

2.1 European funding for the cultural sector, 1993/94    17
2.2 Funding for the cultural sector from the DNH, Scottish, Welsh and Northern Ireland Offices, 1993/94    22
2.3 Other central government funding for the cultural sector, 1993/94    26
2.4 Tax losses resulting from conditional exemption on heritage objects    28
2.5 Local authority funding for the cultural sector, 1993/94    30
2.6 Business support for the cultural sector, 1993/94    32
2.7 Support for the cultural sector from trusts and foundations, 1993/94    35
2.8 Estimated value of volunteer labour in the cultural sector, 1993/94    37
2.9 Funding for the cultural sector, 1993/94    38

## 3 Employment in the cultural sector

3.1 Number of people working in the cultural sector, spring 1994    43
3.2 Distribution of cultural sector employment between industries and occupations    43
3.3 Employment in the cultural sector, by industries and occupations    44
3.4 Regional distribution of cultural employment in the UK    44
3.5 Length of time spent in the same job in the cultural sector    48
3.6 Rates of unemployment in the cultural sector    49

3.7   Gross weekly earnings of employees in the cultural sector        51
3.8   Hours worked by volunteers in the cultural sector,
      converted into full-time equivalents                             55


## 4 Audiences

4.1   Total number of attendances at cultural activities, 1993–94       59
4.2   People attending performing arts events, 1993/94                  60
4.3   Total consumer expenditure on cultural activities, 1993–94        61
4.4   Family expenditure on the cultural sector                         61
4.5   Participation in cultural activities outside the home, by
      social group, 1993/94                                             62
4.6   Participation in cultural activities in the home, by social group,
      1993/94                                                           63
4.7   Percentage of the population participating in selected
      cultural activities, by age                                       64
4.8   Profile of those participating in selected cultural activities,
      by age, 1993–94                                                   64
4.9   Television and radio audiences, by age, 1993                      65
4.10  Family expenditure on the cultural sector, by age of
      head of household, 1993                                           66
4.11  Profile of audiences for cultural activities by geographic
      location, 1991                                                    67
4.12  Importance of cultural events to overseas visitors, 1993          68
4.13  Regional distribution of family expenditure on the
      cultural sector, 1993                                             69


## 5 The performing arts

5.1   Performing arts venues and companies: selected statistics         75
5.2   UK theatres: key statistics, 1993                                 76
5.3   Overseas earnings and payments of the UK music industry, 1993    78
5.4   Employment in the performing arts                                 79
5.5   Funding for the performing arts, 1993/94                          81
5.6   Share of performing arts funding in London, 1993/94               83
5.7   Survey results: performing arts organisations by category         84
5.8   Survey results: regional distribution of performing arts
      organisations                                                     84
5.9   Survey results: performing arts organisations by income           85
5.10  Survey results: performing arts organisations by number
      of employees                                                      85
5.11  Survey results: performing arts organisations by contribution of
      commercial income to total income, and by organisation size       86

5.12 Survey results: performing arts organisations by source
    of support     87
5.13 Survey results: share of income of performing arts organisations
    from arts councils and RABs     87
5.14 Survey results: share of income of performing arts
    organisations from local authorities     88
5.15 Survey results: share of income of performing arts
    organisations from sponsorships     88
5.16 Survey results: share of employees costs in total costs by
    type of performing arts organisation     89
5.17 Survey results: financial outturns of performing arts
    organisations by level of income     90
5.18 Survey results: financial outturns of performing arts
    organisations by importance of public support to total income     90
5.19 Summary of survey results for performing arts
    organisations     91

## 6 Combined arts and arts festivals

6.1   Profile of audience for arts festivals, 1994     96
6.2   Staffing at arts festivals, 1991     97
6.3   Support for combined arts and arts festivals, 1993/94     98
6.4   Arts festivals in the UK: income, 1991     99
6.5   Survey results: all combined arts organisations by category     100
6.6   Survey results: regional distribution of all combined arts
    organisations     100
6.7   Survey results: all combined arts organisations by income     101
6.8   Survey results: all combined arts organisations by number of
    employees     101
6.9   Survey results: all combined arts organisations by
    contribution of commercial income to total income     102
6.10 Survey results: combined arts organisations by source of
    support     102
6.11 Survey results: share of income of combined arts
    organisations from arts councils and RABs     103
6.12 Survey results: share of income of combined arts
    organisations from local authorities     103
6.13 Survey results: share of income of combined arts
    organisations from sponsorships     103
6.14 Survey results: financial outturns of all combined arts
    organisations     104
6.15 Summary of survey results for combined arts organisations     105

## 7 Museums, galleries and the visual arts

| | | |
|---|---|---|
| 7.1 | Types of art trade buyer, 1993/94 | 110 |
| 7.2 | Imports and exports of works of art, antiques, stamps and museums items, 1993 | 112 |
| 7.3 | Employment in museums and galleries, collections, visual arts, crafts and the art trade | 113 |
| 7.4 | Sources of funding for museums and galleries, collections, visual arts, crafts and the art trade | 113 |
| 7.5 | Assistance towards purchase and acquisition of objects by museums and galleries, 1993/94 | 118 |
| 7.6 | Share of visual arts, crafts and museums and gallery funding going to organisations based in London, 1993/94 | 121 |
| 7.7 | Survey results: regional distribution of funded organisations | 123 |
| 7.8 | Survey results: share of funded organisations by size of income | 123 |
| 7.9 | Survey results: funded organisations by number of employees | 123 |
| 7.10 | Survey results: funded organisations by contribution of commercial income to total income | 124 |
| 7.11 | Survey results: funded organisations by source of support | 124 |
| 7.12 | Survey results: share of income of funded organisations from arts councils and RABs | 125 |
| 7.13 | Survey results: share of income of funded organisations from collections funders | 125 |
| 7.14 | Survey results: share of income of funded organisations from local authorities | 126 |
| 7.15 | Survey results: share of income of funded organisations from sponsorships | 126 |
| 7.16 | Survey results: financial outturns of funded organisations | 127 |
| 7.17 | Summary of survey results for museums and galleries, collections, visual arts and craft organisations | 128 |

## 8 The media industries

| | | |
|---|---|---|
| 8.1 | Feature film production in the UK, 1993 | 130 |
| 8.2 | Income to UK broadcasters, 1993–94 | 131 |
| 8.3 | UK publishers' sales, 1993 | 132 |
| 8.4 | New book titles and editions published, 1993 | 132 |
| 8.5 | Estimates of employment within the media industries | 134 |
| 8.6 | Support for the media industries, 1993/94 | 135 |

## 9 The built heritage

9.1 Visitors to historic properties in Great Britain, 1993/94    142
9.2 Number of classified architectural resources in the UK,
     1993–94    144
9.3 Earned income of historic properties through admissions,
     memberships and services, 1993/94    146
9.4 Employment in the built heritage sector, 1993/94    148
9.5 Sources of funding for the built heritage, 1993/94    149
9.6 Value of grants distributed by dedicated heritage bodies,
     1993/94    150
9.7 Breakdown of grant expenditure by type of recipient, 1993/94    151
9.8 Distribution of historic properties in the English tourist regions    153
9.9 Survey results: assets of preservation trusts    155
9.10 Survey results: regional distribution of preservation trusts    155
9.11 Survey results: preservation trusts by contribution of
      commercial income to total income    156
9.12 Survey results: preservation trusts by source of support    156
9.13 Survey results: share of income of preservation trusts from
      local authorities    157
9.14 Survey results: share of income of preservation trusts from
      sponsorships    157
9.15 Summary of survey results for preservation trusts    158

## 10 Conclusions

10.1 Indicators of the importance of the cultural sector, 1993/94    162
10.2 Public support for selected industries and services, 1993/94    163
10.3 Supported organisations by activity: summary characteristics    164
10.4 Share of supported organisations in Greater London,
      compared with resident population    166
10.5 Share of support from selected bodies received by London-
      based organisations, 1993/94    167

## Appendix: survey methodology

A.1 Grants distributed, by category, 1993/94    181
A.2 Sampling ratios and response rates    182
A.3 Survey of preservation trusts: response rates    182
A.4 Confidence intervals for the performing arts    184
A.5 Confidence intervals for combined arts    185
A.6 Confidence intervals for museums and galleries, visual arts etc    185
A.7 Confidence intervals for the built heritage    185

# Abbreviations

| | |
|---|---|
| ABSA | Association for Business Sponsorship of the Arts |
| ACE | Arts Council of England |
| ACGB | Arts Council of Great Britain |
| ACNI | Arts Council of Northern Ireland |
| ACTT | Association of Cinematograph, Television and Allied Technicians |
| ACW | Arts Council of Wales |
| AHF | Architectural Heritage Fund |
| AIL | Acceptance in Lieu |
| AIRC | Association of Independent Radio Companies |
| APT | Association of Preservation Trusts |
| BA | Booksellers Association |
| BADA | British Antique Dealers' Association |
| BAFA | British Arts Festival Association |
| BBC | British Broadcasting Corporation |
| BFC | British Film Commission |
| BFI | British Film Institute |
| BiA | Business in the Arts |
| BML | Book Marketing Limited |
| BPI | British Phonographic Industry |
| BRMB | British Market Research Bureau |
| BSF | British Screen Finance |
| BSIS | Business Sponsorship Incentive Scheme |
| BTA | British Tourist Association |
| BVA | British Video Association |
| CAA | Cinema Advertising Association |
| CAF | Charities Aid Foundation |
| CAVIAR | Cinema and Video Industry Audience Research |
| CC | Crafts Council |

| | |
|---|---|
| CIPFA | Chartered Institute of Public Finance and Accounting |
| CSO | Central Statistical Office (now the Office for National Statistics) |
| DE | Department of Employment |
| DENI | Department of Education Northern Ireland |
| DfE | Department for Education |
| DfEE | Department for Education and Employment |
| DG | Directorate General (of the European Commission) |
| DOMUS | Digest of Museum Statistics |
| DoE | Department of the Environment |
| DoT | Department of Transport |
| DNH | Department of National Heritage |
| DTI | Department of Trade and Industry |
| EC | European Commission |
| EFDO | European Film Distribution Office |
| EH | English Heritage |
| ERDF | European Regional Development Fund |
| ESF | European Social Fund |
| ETB | English Tourist Board |
| EU | European Union |
| EVE | Espace Video Européen |
| FCO | Foreign and Commonwealth Office |
| HEFCE | Higher Education Funding Council for England |
| HEFCW | Higher Education Funding Council for Wales |
| HHA | Historic Houses Association |
| HRPA | Historic Royal Palaces Agency |
| HS | Historic Scotland |
| IMS | Institute of Manpower Services (now the Institute of Employment Studies) |
| ITC | Independent Television Commission |
| LAB | London Arts Board |
| LEC | Local Enterprise Company |
| LEDU | Local Enterprise Development Unit |
| LFS | Labour Force Survey |
| LISU | Library and Information Statistics Unit |
| MCPS | Mechanical-Copyright Protection Society |
| MDA | Museum Documentation Association |
| MEDIA | Measures pour Encourager le Developpement de l'Industrie de Production Audio Visuelle |
| MGC | Museums & Galleries Commission |
| MoD | Ministry of Defence |
| MTI | Museum Training Institute |
| NACF | National Art Collections Fund |
| NAO | National Audit Office |

| | |
|---|---|
| NCA | National Campaign for the Arts |
| NDPB | Non-Departmental Public Body |
| NFER | National Foundation for Educational Research |
| NHMF | National Heritage Memorial Fund |
| NHS | National Health Service |
| NIO | Northern Ireland Office |
| NITB | Northern Ireland Tourist Board |
| NT | National Trust |
| NTS | National Trust for Scotland |
| OPCS | Office of Population Censuses and Surveys |
| PLR | Public Lending Right |
| PPL | Phonographic Performance Limited |
| PRS | Performing Rights Society |
| PSI | Policy Studies Institute |
| PTS | Private Treaty Sale |
| QUANGO | Quasi-Autonomous Non-Governmental Organisation |
| RA | Radio Authority |
| RAB | Regional Arts Board |
| RCAHMS | Royal Commission on the Ancient and Historical Monuments of Scotland |
| RCAHMW | Royal Commission on the Ancient and Historical Monuments of Wales |
| RCHME | Royal Commission on the Historical Monuments of England |
| RICS | Royal Institution of Chartered Surveyors |
| RSC | Royal Shakespeare Company |
| RSGB | Research Surveys of Great Britain |
| SAC | Scottish Arts Council |
| SHEFC | Scottish Higher Education Funding Council |
| SIC | Standard Industrial Classification |
| SLAD | Society of London Art Dealers |
| SO | Scottish Office |
| SOC | Standard Occupational Classification |
| SOED | Scottish Office Education Department |
| SOLT | Society of London Theatre |
| TEC | Training and Enterprise Council |
| TGI | Target Group Index |
| TMA | Theatrical Management Association |
| UDC | Urban Development Corporation |
| VAT | Value Added Tax |
| VPL | Video Performance Limited |
| WAC | Welsh Arts Council |
| WO | Welsh Office |

# Symbols and conventions

| | |
|---|---|
| – | nil |
| * | less than half of the final digit shown |
| ... | not available |
| bn | billion |
| m | million |
| na | not applicable |

Rounded figures: in tables where the figures have been rounded up to the nearest digit, totals may not correspond exactly to the sum of the constituent items.

Non-calendar years: the symbol / represents the financial year (for example 1 April 1993 to 31 March 1994) unless otherwise stated.

# Acknowledgements

The authors should like to thank the members of the reference group: Barclay Price (Crafts Council); Tim Mason and Jeremy Warren (Museums & Galleries Commission); Andy Feist (Arts Council of England); John Sharples (London Arts Board); Irene Whitehead (British Film Institute); Graham Berry (Scottish Arts Council); Neil Smith and John Sankey (Society of London Art Dealers); Ian Brack (English Heritage); Sheila Colvin (Aldeburgh Festival); Helen Auty (The Royal Society of Arts); Christoper Gordon (Engish Regional Arts Board) and Ben Evans (Enigma). We are also grateful to Peter Johnson and Barry Thomas (Department of Economics, University of Durham), Michael Parsonage (HM Treasury) and Russell Southwood for discussions about the study. Our thanks also go to representatives of the sponsors: Michael Pattison and Hugh de Quetteville of the Monument Trust, and Steven Creigh-Tyte, Mary Davies, Hilary Bauer, Margaret Prythergch and Michael Seeney, Department of National Heritage.

We should like to thank all those who responsed to our enquiries, but who are too numerous to name here. They include representatives of the European Commission and the Council of Europe and, nearer home, the Department of National Heritage, the Scottish Office, the Welsh Office and the Northern Ireland Office, in particular the Department of Education, Northern Ireland and the Environment and Heritage Service, Department of the Environment, Northern Ireland. Other government departments which provided us with information include: the Ministry of Defence; the Department for Education and Employment; the Department of the Environment; the Department of Trade and Industry, in particular the Overseas Trade Services; the Foreign & Commonwealth Office; the Home Office, in particular the Voluntary Services Unit and the Central Drugs Prevention Unit as well as the Prison and Probation Services; and the Regional Government Offices. Other bodies include:

local authority leisure and recreation departments; Urban Development Corporations; City Challenge Partnerships; the Higher Education Funding Councils; Training and Enterprise Councils; Local Enterprise Companies; the Local Enterprise Development Unit and the Training and Employment Agency; the Association of Preservation Trusts. We are also grateful to representatives of the the national arts councils and regional arts boards, and numerous charities including the National Trust.

We are indebted to the individuals, arts organisations, building preservation trusts and County Historic Churches Trusts which responded to our surveys, allowing us to examine the workings of the cultural sector.

Last but not least, we are grateful to colleagues at the Policy Studies Institute (PSI) for their support and advice: John Forth, Lydia Maher, Pamela Meadows, Pam Plumer and Philip Taylor. Angela Ruoloto, on placement with PSI from the University of Surrey, assisted with the administration and analysis of the survey. Responsibility for the study and its conclusions, however, lies with the authors.

# Executive summary

## Introduction

*Culture as Commodity? The economics of the arts and built heritage in the UK* provides a comprehensive overview of the operations of the cultural sector.

- The study examines support for the cultural sector from public, private and voluntary sources, and charts its distribution throughout the UK.
- It establishes the relationship between the supported cultural sector and the broader cultural sector (which includes commercial activities), and between these and other areas of the economy. It looks at employment and audiences in the cultural sector as a whole. Furthermore, it outlines the financial operations of supported cultural organisations through their turnover and expenditure, and assesses the relative significance of support to the sector and its earned income.
- Lastly, *Culture as Commodity?* provides a profile of the supported cultural sector intended to serve as the basis of any subsequent investigations which might examine the impact of recent changes to the funding of the cultural sector, in particular the National Lottery.

## Approaches

In order to fulfil these objectives, *Culture as Commodity?* focuses on specific areas of activity:

- the performing arts – drama, opera, dance, orchestras and orchestral music and other music;

- museums, galleries and the national collections, the crafts, the visual arts and the art trade;
- media – including literature, film and video;
- the combined arts, including arts festivals; and
- the built heritage – including historic buildings, monuments and sites.

Common to these activities is the fact that their production at a socially optimal level cannot be wholly ensured by the market. Consequently, the state or other "patrons" step in to support them. *Culture as Commodity?* is concerned primarily with that part of the cultural sector which is in receipt of support, but it seeks to locate that sector within the broader cultural sector where commercial operations prevail. Moreover, it attempts to situate the overall cultural sector within the economy as a whole, and to compare support for culture with support for other sectors.

The research covers the period 1993/94, the financial year before the introduction of the National Lottery and the reorganisation of the national arts councils, and before changes in the organisation of local authorities, which may also impact on arts funding. In this way, the study provides a base line against which to measure the impact of any or all of these changes on the cultural sector.

## Distributing support to the cultural sector

A conservative estimate identifies some £1.7bn in support for the cultural sector from both public and private sources. The Department of National Heritage and the Scottish, Welsh and Northern Ireland Offices provided just over half of this total funding. A further quarter came from local authorities.

However, the study also identifies funding from less obvious sources. Other central government departments, such as the Ministry of Defence and the Department for Education and Employment, contribute support through activities ancillary to their principal purpose. These departments accounted for over 6 per cent of all funding for the sector. Further government assistance is also provided through the waiving of certain taxes in part or full, estimated to be worth at least 7 per cent of total funding. Support from Europe represented a similar proportion of the total, at 5 per cent. Business sponsorship, grant-giving trusts and the voluntary sector together accounted for a further 8 per cent.

## Characteristics of the cultural sector

*Culture as Commodity?* draws together and reanalyses existing data from diverse published and unpublished sources on the sector, creating a unique profile of the broad cultural sector. In particular, it considers employment and audiences.

## Employment

The cultural sector is a significant employer. It accounts for over half a million people, constituting nearly 2 per cent of the total labour force. It employs more people than retail banking and building societies, and nearly twice as many as motor manufacturing. The funded cultural sector is estimated to account for at least a quarter of this employment.

Employment in the cultural sector is characterised by people who are relatively highly educated. Many of the jobs are "non-standard" – a third are self-employed, and a further tenth are in temporary employment. Unemployment levels are relatively high: a number of people in the sector are likely to be living on benefit, and a considerable number need to take on non-cultural occupations to support themselves.

Men and women are employed in approximately equal proportions, but the sector has over three times the average number of people over the state pension age. A third of people working in cultural industries and occupations have jobs based in London. Working in the cultural sector can be a solitary activity – nearly 30 per cent of people work on their own.

Pay in the sector can be poor. However, it appears that the will to work in the sector is not driven by the prospect of pecuniary rewards. Indeed, volunteers provide 8 per cent of the paid labour force (as full-time equivalents).

The survey carried out for *Culture as Commodity?* suggested that, in funded organisations, the performing arts accounted for the largest share of employment (just under 40 per cent). A further third of employment was in museums and galleries and the visual arts. Combined arts represented a quarter of employment in the sector and the remaining activities together, around 5 per cent.

## Audiences

Consumer expenditure on the cultural sector, identified from existing data, can be estimated at £5bn, with 5 per cent of the weekly average family expenditure being spent on cultural products and activities.

The cultural sector is a major part of the leisure industry. There were as many visitors to museums and galleries and historic properties as there were at the cinema. A third of the population went to the cinema, and a fifth each to the theatre or to a museum or gallery. At least as many people attended theatres in London alone as went to Premier League football matches in the 1993/94 season.

The audience for the cultural sector includes not only UK residents but also visitors from overseas. As many as two-thirds of overseas tourists cite aspects of the cultural sector as an important reason for visiting Britain. Among domestic audiences, Londoners tend to attend performing arts events more than people elsewhere in the country. People living in Yorkshire and Humberside are the most likely to attend exhibitions.

Audiences for cultural events outside the home are predominantly from the higher social groups, while the opposite is generally true for home-based cultural activities. The age of audiences for cultural sector activities varies according to particular activities. Younger people are more likely to go to the cinema, whereas dance, drama and opera are more popular with those over 35.

## Characteristics of the supported cultural sector

*Culture as Commodity?* provides a detailed profile of the supported cultural sector. It estimates that some 5,000 cultural organisations and individuals received support in 1993/94. This figure excludes non-cultural organisations (such as community groups and educational establishments) which also received funding for arts and heritage projects. The Policy Studies Institute (PSI) collected detailed data on cultural organisations' incomes, expenditures and level of employment.

About a third of funded organisations operated primarily in the performing arts, and a further third in the combined arts. One fifth were museums and galleries or visual arts organisations, and the media and built heritage sectors accounted for 10 and 5 per cent respectively. The constituents of these groups ranged from large national institutions, for example museums, to individual practitioners, such as potters.

The total turnover of funded organisations was estimated at £2.2bn in the survey year. Funded organisations tend to be small: the study found that over half had incomes of less than £100,000. Only 10 per cent had incomes of more than £1m, and these were marginally more likely to be performing arts organisations.

Funded arts organisations drew, on average, half their income from commercial activities, rather than from public and private support. Combined arts organisations tended to generate slightly less of their income from this source.

The performing and combined arts take the majority of funding from the arts councils and regional arts boards (RABs) (80 per cent), reflecting the major interests of these funders. In the survey year, combined arts organisations received the largest share (nearly half) of local authority funding. Performing arts are the most successful at attracting sponsorship and donations.

Approximately a third of funded organisations in the performing arts, combined arts and the museums, galleries and visual arts sectors ran a deficit in the survey year, and their combined deficit was in the order of £100m. This is approaching the total value of grants given out by the Arts Council of Great Britain in 1993/94 (at £133m). Set against this was a similar-sized total surplus, not available for redistribution within the supported sector.

For all funded organisations, staff costs accounted for a large share of expenditure. For performing arts organisations, they represented around a third, rising to 40 per cent for combined arts organisations and 50 per cent for both museums and galleries and the visual arts, and for the media. However, in line with the broad cultural sector, many funded organisations relied on volunteers and self-employed workers, and recorded no staff costs at all.

Not surprisingly, London accounts for a disproportionate share of funded organisations. This was most noticeable in the performing arts, over a third of which were based in the capital. In stark contrast, the Midlands was under-provided with cultural organisations, with the exception of heritage bodies. In fact, the distribution of heritage bodies tended to be the reverse of that for the rest of the sector, with only 6 per cent located in London and nearly half of the remainder in the rest of the South of England. Scotland is particularly well provided with museums and galleries, and visual arts and crafts organisations – nearly 20 per cent of all such funded organisations were located there.

# Part I
# Introduction and background

# Chapter 1
## Introduction

This study seeks to provide a comprehensive overview of the scope of, and support for, the cultural sector in the UK. It profiles the financial operations of cultural organisations through their turnovers and expenditures, and describes employment in the sector. It assesses the relative significance of support to the sector and its earned income, and establishes the relationship between the supported cultural sector and the commercial cultural sector and other areas of the economy. It does so by an extensive review of literature, of published statistics, of the annual reports of funding bodies and through a survey of organisations and individuals active in the sector.

The study has three, interrelated aims. It seeks to:

- give an overview of the cultural sector (and its constituent areas of activity) in terms of output and employment and, within it, to locate and assess the size of that part of the sector supported by public and private bodies through grants, sponsorship and donations;
- examine the origin of support, the mix of its various components, and their contribution, together with that of earnings from market activities, to the overall income of the supported sector (and its constituent areas of activity); and
- provide a profile of the supported cultural sector to serve as the basis of any subsequent investigations examining the impact of recent policies affecting the funding of the cultural sector, in particular the National Lottery.

# Defining the cultural sector

Many studies start with a definition of key terms. Some terms are widely understood while others evoke different meanings for different people and groups with different interests, or at different times or in different places. "Culture" and thus "cultural" belong to the latter group. Their definition has proved troublesome, indeed controversial. According to Raymond Williams in *Keywords*, "cultural" is that which pertains to "the works and practices of intellectual and especially artistic activity" (1988). From the perspective of economic analysis, therefore, the cultural sector might well be, and indeed has been, viewed as a sub-sector of the broader leisure industry.

The concept of the "cultural industries" started to gain currency in the mid–1980s, thus widening the scope of what might be included in the sector considerably. "Cultural industries" encompassed not only those artistic activities that Williams appeared to be referring to, but also the media and leisure, sport and recreation. However, of concern to the propagators of this broad definition of cultural industries was not merely what they saw as the unifying characteristics of the constituent sectors – their common engagement in the production and distribution of images, concepts, ideas and information, or what was termed at the time "the transmission of meaning" (Garnham, 1987) – but the contribution the overall sector made to the economy and job creation. These extrinsic, rather than intrinsic, qualities of culture were given yet more prominence by the end of the decade in studies of the "arts industries" – taken to include "commercial providers of goods and services which convey to the public cultural ideas and experiences" (Myerscough et al, 1988; see also ACGB, 1985) – and their "economic effect" which looked not only at, for example, orchestras, but also musical instrument manufacturers and suppliers of interval food and drinks[1].

The consequence of so expansive a definition of the sector was that its boundaries became very unclear. Thus, in some analyses, the cultural sector is understood to include the production and distribution of popular culture; in others, it is understood to include only that which is deemed as "lifting the imagination and widening experience" (ACGB, 1985). Differences of opinion on the scope of the sector reflect the wider divisions which Williams describes as "distinctions between 'high' art (culture) and popular art and entertainment" (Williams, 1988)[2].

---

1  This led a reviewer of the work by Myerscough et al to point out that, of all the total revenue generated by the "cultural sector", less than 10 per cent was generated by "conventional arts activities", two-thirds by broadcasting, films, videos, cinemas, books, records and the arts trade, and a quarter by ancillary spending on refreshments, hotels and similar services incurred in attending arts events (Hughes, 1989).
2  It is also worth noting that what was "popular" yesterday might be "high" culture today, for example, Elizabethan folk music or Jacobean dramas.

Although it runs the risk of being branded an elitist approach, the construction of the definition of what constitutes the cultural sector in this study starts in a relatively "conventional", or "traditional", fashion. It takes as its foundation five broad areas of activity which would generally be agreed as being "cultural", namely: the performing arts; fine art; literature; arts festivals; and the built heritage.

## Cultural production and market failure

These five areas of activity have a common feature, which goes beyond their being "cultural". Each comprises a particular sort of production, reproduction or maintenance – that which markets tend, of themselves, to underproduce. And because markets underproduce it, the state, or other "patrons" or philanthropists, step in – either as subsidisers or as producers in their own right – to ensure that output comes nearer to what is considered a "socially optimal" level – ie, the level which is considered "appropriate" or "essential" for a civilised society[3].

Markets may fail to achieve a socially optimal level of output for one or more of four reasons.

- The "output" of "cultural production" might be viewed as beneficial to all because it helps instil a feeling of national pride and identity, and if any one individual refuses to contribute to its costs, she or he can scarcely be excluded from enjoying these benefits. For example, we might all be said to benefit from the acclaim given to the actors and productions of the Royal National Theatre, yet if a single member of society refused to patronise it, she or he would continue to profit from this acclaim.
- Society might value the existence of a given level of artistic activities and is collectively prepared to pay for its survival, and the survival of the institutions which produce it, at a level superior to that which would ensue from the sum of individual consumption. For example, we value having theatres at our disposal, even if we, ourselves, are not frequent visitors.
- It might be recognised that certain artistic activities produce benefits for others than those who are the immediate consumers. For example, the existence of a theatre might make a city a more attractive site for the location of other economic activities or for visitors from outside.

---

3   This has always been so. Prior to the modern state, the nobility and other wealthy people expended a share of their income on luxury items which included cultural products, but rather as a manifestation of their wealth and power than for the benefit of their subjects.

- It might be held that certain artistic activities should be paid for to ensure their production, even if individuals might not recognise their worth. For example, visits to the theatre might improve the well-being of individuals and their ability to interact with one another.

These four arguments draw, respectively, from standard economic theories about "public goods", "option values", "externalities" and "merit goods" (see, for example Hughes, 1989; Peacock, 1976; Cameron, 1991).

This study is concerned primarily with that part of the cultural sector which is supported. It recognises that the support to which it refers can emanate from one or more of a number of sources. Conventionally, the state is thought of as the source of support, but "society" can realise its wishes through the activities of the nation state, the local state (especially, in Britain, the local authorities), or through supra-national organisations (such as the European Commission). In addition, businesses can be important sources of support, and whilst it is to be expected that they derive benefit from the association of their name with the activities in question, the fact that such support entitles them to tax relief, or matching public aid, bears testimony to the belief that they are thereby benefiting society as a whole. Lastly, private foundations, having their founders' and trustees' conceptions of what constitutes an improvement of societal well-being, are important sources of support. So, too, are private individuals, who through inputs of voluntary labour as well as donations and bequests, sustain the upkeep or reproduction of elements of the cultural sector (for example, in the case of the National Trust).

## The relationship between the supported and commercial sectors

By concentrating upon that which receives support and, thus, which is not produced solely by the market, this study considers only briefly much of what is commonly known as "popular culture", whether live or mechanically or electronically produced[4]. However, although it recognises that the supported sector operates within the "context" of the commercial sector, and, as appropriate, describes that context, it also recognises that markets are normally sufficient to assure the production of popular culture – for

---

4   There are practical, as well as theoretical, arguments for concentrating on the supported sector. The make-up, and thus the size, of the commercial sector is difficult to determine. Research based upon surveys would be difficult, since the population is undefined. By contrast, the supported sector is much more easily identifiable, if only because someone, or something, supports it. That someone, or something, can be distinguished relatively easily.

example, in the form of films, music or fiction. This holds true even if the production of some items is associated with a high degree of risk (for example, potential investors in commercial theatre productions are routinely warned of the extremely speculative nature of the enterprise they commit themselves to). Equally, markets operate very satisfactorily in sectors often closely associated with the cultural sector – for example, the trade in artistic objects and antiques, for which London is generally recognised as a world capital, or the television and radio industry where commercial broadcasting is firmly established and the number of channels and providers is expanding.

As well as sometimes being unclear, the boundary between the non-market cultural sector and the market cultural sector can shift, or rather, an activity can shift from one sector to the other. An example of such a shift might be a product which is nurtured in the supported sector subsequently proving robust enough to survive in the commercial sector (as when a play is first staged in the Royal National Theatre and subsequently transfers to the West End). In the language of the economic theories discussed above, in such cases, a "merit" good proves it can survive on equal terms with a "normal" good. However, the risk that it could not was shouldered by society rather than a private person or company[5]. Equally, the survival of one sector might depend upon the existence of the other. Thus, actors might receive their initial on-the-job training in the supported theatre before graduating to the commercial theatre or film, or vice versa. Similarly, the existence of a large number of commercial theatres in London might contribute to a critical mass of theatrical activity that sustains the supported theatre, or the reputation of the quality theatre provided by the supported sector attracts an interest, and level of visits, from which the commercial sector can draw advantage (ACE 1996a).

While the sector to be studied is protected from the full consequences of market forces, it is in no way immune to them, nor does it necessarily seek to isolate itself from them. There can be said to exist a market for support, in that individual "units of production" – be they organisations or individuals – have to compete for assistance and to present a case for it, if not on an annual basis at least at regular intervals. Furthermore, and as importantly, support accounts for only a part of total income for many organisations. For some organisations, admission charges might well be at least as important a source of revenue as grants or sponsorship, and in

---

5   In any particular case, however, it has to be asked if it is the running costs or the set-up costs which are being covered. The latter might remain with the organisation responsible for the production's initiation. The analogy is with the Concorde. British Airways and Air France can profitably operate it, but only because they are not obliged to repay the enormous development costs it incurred. Information on the extent of such cross-subsidy is extremely difficult to obtain, and for this reason no attempt has been made to quantify it in this study.

setting admission prices organisations are obliged to make decisions about what "customers" – audiences or visitors – might be prepared to pay, and what the consequences of an adjustment are, whether or not their pricing policy also requires them to take account of wider "social" objectives such as maximising their accessibility to the general public. Many have trading arms (for example, V&A Enterprises) or retailing and catering operations which operate alongside, and buttress, their supported activities. Moreover, in the 1980s, no doubt under pressure from government, arts funding bodies increasingly came to recognise the requirement that the arts should operate in some degree in relation to the market. For example, the Arts Council of Great Britain (ACGB):

> *enthusiastically adopted the rhetoric of the enterprise culture – promoting business support, insisting on better marketing, business efficiency and matching funds from other sources. (ACGB, 1994)*

Lastly, it is likely that public investment in cultural production generates some additional output and income via "multiplier effects" (for example, the further spending of the income they earn by those involved in constructing a venue or playing in an event, or the effects on a locality of the spending by visitors attending a major event), and that the realisation of these is achieved through the normal play of market forces. Recognition of an extrinsic as well as an intrinsic value to support has spawned an extensive literature aimed at measuring the economic impact of the arts, particularly at the local level, at advocating support for cultural activities as an instrument of local regeneration (see, for example, ACGB, 1988), and a number of attempts to measure the overall contribution of the sector, however defined, to the local or national economy. Oft-cited examples include studies by Myerscough et al (1988) and the Port Authority of New York and New Jersey (1983 and 1993) about Britain and the New York metropolitan area respectively. The validity of some of the claims that have been made, particularly those in the studies which seek to superimpose local multipliers onto national aggregates, is doubtful (for a critical review, see van Puffelen, 1996), but their existence serves as a further reminder that the supported cultural sector does not operate in isolation from the rest of the economy.

## Approach of this study

This study started to define its scope by considering five "traditional" concepts of cultural activity. Having discerned a unifying feature they possess, a vulnerability to market failure, it was determined to direct atten-

8

tion at those activities in receipt of support – from public or private sources, and in the form of capital or revenue funding. A next, and necessary, step is to describe more precisely what the five areas of activity comprise, and which of these constituent elements is likely to be subject to support. This step governs what falls within the core area of concern of the study and what, because it is largely a commercial activity, falls rather into that which has been described as the wider context. This is done in the following table which also makes clear that, sometimes, a certain type of undertaking might be supported and sometimes it might not, and that some undertakings might have both a supported and a commercial component. The first column sets out the five "traditional" concepts; the second column presents their current derivatives – the terms commonly used to refer to them and which will be used throughout this study; the third column spells out the sort of undertaking to be found in the supported sector; and the fourth column spells out the sort of undertaking to be found in the commercial or private sector and in other areas tangential or peripheral to the sector.

| *"Traditional" concepts* | *Area of activity* | *"Core" – supported activities* | *"Wider context" – commercial, private and tangential activities* |
|---|---|---|---|
| Performing arts | Performing arts | Theatre, opera, dance, orchestras and other music | Theatre, opera, dance, orchestras and other music |
| Arts festivals | Combined arts | Combined arts, festivals and service organisations | Arts festivals, service organisations |
| Fine art | Museums and galleries, and the visual arts | Visual arts, crafts, museums and galleries and the national collections | Independent museums, galleries and the art trade |
| Literature | Media | Literature, video, film and broadcasting | Publishing, film and cinema and broadcasting |
| Built heritage | The built heritage | Historic buildings and monuments | Privately owned historic buildings and monuments |

Such an approach leaves out from its core certain activities which are sometimes considered as part of the cultural sector. The most obvious are public libraries and government-funded broadcasting. The exclusion of the former – with the exception of the "national collections", which can be regarded as "museums of books" – is justified on the grounds that they function rather as institutions of education or leisure than as institutions of culture. The exclusion of the latter is justified on the grounds that public service broadcasting competes directly with commercial broadcasters, albeit drawing its revenue from a different source – obligatory licence fees rather than advertising or sponsorship – and operates in the same market. Both activities are, therefore, treated as part of the context of the supported media sector rather than as part of it. Largely ignored in the study are tangential activities which relate to all of the areas of activity, in particular tourism and education, although it is recognised that on occasion these can overlap with the cultural sector, both supported and not supported.

No distinction is made between voluntary and paid activities, or between amateur and professional activities. If amateur activities, or those staffed wholly by volunteers, are in receipt of support they are included in the core of the study.

The study takes as its reference year the financial year 1993/94, for two reasons. First, when the research began, that year provided a more comprehensive set of data than would have been available for later years. Second, it was recognised that a study of the 1993/94 financial year would provide a useful basis for potential comparisons with subsequent investigations of the economics of the cultural sector. Since 1993/94 various changes have taken place in the funding structure and sources of funding of the sector. With respect to the former, the Arts Council of Great Britain has been succeeded by the Arts Council of England, and funding for the Scottish Arts Council and the former Welsh Arts Council (since renamed the Arts Council of Wales) has been channelled through the Scottish and Welsh Offices respectively. In addition, the reorganisation of local government in Scotland, Wales and England is likely to affect their support for the arts. With respect to changes in funding for the sector, the National Lottery which began providing funds in 1995, has among its "good causes" the arts and heritage and established dedicated distributing bodies to that effect. According to the Arts Council's 1994 lottery application pack, it is hoped that the lottery will lead to an increase in the quality of the infrastructure of the sector. However, it is also feared, in some quarters, that it might lead to a diminution of the value of support available from the Treasury (see, for example, *Financial Times*, 30.10.96).

## Research strategy

In carrying out the research a fourfold strategy was adopted:

- a review of literature, which examined both published and unpublished documents on how the cultural sector as a whole – both supported and commercial – and various areas of activity within these two parts of the sector, operate and raise revenue;
- existing data sets covering organisations, audiences and employment were investigated and analysed;
- data on support for cultural activities from public (supra-national, national and local government) and private (business, trusts and foundations and individuals) sources[6], enabling quantification of the level of support, it nature and its recipients, were collected and collated;
- organisations and individuals in receipt of support from public and private sources were surveyed, paying particular attention to understanding the level and the mix of support received and the relationship of support to earned income.

## Structure of this book

The study itself is organised into three parts.

### Part I Introduction and background

Part I is divided into four chapters, the first of which is the present Introduction. Chapter 2 charts the funding structure of the cultural sector in the UK, looking at the contribution of the European Commission, the Department of National Heritage and other central government departments, local authorities, and the private and voluntary sectors. Chapter 3 considers the importance of the cultural sector, whether supported or commercial, as a source of employment. Chapter 4 examines the audiences and visitors for different cultural activities, again both supported and commercial.

### Part II Cultural activities

Whereas Part I examined the providers of funds, in Part II the activities

---

6   The research drew primarily on sources which refer to national constituencies rather than those with smaller, local remits (for the latter, see, for example, Myerscough, 1996 and Kellaway, 1996).

themselves and the organisations and individuals in receipt of support are scrutinised. The five areas of activity are examined in detail: Chapter 5 considers the performing arts; Chapter 6 combined arts and arts festivals; Chapter 7 museums and galleries, collections, the visual arts, crafts and the arts trade; Chapter 8, the media industries; and Chapter 9, the built heritage. Each chapter includes a sketch of the wider context of the supported areas of activity with which it is concerned, covering number of organisations, commercial activities, details of employment and, where appropriate, audiences. It goes on to consider the core of each area of activity, looking at sources of support and then their earned incomes and turnover, drawing from the results of the special survey of supported organisations.

## Part III Conclusions

Part III, Chapter 10, summarises and compares the five areas of activity examined, and presents the most salient features of the study and relates the supported cultural sector to other supported sectors within the economy.

An appendix describes the techniques used in the survey, carried out for this study.

# Chapter 2
# Distributing funding to the cultural sector

This chapter considers how, and how much, funding is distributed to the cultural sector in the UK. Support for the sector derives from a variety of institutions, operating at a number of levels and sometimes, but not always, in conjunction with one another. They include:

- European sources;
- central government sources;
- local government sources;
- business sector sources;
- trusts and foundations and private donors; and
- volunteer workers.

Individual sections of this chapter deal in detail with each source. A concluding summary shows the overall level of support to the cultural sector and the relative contribution from each of the above sources.

Data are drawn from the reports of government departments and specialised funding bodies, from surveys carried out by bodies with an interest in either the sector or one or more of its funders, from extensive correspondence with individual authorities and organisations and from surveys conducted by researchers at PSI. As described in Chapter 1, the reference year is, as often as possible, the fiscal year 1993/94. However, some data refer to the calendar year 1993, and some to organizations' financial years most closely approximating to 1993/94[1].

# European sources

The European Union (EU) is the most important source of European funding for the cultural sector in the UK. As such it is discussed before other sources from which UK cultural sector projects have received support.

## The European Commission

The vast majority of EU support comes through three Directorates General of the European Commission (EC): Audio Visual Information, Communication and Culture (DGX); Employment, Industrial Relations, Social Affairs (DGV) and Regional Policy (DGXVI). Only DGX has a specific remit to promote cultural objectives. However, aid is also channelled to projects with a greater or lesser cultural dimension through the so-called "structural funds" – especially the European Social Fund (ESF, through DGV) and the European Regional Development Fund (ERDF, through DGXVI) – in fulfilment of such objectives as the training of young unemployed people, or the support of heritage conservation projects and tourism development initiatives designed to create jobs in areas of high unemployment. In almost all cases, a condition for receipt of community funding is that the sponsored project raises matching finance elsewhere.

Precise details of EC funding to the cultural sector are difficult to obtain. The fullest account to date is Bates and Wacker (1993) undertaken for DGX at the request of the Ministers of Culture, and summarised by the Arts Council of Great Britain (ACGB) in its *International Update* (1993). The study suggested that EC funding for the cultural sector from all sources during the five-year period 1989–93 was £1.87bn, or about £374m per year. This represented 0.8 per cent of the EC budget.

The activities of DGX have been relatively modest in size compared to those of the directorates not directly concerned with culture, providing £1.4m to the UK cultural sector. With respect to the UK, three

---

1   Administrative and overhead costs have only been included where the body concerned operates only in the cultural sector. For example, these costs are included when considering the total expenditure of the Arts Council of Great Britain (ACGB), but have not been calculated in relation to the expenditure of the Scottish Office on the cultural sector. Furthermore, administrative costs have not been calculated pro rata for separate cultural activities: thus, for example, the figure given for ACGB funding of the performing arts represents only grants and other direct expenditure and not any other costs or contributions.

programmes, or areas of activity, stand out. The largest sum of support came from the MEDIA programme (*Measures pour Encourager le Developpement de l'Industrie de Production Audio Visuelle*), supporting the film and television sector through the provision of training and enhancing production and distribution opportunities. Nearly £1m in grants came to the UK from this source in 1993/94[2]. In addition, UK projects received just over £0.25m through the Kaleidoscope programme, which aims to promote greater public access to, and familiarity with, the culture and history of the European peoples, and to encourage artistic and cultural collaboration. Lastly, the UK has received a further £0.3m under funds set aside for the conservation and promotion of architectural heritage and historic sites.

The vast majority of EC funding to the sector originated from programmes designed to meet economic and social objectives rather than cultural objectives, that is to say from the "structural funds". These accounted for over £82m of the £84m total received from the EC in 1993/94. By far the most important of these funds is the ERDF which gave £53m to infrastructural projects with a cultural content, in particular projects concerned with the conservation of cultural heritage as a support to the development of tourism. Most of this went to the construction or restoration of theatres, concert halls, galleries and museums, or the restoration of sites of historical or architectural importance, under programmes designed to regenerate inner-city areas[3]. Similar projects were also supported under the separate Rechar programme, directed at former coal-mining districts. Underdeveloped or disadvantaged rural areas benefited from a dedicated programme, Leader. The latter provided support to infrastructural programmes analogous to those described for urban areas including assistance to craft producers and promotion of arts festivals. Scotland received at least £0.5m in Leader funds in 1993 and Northern Ireland £1.8m.

The ESF, which seeks to reintegrate unemployed people into work by offering training and subsidies to employers, sponsored a number of cultural sector projects in 1993/94. These were directed towards producing performing arts, audio-visual and design skills (the last of which lies outside the remit of this study). Merseyside stands out as having particu-

---

2   A number of European programmes or bodies provide assistance to the film industry in the form of cheap loans for production or distribution. Of note are CARTOON, EVE (Espace Video European) and EDFO (European Film Distribution Office). The list of those supported by the EFDO in 1993/94 included, *The Snapper, Baji on the Beach, Leon the Pig Farmer* and *Naked*.
3   ERDF-funded cultural projects in the UK in 1993/94 included the Merseyside Philharmonic Hall, Manchester City Art Gallery and Museum of Science and Industry, the Mid-Wales Centre for the Arts, and the National Centre for Literature in Industrial South Wales.

larly benefited in this respect – of the £0.7m spent in England in 1993 for this type of ESF project, £0.3m was spent in Merseyside.

For the UK, a very minor source of funds for projects with an incidental cultural dimension, has been DGXXII, concerned with Education, Training and Youth. The latter has provided small sums for the promotion of lesser used languages (Gaelic and Welsh) and cross-country exchanges. Other minor sources of funding were identified from Cedfop, the European Centre for the Development of Vocational Training, through the Petra programme for vocational training for young people, and DGXIII (Telecommunications, Information Market and Exploitation of Research).

### Other European sources

A number of other European funding bodies also support cultural objectives. They include: the European Cultural Foundation, an independent, non-profit organisation promoting social and cultural activities of a multinational and European nature; Eurocreation, providing financial and technical aid for transnational projects within EU member states (usually involving a French partner) by young European creators or entrepreneurs; EUCREA (European Creativity for Disabled People), a non-governmental organisation funded by the EC; and Eurimages, a pan-European fund established by the Council of Europe, providing low-cost loans to film-makers. The Council of Europe also provides non-repayable assistance, both to promote interregional cultural cooperation and to enable training in cultural administration, and UK organisations have been recipients of such assistance.

Total European funding for the cultural sector in the UK is summarised in Table 2.1

## Central government

UK government support is distributed to the cultural sector through several departments, in particular the Department of National Heritage (DNH). However, funds from other government departments benefit the cultural sector in the fulfilment of other objectives, such as higher education, military training, urban regeneration and support for local authorities.

Table 2.1 European funding for the cultural sector, 1993/94 (£m)

| | Living arts (performing and combined arts, and festivals) | Visual arts and collections (including the national libraries) | Media (the moving image industries and literature) | Built heritage | Other | Total | Percentage down |
|---|---|---|---|---|---|---|---|
| European Commission | | | | | | | |
| DGX | 0.2 | 0.1 | 0.8 | 0.3 | – | 1.4 | 1.6 |
| Structural funds | 27.6 | 12.6 | 4.8 | 36.8 | 0.4 | 82.2 | 98.2 |
| Other DGs | 0.1 | – | – | – | – | 0.1 | 0.1 |
| Subtotal | 27.9 | 12.7 | 5.6 | 37.0 | 0.4 | 83.6 | 99.9 |
| Council of Europe | * | – | – | – | * | * | * |
| Total | 27.9 | 12.7 | 5.6 | 37.0 | 0.4 | 83.7 | 100.00 |
| *Percentage across* | *33.4* | *15.1* | *6.7* | *44.3* | *0.5* | *100.0* | *–* |

Sources: The Scottish, Welsh, and Northern Ireland Offices; Regional Government Offices; DfEE European Social Fund Unit.

## The Department of National Heritage

The DNH was formed in April 1992 with responsibility for the arts, museums and galleries, heritage, libraries, broadcasting, film and media, tourism, sport and recreation, the National Lottery and international cultural relations with the EU and Council of Europe[4]. Some of the DNH's responsibilities are for the whole of the UK, but others – including the arts – are for England only, with responsibility for their areas falling to the Welsh Office, the Scottish Office (Education, Environment and Industry Departments) and the Northern Ireland Office (Departments of Economic Development, Education and Environment). Although the division of tasks and funding has since changed, reference is made here to the system operative in the year for which data were collected.

Some 85 per cent of the DNH's expenditure – or a total of £794m in 1993/94 – is committed to the cultural sector as defined in this study. Some is distributed directly through the Department, but a large part is distributed through a network of self-standing public bodies and agencies, including QUANGOs, "next step" agencies and non-departmental public bodies (NDPBs) – each operating in a particular sector. Some of these operate in conjunction with regional bodies, of which they are the principal source of funding.

The DNH is the direct funder of 11 national museums and galleries and their branch museums in England, namely the British Museum, the Natural History Museum, the Imperial War Museum, the National Gallery, the National Maritime Museum, the National Museums and Galleries on Merseyside, the National Portrait Gallery, the Science Museum, the Tate Gallery, the Victoria and Albert Museum and the Wallace Collection. It also funds five non-national museums – the Horniman Museum, the Geffrye Museum, the Manchester Museum of Science and Industry, the Sir John Soane's Museum and the Museum of London.

The Department also directly sponsors the British Library, the Occupied Royal Palaces and other properties, the Royal Armories, Historic Royal Palaces and the Royal Parks (the last two of which are administered by dedicated "next steps" agencies).

In furtherance of its support of the national collections and libraries, the DNH reimburses the Inland Revenue Commissioners for tax forgone when it accepts works of art or property in lieu of capital transfer tax and

---

4   The functions of the DNH were  formerly the responsibilities of six other departments: the Office of Arts and Libraries was responsible for museums, galleries, the arts, libraries and some aspects of film. Heritage was the responsibility of the Department of the Environment; film and export licensing of art, antiques and collectors' items, the Department of Trade and Industry; tourism, the Department of Employment; broadcasting and press, the Home Office. Sport, and safety at sports grounds, which fall outside the remit of this study, were the responsibilities of the Department of Education and Science and the Home Office.

inheritance tax. The DNH also gives grants to encourage business spon-sorship of the arts. Both these functions are described in more detail below.

## Arms' length bodies funded by the DNH

A number of arms' length bodies redistribute money to the cultural sector from the DNH, and the most important of these are described in the following paragraphs. They include the national arts councils which are responsible for the performing arts, visual arts, literature and media. As described in Chapter 1, until April 1994, the principal element of the arts council structure was the ACGB which directly funded arts organisations and individuals. It also allocated funding to ten regional arts boards (RABs) in England, the Scottish Arts Council (SAC) and the Welsh Arts Council (WAC). The ACGB's expenditure in 1993/94 was some £217m. The Scottish, Welsh and Northern Ireland arts councils spent £22m, £12m and £6m respectively in 1993/94.

In contrast to certain of the European sponsors described above, the arts councils and RABs do not, as a rule, operate rigid "matching" formu-lae, and each application is treated on its merits. Applications for, or the achievement of, funding from other sources – for example, the appropri-ate local authority – might well enhance the likelihood of winning assistance, but they are not a necessary condition for support. However, sole funding can and does occur, although infrequently.

Alongside the arts councils is the Crafts Council (CC) which spent £4.6m in 1993/94 (including its grants to the Scottish and Welsh Arts Councils and the RABs). In Scotland, support for the crafts is included in the general support given by the Scottish Office to SAC, which makes payments to the CC for activities which benefit Scotland. In Northern Ireland, crafts are the largely the responsibility of the Department of Economic Development's agency, the Local Enterprise Development Unit (LEDU).

The Museums & Galleries Commission (MGC), funded by the DNH, is the government's advisor on museums, and the advisory body for museums in the UK. The MGC funds seven English Area Museum Councils, provides grants for museums and galleries in England and also funds the Museum Documentation Association. The MGC is the leading standards-setting body for museums in the UK, and is responsible for the museums' Registration Scheme. It administers the Government Indemnity Scheme (insuring objects in transit or display when they are on loan) and the Acceptance in Lieu scheme on behalf of the DNH. The MGC's expen-diture in 1993/94 was £9.1m of which £7.6m was passed on in the form of grants.

English Heritage, an NDPB supported by the DNH, is responsible for over 400 historic properties in England and also gives out grants for the conservation of the built heritage. The DNH also funds the National Heritage Memorial Fund (NHMF). Expenditure by these two bodies in 1993/94 was £116m and £11m respectively.

The DNH provides just over half of the British Film Institute's (BFI) income. In pursuit of its remit to promote film and television, the BFI spent nearly £28m in 1993/94. Some of this took the form of grants to the RABs and WAC, rather than direct sponsorship, or the pursuit of its own activities.

## The Scottish Office

In 1993/94, the Scottish Office's (SO's) responsibilities for the cultural sector were divided between its Education and Environment Departments[5]. It was also responsible for the regulation of grant aid to Scottish regional and local authorities (see below).

The Education Department promoted the living arts in Scotland[6], collections and also funded media activities. It did so through the SAC, Gaelic broadcasting and via direct support for the National Museums of Scotland, the National Galleries of Scotland and the National Library of Scotland. It also supported the Scottish Museums Council, the Scottish Film Council and the Scottish Film Production Fund. Historic Scotland, an agency of the SO, is primarily responsible for expenditure on the built heritage. It is also responsible for sponsoring the Royal Commission on the Ancient and Historical Monuments of Scotland (RCAHMS), which is funded directly by the SO. The SO also supports the Royal Fine Art Commission for Scotland.

Total Scottish Office expenditure on the cultural sector in 1993/94 was about £64m.

## The Welsh Office

Since April 1994 the Welsh Office has been responsible for the newly established Arts Council of Wales (ACW). It also supports the National

---

5   In 1995 responsibility for arts activities passed to the Education and Industry Department, Arts and Cultural Heritage Division, and to the Development Department for the built heritage.

6   In this chapter, the "living arts" is used to refer to the performing arts, combined arts and art festivals. This was made necessary because funding for these activities could not always be disaggregated. This term is not used in subsequent chapters.

Museum of Wales, National Library of Wales and Council of Museums in Wales and contributed to the Museums and Galleries Improvement Fund, Cadw: Welsh Historic Monuments Executive Agency, and the Royal Commission on the Ancient and Historical Monuments of Wales[7].

The Welsh Office spent about £38m on the cultural sector in 1993/94.

## The Northern Ireland Office

The Northern Ireland Office's direct responsibilities for the cultural sector were divided between two departments: Education (DENI) and Environment Service[8]. Heritage is the responsibility of the Environment Service and the living arts. Collections are the responsibility of DENI which supports the Arts Council of Northern Ireland (ACNI) (reconstituted in April, 1994), the two national museums – the Ulster Museum and the Ulster Folk and Transport Museum, as well as the Ulster-American Folk Park. It has supported the Northern Ireland Museums Council since 1993/94.

Spending by the Northern Ireland Office on the cultural sector was some £32m in 1993/94.

## Summary of funding in England, Scotland, Wales and Northern Ireland

Total funding of the cultural sector by the DNH and its equivalents in Scotland, Wales and Northern Ireland was some £870m in 1993/94 (Table 2.2). A quarter of this (£238m) was distributed through the arts councils, either nationally or regionally. Museums, galleries and collections absorbed up to £420m, or nearly half of the total DNH and equivalent spend, and heritage a further fifth – £163m. The media was, in relation to the three broad areas described so far, very much a residual category[9].

---

7   The National Museum of Wales is now known as the National Museum and Galleries of Wales, and the Museums and Galleries Improvement Fund is no longer operating.

8   From 1996 the Environment Service's functions were taken over by the Environment and Heritage Service, a "next steps" agency.

9   These calculations assume, of course, that all of the expenditure recorded in the visual arts, museums and galleries column went to museums and galleries, and it adds to this sum expenditure on national libraries recorded in the libraries and literature column. This simplification is necessary because visual arts expenditure cannot always be separated out from museums and galleries expenditure and because not all pending on libraries can be separated out from expenditure on literature.

*Table 2.2 Funding for the cultural sector from the DNH, Scottish, Welsh and Northern Ireland Offices, 1993/94 (£m)*

| | National and umbrella funding bodies (a) | Living arts (performing and combined arts, and festivals) | Visual arts and collections (including the national libraries) | Media (the moving image industries and) literature | Built heritage | Other | Total | Percentage down |
|---|---|---|---|---|---|---|---|---|
| Department of | | | | | | | | |
| National Heritage | 230.3 | 1.3 | 334.1 | 30.7 | 139.3 | – | 735.7 | 84.7 |
| Scottish Office | – | 1.0 | 46.1 | 10.6 | 5.8 | – | 63.5 | 7.3 |
| Welsh Office | – | – | 24.3 | * | 13.4 | – | 37.8 | 4.3 |
| Northern Ireland Office | 7.5 | 3.8 | 14.5 | * | 3.5 | 2.6 | 31.8 | 3.7 |
| Total | 237.8 | 6.1 | 419.0 | 41.3 | 162.0 | 2.6 | 868.8 | 100.0 |
| *Percentage across* | *27.4* | *0.7* | *48.2* | *4.8* | *18.7* | *12.6* | *100.0* | *–* |

Sources: Department of National Heritage, Scottish Office, Welsh Office, Northern Ireland Office.
(a) Core activities, not including special initiatives such as LEDU.

## Other government departments

A number of other government departments contribute to the cultural sector through activities which are ancillary to their principal purpose. Examples are given in the following paragraphs.

The Ministry of Agriculture, Fisheries and Food funds the Royal Botanic Gardens, Kew – the national botanical reference collections. Its grant-in-aid during 1993/94 was £15m.

In 1993/94, the Ministry of Defence (MOD) directly and indirectly supported military music schools and over 200 military museums at an annual cost of about £13m. The Ministry is directly responsible for six devolved museums – the National Army Museum, the Royal Air Force Museum, the Royal Naval Museum, the Royal Marines Museum, the Royal Navy Submarine Museum and the Fleet Air Arm Museum. There are also 70 non-devolved museums and galleries that receive support from the MOD. The Ministry also indirectly supports many small regimental museums through its funding of the regiments themselves. In 1993/94, the bulk of military musical training was carried out at the Royal Marines' school of music at Deal and at the army's military school of music at Kneller Hall, which together represented an expenditure of around £9m.

The Department for Education (DfE), which was amalgamated with the Department of Employment in 1995 to form the Department for Education and Employment (DfEE), funds universities and, thereby, approximately 300 university museums and galleries, theatres and art centres. However, since regular expenditure for many such collections and centres is through staff salaries, which are rarely separately identified, little is known about their actual cost. Only the museums and collections deemed of "undoubted national distinction" are funded in their own right. In 1993/94, 18 such collections in 12 English universities received £7m from the Higher Education Funding Council for England (HEFCE). The Scottish Higher Education Funding Council made similar grants worth £0.6m to three universities[10]. DENI gave £0.2m to the two universities in Northern Ireland, for the visual and performing arts.

Through its funding of the grants scheme for National Voluntary Youth Organisations, the DfE also provided support to the National Youth Choir, the National Youth Dance Trust, the National Youth Orchestra, the National Youth Theatre and the UK Federation of Jazz Bands. Overall, the amount of identifiable grant was in the order of £0.2m.

The Department of Employment (DE) has had a peripheral involvement in the cultural sector through the employment and training programmes run on its behalf by (in England and Wales) Training and Enterprise Councils (TECs) and (in Scotland) Local Enterprise

---

10   The Higher Education Funding Councils for England and Scotland have since reviewed their non-formula funding.

Companies (LECs). Examples of projects supported are local community arts organisations offering work experience and training to young people who have been unemployed for a long period. Merseyside TEC appears to have been particularly active in the provision of such training, spending £0.7m in 1993/94, far in excess of any other TEC. Total TEC spending in 1993/94 was in the order of £1.1m. A number of LECs – but particularly the Glasgow Development Agency and Western Isles Enterprise – have contributed to projects in the cultural sector through small-business support programmes, heritage and tourist programmes and training programmes. Alone their contribution was £0.6m, against total LEC spending of £1m.

A functional equivalent of TECs and LECs in Northern Ireland is the Training and Enterprise Agency, which runs its Action for Community Employment programme, and projects involving the cultural sector worth £1.6m were carried out in 1993/94. The vast majority of projects – worth £1.2m – involved the restoration of heritage sites. LEDU also made small grants – under £0.2m in total – to promote craft activities. The DE also contributed to the industry lead bodies for training and development[11].

The Department of the Environment (DoE) provides grants to local authorities, part of which go towards the support of cultural activities (see below). Along with the Scottish and Welsh Offices, it has been responsible for a succession of "urban programmes"[12], intended to rebuild inner cities, and these have provided a potential source of funding for cultural-sector projects insofar as they contributed to improving the quality of life of districts as places of residence and business. The City Challenge scheme, launched in 1991, made explicit reference to improvements to the cultural environment in eliciting bids for funds. Projects funded by City Challenge with a cultural component – most concerning the living or visual arts – worth some £5.4m were supported in 1993/94. Projects in Merseyside made up £2.3m worth of these. A further £8.3m came to cultural-sector projects through other "urban programme" schemes, again with half going to living or visual arts projects. Under both City Challenge and other urban programme schemes, grants largely took the form of assistance for capital projects such as the renewal or construction of venues and museums.

The Foreign and Commonwealth Office (FCO) supports the British

---

11   Industry lead bodies for training and development and industry training organisations concerned with the cultural sector include the Museum Training Institute (for the museums and heritage sectors); Skillset (broadcasting and film) and the self-explanatory Arts and Entertainment Training Council; the Book House Training Centre; the Booksellers Association of Great Britain; the Council for Dance Education and Training, and the Craft Occupational Standards Board.

12 Counted under this heading are, inter alia, the activities of Urban Development Corporations (UK), City Challenge, City Grant (now English Partnership), Task Forces, City Action Teams (all England only), Urban Aid (Scotland), Urban Programme and Rural Initiative (Wales) and Local Economic Development Unit projects (Northern Ireland).

Council and most overseas cultural relations except those with the EU and Council of Europe. The most important of these institutions is the British Council. Its objective is the promotion of cultural, educational and technical cooperation between Britain and other countries through teaching, publishing, the provision of grants and staging and supporting events. About 5 per cent of the British Council's expenditure, or some £21m, was committed to the arts in 1993/94. A small part of this is given in direct subsidy – largely in the form of contributions to expenses involved in the presentation of arts events abroad. The Commonwealth Institute, which operates a museum and library, received a further £3.7m.

The Department of Health is estimated to support about 50 museums in hospital and medical research institutes as well as a number of artists in residence. In recent years, there have been increasing numbers of arts projects in hospitals reflecting concern for the design of health-related buildings. Art is often considered to make a significant contribution to the quality of care in hospitals and many National Health Service hospitals have arts projects – usually in the form of the visual arts and crafts. The Arts for Health agency, established in 1988, estimates that there were then about 50 to 60 full-time arts coordinators in the National Health Service whose job was to devise strategies and raise funds from grants and donations.

The Home Office supports prison and police museums and also enables arts activities in prisons and within the Probation Service (Peaker and Vincent, 1993). These include residencies, performances, workshops, and exhibitions. Expenditure of some £0.7m by the prison and probation services on such activities has been identified for 1993/94. An additional £0.3m in grants was made by the Home Office Central Drugs Prevention Unit to a number of projects which had an arts component – in either the performing or visual arts or the media sub-sectors.

Assistance to UK exporters, including those coming from industries such as crafts, arts and antiques, books and films and media, can be gained from the Department of Trade and Industry (DTI). Such assistance takes the form of grants towards the rental of space and set-up costs for attendance at trade fairs and on trade missions outside Europe. Of the total of £135m granted to potential exporters under this provision, £1.7m went to firms working in the cultural sector.

The Department of Transport (DoT) is responsible for the London Transport Museum. Its income and expenditure are contained within the accounts of London Transport, but the museum has no specific allocation from the DoT and expenditure on it cannot be identified.

Overall, expenditure on the cultural sector by central government departments without a principal or specific responsibility for culture was some £168m (Table 2.3). This is the equivalent of just under one eighth of the combined expenditure on culture of the DNH and the Scottish, Welsh and Northern Ireland Offices together.

*Table 2.3 Other central government funding for the cultural sector, 1993/94 (£m)*

| | Living arts (performing and combined arts, and festivals) | Visual arts and collections (including the national libraries) | Media (the moving image industries and literature) | Built heritage | Other | Total | Percentage down |
|---|---|---|---|---|---|---|---|
| MAFF | – | 14.9 | – | – | – | 14.9 | 8.9 |
| MOD | 0.9 | 11.7 | – | – | – | 12.6 | 7.5 |
| DfE | 0.2 | 7.2 | – | – | – | 7.4 | 4.4 |
| DE | 2.1 | 0.2 | 0.8 | 1.4 | 1.4 | 5.9 | 3.5 |
| DoE | 19.6 | 3.1 | 0.5 | 10.7 | 5.4 | 39.3 | 23.4 |
| FCO | 11.2 | 7.8 | 3.5 | – | 2.7 | 25.2 | 15.0 |
| HO | 0.6 | 0.1 | 0.1 | – | 0.3 | 1.1 | 0.7 |
| DTI | 0.2 | 0.6 | 0.9 | – | – | 1.7 | 1.0 |
| Treasury | – | – | – | – | 60.0 | 60.0 | 35.7 |
| Health | – | 0.1 | – | – | – | 0.1 | 0.1 |
| Total | 34.8 | 45.7 | 5.8 | 12.1 | 9.8 | 168.2 | 100.0 |
| *Percentage across* | 20.7 | 27.2 | 3.4 | 42.9 | 5.8 | 100.0 | – |

Sources: Individual government departments; Royal Botanic Gardens (1994); British Council; British Commonwealth Office; English Partnerships; City Challenge Partnerships; TECs; LECs; Action for Community Employment; individual organisations in receipt of funding; Inland Revenue Statistics; O'Brien and Feist (1996).

## Tax relief

As well as promoting or assisting a project, organisation or institution by making grants, government can support the cultural sector by waiving, in part or in full, the obligation to pay tax. Charities and other non-profit-making bodies are exempt from paying corporation taxes. Special corporation tax provisions apply to film-making companies. These allow them to defer writing off production costs for up to three years, giving time for the project to generate profits, and also allow them to set off costs of any one project against other, more profitable projects[13].

The most extensive direct tax reliefs supporting the cultural sector are those directed toward the heritage. The built heritage sector benefits through zero-rated VAT for alterations to listed buildings. A briefing paper by the Historic Houses Association, English Heritage and the National Trust estimated that the value of the total non-recoverable VAT on repairs to historic buildings in 1993/94 was £64m. Property, in the form of land, buildings or movables[14], is subject to inheritance tax when transferred at death to other than the spouse of the deceased. In order to meet inheritance tax payments, the liable owner can transfer property of equivalent value to the nation or a charity – for example, to a museum or trust – if it is accepted by the Secretary of State for National Heritage following the MGC's recommendations (see above). In this case the DNH reimburses the Inland Revenue to the value of the transfer. The value of works accepted "in lieu" were valued at £3m in 1993/94[15].

Not dissimilar to the Acceptance in Lieu scheme is the Private Treaty Sale provision, whereby capital tax can be avoided through the sale of a heritage property to a recognised charity, trust or government body. The seller receives (on top of the net price) a share of the tax otherwise payable and the purchaser pays only this amount rather than the gross price. The property, rather than being physically moved to a new location as with the Acceptance in Lieu scheme, remains in situ. The NHMF assisted purchases worth £1.7m in 1993/94 under Private Treaty Sales. However, this would have represented only a fraction of the total value of Private Treaty Sales for that year, since not all would have been assisted by the NHMF.

---

13  See *Accountancy Age* 23 May 1996. The Advisory Committee on Film Finance (the Middleton Committee), report in mid-1996, suggested allowing film-makers to write off 100 per cent of production costs in the year in which they are incurred, arguing that "tax relief played an important part in the resurgence of the US film industry and it could play a similar role here". The DNH, which established the committee, had not responded in detail at the time of writing.

14  These movables are considered as heritage items for this form of tax relief.

15  The DNH budget for Acceptance in Lieu is £2m. When the value of acceptances exceeds this figure access may be sought through the Public Expenditure Reserve. The £3m figure for 1993/94 was comparatively low. In 1994/95 and 1995/96 the figures were £6m and £9m respectively.

Most important, in financial terms, is the Conditional Exemption scheme. Property which is deemed to be "heritage property" of "outstanding importance" can be relieved of inheritance tax, at least with respect to those parts deigned to meet this criterion. In return for conditional exemption the owner has to make the property, including any designated contents, accessible to the public for a minimum of 28 days per year and to undertake necessary maintenance[16]. The level of inheritance tax to be paid, and thus the level of exemptions, fluctuates considerably on a year-by-year basis as the pattern of deaths among heritage property owners varies. Table 2.4 illustrates this. For 1993/94, the Inland Revenue estimates tax forgone of £60m due to conditional exemptions for heritage property.

*Table 2.4 Tax losses resulting from conditional exemption on heritage objects*

| Tax year | £m |
|---|---|
| 1987/88 | 28.5 |
| 1988/89 | 46.7 |
| 1989/90 | 183.4 |
| 1990/91 | 44.4 |
| 1991/92 | 21.2 |
| Average | 64.8 |

Source: Inland Revenue Statistics (various years).

## Local government

Local authorities in the UK are funded by a mixture of charges they raise on residents and businesses and, quantitatively far more important, grants from cental government. They are empowered to give assistance to cultural sector projects – in the form of both revenue grants and capital grants. However, only in Scotland and Northern Ireland is such assistance statutory.

In three cases, groups of English authorities act collectively under the terms of what are called Section 48 schemes – grant schemes set up under Section 48 of the 1986 Local Government Act to provide for voluntary bodies the activities of which extend beyond the area of one district or borough. The joint arrangements in question are the Association of

---

16  Conditional exemption remains effective only so long as the property is not disposed of. If an object is sold on the open market, the full tax charge will then apply. Not all applications are accepted. Only 49 per cent of the 545 applications submitted between 1986 and 1992 had been accepted by the end of the period. Nor are the terms of the exemption always fulfilled, in so far as access is not granted or exempted items are sold (see NAO, 1992).

Greater Manchester Authorities, the West Yorkshire Grants Scheme and the London Boroughs Grants Scheme. The expenditure on cultural sector projects of these was just under £6m in 1993/94, with the London scheme accounting for just over £3m and the Manchester scheme for about £2m. Further support by English local authorities for activities which occur in wider geographical areas than defined by their individual political boundaries occurs through their subscriptions to the RABs. From the English local authorities these totalled some £3m in 1993/94.

Through their leisure and recreation (or equivalent) departments, UK local authorities spent about £370m on the cultural sector in 1993/94[17]. They maintain over 800 local museums and art galleries as well as theatres and concert halls. Their contribution takes the form of either mounting their own events or making grants to organisations and individuals. A special analysis of the English authorities' revenue expenditure for the year 1993/94 showed that the largest share of support – nearly two-thirds – went on their own venues, and that most of these were managed by themselves (Marsh and White, 1995).

Per capita spending by leisure and recreation departments is rather higher in Scotland (£7.30) and rather lower in Wales (£5.70) than in England (£6.40). Northern Ireland recorded a yet lower figure, but this can in part be explained by different funding structures and greater importance of central government sources. Within England, London local authorities make substantially greater provision than do authorities elsewhere – over £9 per capita. The Corporation of the City of London has promoted itself as the third largest sponsor of the arts in the country after the government and the BBC. In 1993/94 it provided support of £21m for the Barbican Centre and committed £9.7m to the centre's refurbishment. It also supports the Museum of London, various libraries and the proposed Guildhall Art Gallery, due to open at the end of 1996 (Corporation of London, 1994). The cultural sector in London, of course, serves a far wider constituency than London resident and working populations. It is heavily visited by visitors from outside London and from overseas. Over 50 per cent of overseas tourists to the UK in 1993 stayed in London (BTA/ETB, 1994b).

Local authority support for the cultural sector also comes from departments other than leisure and recreation, but such support is much more

---

17   Data for England and Wales are drawn from the annual survey carried out by CIPFA. This source has been criticised, especially for its treatment of non-responding authorities and for what is understood as "the arts sector" by those making returns. Some alternative estimates have been made for some of the totals it produces (see Feist and Dix, 1994; Marsh and White, 1995). However, alternative studies have been one-off and/or limited to particular regions (those cited refer only to 1994/95 and only to England). For the purposes of consistency, CIPFA figures are used, but this should not be taken as a judgement of their quality relative to that of alternatives.

difficult to identify and disaggregate. For example, some aspects of local education authorities' spending might have a cultural component, while planning and environment departments might fund public art projects, or contribute to heritage restoration projects. More recent (1994/95) Chartered Institute of Public Finance and Accounting (CIPFA) statistics on spending by planning and development departments allow expenditure on the conservation of historical buildings to be identified and thus permit estimates to be made for earlier years. Expenditure by authorities in England and Wales for this purpose is estimated to have totalled some £32m in 1993/94 (see Chapter 9), while Scottish local authorities spent a further £1m. Data on spending by district councils in Northern Ireland on the conservation of the built heritage are not centrally collected.

Total local government expenditure on the cultural sector was just over £400m in 1993/94 (Table 2.5). This was approximately half the amount spent by the DNH. The largest share of local authority expenditure went to the performing arts, combined arts and festivals, both in local authority theatres and elsewhere. Most of the remainder went to the support of local authority galleries and museums.

*Table 2.5 Local authority funding for the cultural sector, 1993/94*
*(£m and £ per capita)*

| | Museums and galleries | Built heritage (a) | Other spend | Total | £ per head of population | Percentage down |
|---|---|---|---|---|---|---|
| County councils | 20.0 | .. | 15.6 | 35.6 | 1.2 | *8.8* |
| Metropolitan district councils | 36.1 | .. | 38.1 | 74.3 | 6.6 | *18.3* |
| Non–metropolitan district councils | 49.0 | .. | 84.4 | 133.4 | 4.0 | *32.9* |
| London authorities | 5.2 | .. | 58.3 | 63.4 | 9.2 | *15.7* |
| Section 48 schemes | 0.5 | .. | 5.2 | 5.6 | .. | *1.4* |
| England | 110.7 | 32.0 | 201.7 | 344.3 | 7.1 | *85.0* |
| | | | | | | |
| Wales | 7.4 | .. | 9.0 | 16.5 | 5.7 | *4.1* |
| Scotland | 30.2 | 1.0 | 7.3 | 38.5 | 7.5 | *9.5* |
| Northern Ireland | 1.7 | .. | 4.1 | 5.8 | 3.6 | *1.4* |
| Total UK (b) | 150.1 | 33.0 | 222.1 | 405.1 | 7.0 | *100.0* |
| *Percentage across* | *37.0* | *8.1* | *54.8* | *100.0* | *–* | *–* |

Sources: CIPFA, Leisure and Recreation Statistics, estimates, 1993/94; Scottish Office; The Forum for Local Government and the Arts / The Arts Council of Northern Ireland.
(a) England total represents both England and Wales.
(b) The total may differ from that in Table 2.9 as some local authority heritage spend is there accounted for under central government expenditure.

# The business sector

The private sector contributes to the arts in various ways – through business sponsorship and corporate membership schemes, including those encouraged by the government, through donations, the provision of secondees and help "in kind".

## Business sponsorship

Businesses sponsoring the arts normally expect certain benefits in return. These include promotion and advertising opportunities, such as entertaining clients and VIPs, access to specific markets, the enhancement of their corporate image by association with a prestigious event, and the possibility of boosting staff morale by providing free or discounted tickets. Sponsorship is generally regarded as part of a company's promotional expenditure and is normally allowable for tax purposes.

The Association for Business Sponsorship of the Arts (ABSA) specifically exists to promote and encourage partnerships between the private sector and the cultural sector. In 1993/94 it administered the Business Sponsorship Incentive Scheme (BSIS) on behalf of the DNH, which was relaunched as the National Heritage Arts Sponsorship Scheme: the Pairing Scheme for the Arts, in 1995 (see below). It also carries out an annual national survey of business sponsorship for the culture sector. Some 70 per cent of the total £70m raised in 1993/94 took the form of cash sponsorship – sponsorship of events, of capital projects and of awards and prizes. The remainder was divided almost equally between corporate membership[18], corporate donations and assistance in kind.

Since 1989 ABSA has also administered the Business in the Arts (BiA) programme which seeks to improve the quality of arts management by providing arts managers with access to private-sector training. This programme has two facets to it: the Placement Scheme and Arts Management Development schemes. The former involves recruiting and training experienced business people to act as voluntary advisors to cultural sector organisations. The latter provides advisory seminars, arranges access for arts managers to companies' in-house management courses and gives bursaries to senior arts managers to attend short courses at business schools. For 1993/94 this was estimated to have a commercial value of approximately £0.7m.

Business support for the cultural sector was worth at least £70m in 1993/94[19], largely in the form of sponsorship of events, organisations and

---

18  Corporate memberships are, as their names implies, recurrent sums paid by corporate bodies to cultural organisations, which provide particular benefits such as free or discounted tickets and the opportunities for corporate entertainment.

19  This figure may be an underestimate, because ABSA's data are solely based on recipient organisations which respond to its survey.

Table 2.6 Business support for the cultural sector, 1993/94 (£m)

| | Living arts (performing and combined arts, and festivals) | Visual arts and collections (including the national libraries) | Media (the moving image industries and literature) | Built heritage | Service provision | Total | Percentage down |
|---|---|---|---|---|---|---|---|
| Cash sponsorship | 36.7 | 8.3 | 3.0 | 0.6 | 0.1 | 48.8 | 70.1 |
| Sponsorship in kind | 4.1 | 1.6 | 0.4 | 0.1 | 0.2 | 6.2 | 8.9 |
| Corporate membership | 6.3 | 1.1 | 0.2 | * | * | 7.6 | 11.0 |
| Corporate donations | 3.8 | 1.3 | 1.6 | 0.3 | 0.008 | 7.0 | 10.0 |
| Total | 51.0 | 12.2 | 5.3 | 1.0 | 0.1 | 69.6 | 100.0 |
| *Percentage across* | *73.3* | *17.5* | *7.6* | *1.4* | *0.2* | *100.0* | *–* |

Source: ABSA (1994).

individuals (Table 2.6). Half of this business support went to the performing arts, and this combined with arts festivals accounted for nearly two-thirds of the total.

### Private-sector schemes in partnership with the government

In 1993/94 the government had three major schemes which fostered private support for the cultural sector.

The BSIS, described above, functioned as an incentive to increase the level of business sponsorship of the cultural sector in the UK. It offered cultural sector organisations financial awards of between £11,000 and £50,000 to match funds from businesses sponsors, whereby first-time sponsorship is matched on a 1:1 basis, second-year sponsorship on a 1:2 basis and subsequent sponsorship on a 1:4 basis. A scheme similar to BSIS was in operation in Northern Ireland, also administered by ABSA, but on behalf of the Department of Education for Northern Ireland. In 1993/94 ABSA made BSIS awards totalling £4m. These complemented a total of £8m raised in sponsorship. Nearly a third of award money, and over 40 per cent of sponsorship money, went to organisations in London (ABSA, 1994).

The DNH's two other schemes, the Theatres Restoration Fund and the Museums and Galleries Improvement Fund, were short-term.They matched central government funds to grants from charitable trusts and made awards to projects submitted by organisations from within the relevant sub-sectors. Between 1992/3 and 1993/94, the first of these two funds disbursed nearly £4m, while from 1993/94 until 1995/96, the second has had an annual budget of the same amount.

## Trusts and foundations

Cultural organisations also receive funds from trusts and charities, of which several thousand operate in the UK. They are, however, relatively low on their priorities. One source (Leat, 1992) estimated that only about 4 per cent of grants from the 400 largest trusts goes to the cultural and the environment sectors combined. A more recent guide to arts funding (Doulton, 1994) listed about 250 grant-making trusts that give grants, of which the National Arts Collections Fund (NACF), the Calouste Gulbenkian Foundation and the Foundation for Sport and the Arts were among the largest supporters. But whereas the NACF is exclusively dedicated to assisting the arts, the others are also concerned with other causes. During 1994 the Gulbenkian, for example, gave grants worth over £2m of which over half went to the arts and cultural activities.

## Grants

ABSA (1994) reported that trusts and foundations granted nearly £22m to the cultural sector in 1993/94 The largest single share of this (38 per cent) went to museums, and the second largest share (15 per cent) to theatres. However, ABSA's reliance on collecting data from recipient organisations left it open to bias because of the lack of responses from organisations which were, nevertheless, major beneficiaries of charitable giving.

Accordingly, PSI carried out its own survey, directed toward grant-making trusts identified as supporting the cultural sector in the Charities Aid Foundation (CAF) *Directory of Grant Making Trusts* (1993 edition). The trusts were asked to provide a copy of their annual report and accounts, and a schedule of the organisations that had received funding for an arts-based activity in the period in question[20]. A total of £40m was identified for funding of the arts and built heritage in 1993/94, over 80 per cent more than suggested by ABSA (Table 2.7)[21].

PSI found that 40 per cent of grants went to museums, galleries and the visual arts, and a further 32 per cent to the performing arts. The built heritage, including the preservation of churches, which scarcely featured in the ABSA survey, received 6 per cent of grant money. The survey could not, however, identify the regional distribution of funds, something which the ABSA survey, by concentrating upon recipients, could. The latter suggested that a disproportionate share of grants from trusts went to London. The capital absorbed nearly half of funds disbursed in 1993/94, while the next most important recipient was Scotland, with 15 per cent.

## Friends and membership organisations

The National Campaign for the Arts (NCA) describes "Friends" organisations as bodies supporting particular venues or companies, usually in return for priority booking arrangements, reduced ticket prices or free admissions, discount on merchandise, dress rehearsal tickets and oppor-

---

20   A total of 117 grant-making trusts were surveyed. The response rate to the survey was 59 per cent. It can be assumed that some of those that did not respond do not give money to the arts on a regular basis, and may have been listed by CAF on the basis of a one-off grant. Also excluded from the final response rate were those that declined to provide information on the recipients of grants on the grounds of confidentiality.

21   This sum represents a highly conservative estimate because the survey was necessarily based on the schedules of recipients of funding supplied by trusts identified as serving the sector. These schedules did not always clearly identify recipients as belonging to the sector. For example, six Sainsbury Family Trusts were estimated to have given £1.8m to the cultural sector on the basis of the survey. Of these, it has subsequently been confirmed that five, in fact, gave a total of £11.8m.

Table 2.7 Support for the cultural sector from trusts and foundations, 1993/94 (£m)

| | Living arts (performing and combined arts, and festivals) | Visual arts and collections (including the national libraries) | Media (the moving image industries and literature) | Built heritage | Service provision | Unclassified | Total |
|---|---|---|---|---|---|---|---|
| Charities who provided detail | 22.4 | 10.0 | 1.0 | 2.4 | 0.3 | 0.2 | 36.3 |
| Charities who provided total only, pro rata | 2.0 | 0.9 | 0.1 | 0.2 | * | * | 3.2 |
| Subtotal | 24.4 | 10.9 | 1.1 | 2.6 | 0.3 | 0.3 | 39.6 |
| Additional funding identified as received by funding bodies (a) | .. | .. | .. | .. | .. | | 0.153 |
| *Total* | 24.4 | 10.9 | 2.2 | 2.6 | 0.3 | 0.3 | 39.7 |
| *Percentage across* | 61.5 | 27.4 | 2.8 | 6.4 | 0.8 | 0.7 | 100.0 |

Source: PSI survey.
(a) Charities which did not respond to, or were not included in, the survey.

tunities for closer contact with a venue or company, and playing a role in fundraising and winning sponsorship (NCA, 1995). The diversity and scale of their activities varies enormously and includes mounting lecture programmes, arranging visits, operating museum services, and providing volunteers. A study published in 1992 lists 225 organisations which were affiliated to the British Association of Friends of Museums (Heaton, 1992). Their memberships ranged from just 20 to 70,000 (the largest being the Friends of the Royal Academy).

## Donations

In addition to the corporate donations referred to above, mention should be made of giving by members of the public, often in response to a special appeal. Thus, in 1994 Canova's *The Three Graces* – which had been sold to a foreign bidder for £7.6m in open auction – was "saved for the nation", being bought by the Victoria and Albert Museum and the National Galleries of Scotland after a major fundraising campaign. As well as obtaining a substantial grant from the NHMF, the campaign elicited large donations from JP Getty II and Baron Thyssen, £0.5m from the NACF and £0.1m in small-scale public and private donations. The NACF itself raises about half of its funds from a combination of subscriptions, donations and legacies, largely from private individuals (NACF, 1995).

## Volunteering

As well as depending upon the financial contributions of private bodies and individuals, the cultural sector is also a substantial user of voluntary labour. This enables the staffing up of everyday activities, the bringing in of special skills and the undertaking of exceptional activities, as well as providing general oversight and direction through membership of management committees and boards of trustees. Unfortunately, other than broad aggregates, very little is known about the extent of voluntary activity in the UK, and few individual organisations provide details in their own reports.

A special study for the ACGB (Martin, 1994) of the living arts and media sector found that, in 1994, some 65 per cent of surveyed organisations used volunteers, and those doing so had between two and three volunteers for every paid member of staff. However, over half of the users of volunteers estimated that these met under 10 per cent of their staffing requirements. Grossing up this study's results is difficult, but based upon the employment information given in the study, and assuming that non-respondents were similar to respondents, the annual input of volunteers to the sector could be as much as 5 million hours.

The British Tourist Authority/English Tourist Board Research Services (BTA/ETB) have estimated the number of volunteers in historic properties and museums and galleries at 20,000 and 16,000 respectively for 1993 (BTA/ETB, 1993). The independent organisation, the National Trust (NT), which preserves buildings of historic interest and places of natural beauty, is heavily reliant on volunteers. It reported that, in 1993, nearly 28,000 people contributed just over 1.6 million unpaid hours to its work, accounting for about one sixth of its total labour input (NT, 1994). Using BTA/ETB estimates for the number of volunteers, and NT estimates for the hours worked per year by each volunteer, it can be calculated that volunteers contributed some 1.1 million hours to the historic properties sector and another 0.9 million hours to the museums and galleries sector.

If hours contributed by volunteers are priced, the support they contribute can be entered into the calculation of the total value of support within the cultural sector. Valuing labour inputs depends upon the assumptions made about productivity. Here a conservative estimate is made, whereby it is assumed that hours are paid at the average rate for part-time women working in the service sector (£3.89 in April 1993). Table 2.8 displays the results. Total support in the form of voluntary labour might be as much as £27m, but the contingent nature of the calculation should be recognised.

*Table 2.8 Estimated value of volunteer labour in the cultural sector, 1993/94*

|  | Number of volunteers | Hours worked per year (millions) | Value (£m) |
|---|---|---|---|
| Living arts and media | .. | 5.0 | 19.0 |
| Museums and galleries | 16,000 | 0.9 | 3.6 |
| Historic properties | 20,000 | 1.1 | 4.4 |
| Total | .. | 7.0 | 27.0 |

Sources: Estimates based upon BTA/ETB (1995b); Martin (1994); and NT (1994).

## Summary

On the basis of the information reported in this chapter, it is possible to make a broad estimate of the total value of support flowing to the cultural sector from public and private sources. Table 2.9 aggregates Tables 2.1 to 2.8 from the preceding sections of this chapter. The totals that it gives represent lower bounds, in so far as insufficient detail is available with respect to EC funding, other central government department funding

Table 2.9 Funding for the cultural sector, 1993/94 (£m and percentages)

| | Umbrella funding bodies (a) | Living arts (performing and combined arts, and festivals) | Visual arts and collections (including the national libraries) | Media (the moving image industries and literature) | Built heritage | Service provision | Other | Total | Percentage down |
|---|---|---|---|---|---|---|---|---|---|
| European funding | – | 27.9 | 12.7 | 5.6 | 37.0 | – | 0.4 | 83.7 | 4.8 |
| Central government | | | | | | | | | |
| Department of National Heritage (b) | 230.3 | 1.3 | 334.1 | 30.7 | 139.3 | – | – | 735.7 | 42.6 |
| Scottish Office | – | 1.0 | 46.1 | 10.6 | 5.8 | – | – | 63.5 | 3.7 |
| Welsh Office | – | – | 24.3 | * | 13.4 | – | – | 37.8 | 2.2 |
| Northern Ireland Office | 7.5 | 3.8 | 14.5 | * | 3.5 | – | 2.6 | 31.8 | 1.8 |
| Other government departments (c) | – | 34.8 | 45.7 | 5.8 | 12.1 | – | 9.8 | 108.2 | 6.3 |
| Tax relief | – | – | – | – | 125.0 | – | – | 125.0 | 7.2 |
| Local authorities (d) | 3.1 | 219.0 | 150.1 | : | 33.0 | 0.7 | 0.6 | 405.1 | 23.5 |
| Charities (e) | – | 12.7 | 18.7 | 1.3 | 5.6 | 0.1 | – | 39.6 | 2.3 |
| Business (f) | – | 51.0 | 12.1 | 5.3 | 1.0 | – | – | 69.5 | 4.0 |
| Volunteer contributions | – | 19.0 | 3.6 | (g) | 4.4 | – | – | 27.0 | 1.6 |
| Total | 240.9 | 370.5 | 661.9 | 59.2 | 380.2 | 0.9 | 13.3 | 1,726.9 | 100.0 |
| *Percentage across* | *13.9* | *21.5* | *38.3* | *3.4* | *22.0* | *\** | *0.8* | *100.0* | *–* |

Sources: Tables 2.1 to 2.8

(a) That cover more than one sector, such as the arts councils and regional arts boards.
(b) Excluding funding of £58m to S4C.
(c) Excluding Foreign and Commonwealth Office funding of £175.7m for the BBC World Service.
(d) Including Section 48 grant schemes and public library provision in England, Wales and Scotland. Some of the expenditure shown under performing arts for local authorities may belong in one of the other, more specific categories. However, information was not available in sufficient detail. Contributions to RABs (column one) calculated from the annual reports of the RABs.
(e) Minimum figures.
(f) Derived from the ABSA survey. Again, these figures represent the minimum limit. Includes the BSIS scheme.
(g) Incorporated into the figure for the performing arts.

and local government funding to identify support for projects under programmes not classed as cultural (in particular, training programmes, business support schemes and urban regeneration programmes). Despite its approach being handicapped, this study has identified some £1.7bn of support and patronage flowing to the cultural sector.

The DNH and its Scottish, Welsh and Northern Ireland equivalents appear to be the largest funders of the cultural sector, their share constituting just over one half of the total. Local authorities contribute a little under a quarter of the total support. The contribution of other sectors is dwarfed by that of both the national and the local states. Corporate sponsorship contributes under 5 per cent, and the share of charitable trusts and volunteers taken together is of a similar size. Sources not conventionally considered as supporters of the cultural sector – the European structural funds and "other" UK government departments – are responsible for one fifth of total support for the sector.

# Chapter 3

# Employment in the cultural sector

## Introduction

This chapter focuses on employment in the cultural sector, the earnings of those who work in the sector and the contribution of volunteers to it. Because it draws from established data sources, it is determined by the categorisations these use, with respect to both industries in which people work and their occupations.

For the purposes of this chapter, employment in the cultural sector comprises people working in a cultural industry or in a cultural occupation. Thus, it includes people working in a cultural industry but not having a cultural occupation, and people having a cultural occupation but not working in a cultural industry. An example of the former might be an accountant working in a theatre; an example of the latter is a curator

---

1   Other studies have adopted rather different definitions of cultural-sector employment. Thus, *Cultural Trends* (1994), no 20, also concerned with employment, looked only at certain industries which were direct producers of "culture". Its remit included film production and distribution, radio and TV as well as theatre, libraries and museums. On the other hand, a recent study by the Arts Council of England (O'Brien and Feist, 1995), concentrated upon people in cultural occupations, although its definition of the latter included journalists, architects, clothes designers and industrial designers, as well as people making musical instruments – ie people directly involved in the production of an input to the cultural sector. An appendix to the chapter on employment in *Cultural Trends* (1997), no 25, presents a detailed reconciliation of findings from the Labour Force Survey given in the definitions used there and those used in O'Brien and Feist (1995) and other studies.

working in a corporate art collection[1]. Inclusion in the "cultural sector" by reference to industry and occupation says nothing about the status of the organisations where the individuals work. These organisations might be one person organisations or much larger corporations, can be in the public, private or voluntary sectors and may be commercial, or non-profit-making organisations.

The principal data source for this chapter is the Labour Force Survey (LFS), conducted each quarter from a sample of the UK population[2]. The sample used in this chapter is that for spring 1994, which corresponds most closely to the period covered in this study (1993/94). Industries are identified by reference to the 1992 Standard Industrial Classification (SIC), 12 of which most closely conform to the definition of the cultural sector used here[3]. Occupations are identified by reference to the Standard Occupational Classification (SOC), of which eight are included here[4]. Because the number of people in particular, narrowly defined industries or occupations from which the survey collects information is relatively small, it has been necessary to group the industries and occupations referred to above. Thus the cultural industries include:

- publishing (SICs 22.11 and 22.14);
- recording (SICs 22.31 and 22.32);
- films (SICs 92.11, 92.12 and 92.13);
- radio and TV (SIC 92.20);
- visual, literary and performing arts (SICs 92.31 and 92.32);

---

2 The LFS collects information from about one person in 350, unlike the census which collects information from everybody. As a consequence, the LFS collects information from only a relatively small number of any narrowly defined group of people who are not particularly common – for example, actors. Since estimates about the population made on samples which are small are subject to quite wide margins of error, highly detailed analysis, such as is possible with a census, cannot be made. To undertake analysis it is often necessary to use wider groupings, and thus groupings which contain information from a larger number of people, than would be the case if a census were being analysed.

3 These SIC codes refer to: book publishing (22.11); music publishing (22.14); production of gramophone records (22.31); production of video tapes (22.32); motion picture and video production (92.11); motion picture and video distribution (92.12); motion picture projection (92.13); radio and television activities (92.20); artistic, literary and creation activities (92.31); arts facilities (92.32); library and archive activities (92.51); museum activities (92.52). Libraries are included here because they are compounded in SIC 92.51 with archive activities.

4 The SOC codes referred to are: entertainments and sports managers (176); librarians (270); archivists and curators (271); authors, writers and journalists (380) (excluding people working in newspaper publishing, journal and periodical publishing and news agency activities); artists, commercial artists and graphic designers (381); actors, entertainers, stage managers and producers (384); musicians (385); photographers, camera, sound and video equipment operators (386).

- museums, libraries and archives (SICs 92.51 and 92.52);

and the cultural occupations include:

- managers (SOC 176);
- librarians and archivists (SOCs 270 and 271); and
- artists (SOCs 380, 381, 384, 385 and 386)[5].

The LFS captures data on unemployment, which are complemented by the data provided by the Employment Service. Quarterly data from the latter on unemployment by occupation were made available to PSI. This refers to people who are in receipt of benefit and available for work, a different definition to that used in the LFS which concentrates upon people available for work and actively seeking it, regardless of their benefit status[6].

Data on earnings are more limited in scope and were analysed less extensively than the above. The principal source of these data is the annual *New Earnings Survey*, carried out in April each year. It publishes data by both industry and occupation. Although data are published when the sample size for the category is small (as few as ten), this level was reached for only relatively few cultural occupations and for even fewer cultural industries. A second shortcoming of the *New Earnings Survey* is that, by definition, it records earnings not income, thereby excluding self-employed people. This chapter draws on the April 1995 *New Earnings Survey*.

The importance of volunteer workers in the cultural sector has already been noted in Chapter 2, and here some estimates have been made of their number, drawing from a variety of partial sources. Statistics on volunteering are collected in an occasional and idiosyncratic fashion, and the definitions used, and the way in which data, if any, are presented, differ from source to source. Nevertheless, some indication of the importance of such workers can be given.

# Employment

In spring 1994, a total of 560,000 people were working in either a cultural sector industry or a cultural sector occupation, or both. This total includes both people whose first, or main, job was in the sector and people whose second, or subsidiary, job was in the sector (for example, a teacher who

---

5   The number of cases counted in the recording industry and among managers is too small for proper analysis.

6   This difference is particularly poignant in the cultural sector. According to *Hansard* (House of Lords, 28/3/1996), only 3,000 of the 14,000 individuals who were registered as unemployed and who gave their last occupation as "actors, entertainers, etc" were actually eligible to claim unemployment benefit.

*Table 3.1 Number of people working in the cultural sector, spring 1994*

| People working in the cultural sector | Numbers and percentages |
|---|---|
| Main job only | 496,000 |
| of which, both main and second job | 12,000 |
| Second job only | 63,000 |
| Total | 559,000 |
| | |
| Main job, all sectors | 25,546,000 |
| Cultural sector main jobs as a percentage of all main jobs | 2 |

Source: Labour Force Survey, spring 1994.

writes television plays when not teaching). The breakdown between these categories is shown in Table 3.1.

These statistics enable the relative importance of the cultural sector to be compared with that of other sectors. For example, the motor industry employs some 282,000 persons and retail banking (including building societies) some 473,000 persons. In other words, the cultural sector is about as important, in employment terms, as the latter industry and nearly twice as the important as the former.

The distinction has been made between cultural industries and cultural occupations, and the distribution of the 496,000 people working in the cultural sector between industries and occupations is shown in Table 3.2.

*Table 3.2 Distribution of cultural sector employment between industries and occupations*

| | Thousands | Percentage |
|---|---|---|
| Cultural industry | 187 | 37.7 |
| Cultural occupation | 173 | 34.9 |
| Both | 136 | 27.4 |
| Total | 496 | 100.0 |

Source: Labour Force Survey, spring 1994.

Table 3.3 shows the distribution of this employment for those people with a main job in the cultural industries and occupations summarised above.

## Regional distribution

The half a million people working in the cultural sector are concentrated very strongly in the metropolitan areas of the country, and especially in

*Table 3.3 Employment in the cultural sector, by industries and occupations*

|  | Thousands (a) |
| --- | --- |
| Cultural industries | |
| Publishing | 38 |
| Recording | 8 |
| Films | 32 |
| Radio and TV | 60 |
| Visual, literary and performing arts | 94 |
| Museums, libraries and archives | 90 |
| Cultural occupations | |
| Managers | 22 |
| Librarians and archivists | 24 |
| Artists | 262 |

Source: Labour Force Survey, spring 1994.
(a) These categories cannot be summed, as some people fall into more than one category.

*Table 3.4 Regional distribution of cultural employment in the UK*

|  | Percentages |
| --- | --- |
| Greater London | 33 |
| Rest of South East England | 16 |
| Other metropolitan areas (a) | 19 |
| Rest of UK (b) | 33 |
| Total | 100 |

Source: Labour Force Survey, spring 1994.
(a) Tyne and Wear, West Yorkshire, South Yorkshire, the West Midlands, Greater Manchester, Merseyside and Strathclyde.
(b) Only one per cent of people work in the cultural sector in Northern Ireland, four per cent in Wales and seven per cent in Scotland.

London (Table 3.4). By comparison, 13 per cent of the working population have jobs in London, and a further 18 per cent have jobs in the rest of the South East.

The importance of London is intensified when particular cultural industries are examined. Thus, of people with a main job in the sector, 58 per cent of those working in radio and TV were based in London, as were 47 per cent in publishing (but only 21 per cent from museums, libraries and archives).

## Basic demographics

The cultural sector employs men and women in approximately equal proportions – 55 per cent of people with a main job in the sector are men and 45 per cent are women, reflecting the distribution in the economy as a whole. However, in relation to the cultural sector as a whole, there is a strong over-representation of women in the museums, libraries and archives sector (67 per cent) and a strong under-representation of women among people with artistic occupations (33 per cent). More remarkable is the major difference in the age structure between various cultural industries. For example, 22 per cent of people in films, but only 7 per cent in visual, literary and performing arts were under 25. Only six per cent of people in films, but 28 per cent in visual, literary and performing arts and 30 per cent in museums, libraries and archives were 50 or over. Indeed, as many as 10 per cent of people working in visual, literary and performing arts were aged over the state pension age, and this compares with only three per cent across all industries.

It is notable that the sector involves people who are relatively highly educated. Nearly a third (31 per cent) are qualified to degree level, and a further 12 per cent passed through some other form of higher education. In the economy as a whole, the equivalent shares are only 13 per cent and 9 per cent respectively. In the radio and TV sector, half (47 per cent) had completed higher education.

Only one in ten (11 per cent) of people working in the sector as a whole had qualifications below O-level standard (NVQ2 equivalent) or had no qualifications at all. However, in the museums, libraries and archives sector this rose to one in five (20 per cent).

## The nature of employment relationships

Self-employment is an important characteristic of cultural sector employment. Overall, 34 per cent of people with a main job in the sector work on a self-employed basis. This compares with 13 per cent in the economy as a whole.

Self-employment is more pronounced in some cultural industries than in others, standing at 2 per cent in museums, libraries and archives, 28 per cent in films and 67 per cent in visual, literary and performing arts. Where the job is a second job, the share of self-employment is, not unexpectedly, much higher. Two-thirds (65 per cent) of such jobs are self-employment jobs.

Jobs in the cultural sector are often temporary, being seasonal or otherwise short-term – examples are work in historical buildings open only part of the year and in plays with a limited production run. For some people, the only "cultural" jobs that are available might be part-time or seasonal. Of employees (but not self-employed people)[7] in the sector, one in eight (13 per cent) are in temporary jobs – twice as many as in the generality of industries. Again, substantial differences are apparent within the sector. The level of temporary employment in radio and TV was 23 per cent and in museums, libraries and archives, 19 per cent. In contrast, temporary employment in publishing represented only 4 per cent.

Since a self-employed job can finish at the end of a season or run, or once a commission has been fulfilled, self-employment can be considered as, in many ways, a functional equivalent of temporary employment. If this is so, the overall level of "flexible" employment within the sector rises yet more. As many as four in ten people with a main job in the cultural sector are either self-employed or in a temporary job, especially: 36 per cent in films; 37 per cent in radio and TV; and 70 per cent in visual, literary and performing arts.

Second jobs in the sector are much more likely to be temporary, in the sense of being occasional or seasonal, than are main jobs. Only half of people with a second job claim it to be a regular one.

Part-time working is widespread in the sector, but not more widespread than in the economy as a whole (part-time workers as self-defined). Approximately one in four people (24 per cent) work part-time. However, there are some differences between the different cultural industries, with, for example, only 15 per cent in radio and TV and in publishing, but 42 per cent in museums, libraries and archives.

Some people, despite regarding their cultural-sector job as their main job, work relatively few hours in it. Nearly a fifth (19 per cent) worked no more than 10 hours in their main job in the survey week. This share was higher in visual, literary and performing arts, where it stood at 27 per cent and lower in films, where it stood at 13 per cent. At the other end of the spectrum, one in ten in the sector worked over 50 hours in their main job. This share was higher in radio and TV, where it stood at 16 per cent, and lower in museums, libraries and archives, where (given the high level of part-time working) it stood at two per cent.

Second jobs tended to involve very few hours, such that one in eight with a second job had done no work at all in that job in the survey week and two-thirds had done no more than eight hours.

## Nature of employer

By far the largest share of people working in the cultural sector work in the private sector (in other words, in commercial organisations as opposed

---

7   The LFS does not ask a question about temporary working of the self-employed.

to those run by local or central government or in the voluntary sector). Most of the remainder work for central or local government. Overall, 68 per cent work in the private sector, 25 per cent work in the public sector and six per cent work in the voluntary or "other" sectors.

The incidence of private-sector employment is highest in films (96 per cent) and visual, literary and performing arts (85 per cent) and lowest in museums, libraries and archives (34 per cent). Almost all (94 per cent) of those employed in the latter cultural industry work for central or local government. One in five of those working in the visual, literary and performing arts are in the voluntary sector.

Nearly half (45 per cent) of people working in the private sector are self-employed, and one in five of those working in the public sector are on a temporary contract.

Workplaces in the cultural sector tend to be small – a product, in part, of the high level of self-employment involving people working on their own. The proportion of people with main jobs in workplaces varies, such that: 28 per cent are self-employed and work on their own; 28 per cent work in workplaces with fewer than 25 employees; 43 per cent work in workplaces with more than 25 employees. In the overall economy the equivalent shares are, respectively, 10 per cent, 32 per cent and 57 per cent.

Larger workplaces (25 or more employees) were more prevalent in radio and TV (73 per cent) and publishing (63 per cent), but nearly two-thirds (62 per cent) of people in the visual, literary and performing arts industry were self-employed and worked on their own, while 48 per cent of people working in museums, libraries and archives were in workplaces with under 25 employees.

## Employment stability

Given the prominence of temporary jobs and self-employment in the cultural sector, it might have been expected that the employment patterns of people in it would be relatively unstable. However, this was not the case. Three out of four (74 per cent) people with main jobs in the sector were working for the same organisation and in the same occupation in 1994 as they were in 1993. The difference between those who were employees and those who were self-employed was minimal. Moreover, while nearly one in five had been in their present job less than a year, nearly a third had been in it for ten or more years (Table 3.5).

The longest job tenures were found in the museums, libraries and archives, and the visual, literary and performing arts sectors – where over one third (35 per cent and 41 per cent respectively) had job tenures in excess of ten years. The shortest tenures were in films – where under a quarter (23 per cent) had such tenures.

*Table 3.5 Length of time spent in same job in the cultural sector*

|  | Percentages |
|---|---|
| Less than 1 year | 18 |
| Between 1 and 5 years; | 32 |
| Between 5 and 10 years | 19 |
| 10 years or more | 32 |
| All | 100 |

Source: Labour Force Survey, spring 1994.

Switches in status between self-employment and dependent employment necessarily occur in the sector, but to a lesser extent than might be imagined. Thus, of people who were employees in 1994, 86 per cent were employees one year previously and only two per cent had been self-employed (the remaining 12 per cent had not been working). Equally, of those who were employees in 1993, 97 per cent were employees one year later and only 3 per cent had become self-employed. Turning the point of examination around, of those who were self-employed in 1994, 77 per cent had been self-employed one year previously and only five per cent had been employees. Of those who were self-employed in 1993, 95 per cent were self-employed one year later and only five per cent had become employees.

People coming into self-employment were more likely to have been unemployed or inactive than those coming from dependent employment. One in eight (12 per cent) of those who were currently self-employed had not been working one year previously, compared to one in ten (9 per cent) of dependent employees.

## Unemployment

In spring 1994, there were nearly 63,000 people whose last job had been in the cultural sector (in either a cultural industry or a cultural occupation) and who were, at that time, unemployed. This gives an unemployment rate for the sector of some 11 per cent[8]. The whole economy unemployment rate in spring 1994 was rather lower, at 9.5 per cent.

Stark differences in unemployment are apparent across different cultural industries (Table 3.6). In addition to the 63,000 people who were unemployed, there were a further 29,000 people from the sector who did want to work, but were either currently unavailable or not currently

8   The unemployment rate is calculated by dividing the number of people unemployed according to the ILO definition – actively seeking work and available for work – and having had their last job in a cultural industry or occupation by the number of people unemployed from the sector plus the number of people working (either as employees or self-employed) in the sector.

*Table 3.6 Rates of unemployment in the cultural sector*

|  | Percentages |
|---|---|
| Publishing | 3 |
| Radio and TV | 12 |
| Films, visual, literary and performing arts | 13 |
| Actors, entertainers, stage managers, producers and directors | 23 |

Source: Labour Force Survey, spring 1994.

seeking work. On this basis, the jobless rate rises to 16 per cent. In both cases, the share of people without work is rather higher than for the economy as a whole.

Unemployment durations among people who had lost their jobs from the sector (or whose self-employment jobs had come to an end) could be quite long. Among all who wanted to work, whether or not they were to be counted as "unemployed", four in ten (42 per cent) had been without a job for less than a year. However, an identical percentage had been without a job for more than two years.

Quarterly data of claimant unemployment showed that, among actors and entertainers, unemployment was highest at the very beginning of the year and declined thereafter, to be at its lowest in the summer. This pattern might reflect the labour market consequences of, first, the end of the pantomime season and, second, the start of the summer season.

# Earnings and income

The earnings of employees are the usual measure of how well people are performing in the labour market. As noted above, a disproportionate share of people working in the cultural sector do so on a self-employed basis. Although some surveys of the earnings of artists in particular areas of the cultural sector do exist (see, for example, Towse, 1993; Knott, 1994; and SAC, 1995), specific data on the income of the self-employed, regardless of their occupation or industry, are particularly hard to obtain[9].

The most important series of data on employees is the *New Earnings Survey*, conducted in April each year. It produces detailed information about full-time adult workers and, where sample numbers permit it, about part-time women workers. The sampling fraction of the *New Earnings Survey*, however, is such that by no means all cultural occupations or indus-

---

9   Broad, but not necessarily accurate, aggregates are available from the General Household Survey and the Family Expenditure Survey, but sample sizes are far too small to permit analysis by occupation. Even the data published by the Inland Revenue refer only to very broad "industrial groups".

tries can be identified. Even where they are, they are identified in rather broader terms than is the case with the LFS. Categories yielding a large enough sample for results to be published include five occupations (entertainment and sports managers; librarians and archivists, including curators; authors and journalists; artists and graphic designers; and actors, entertainers and producers) and three industries (publishing of books and newspapers; radio and TV; and libraries and museums).

The picture which this presents is of relatively high pay, at least among people in cultural occupations. In general, earnings are at, or above, the average for all employees and the average for all white-collar (non-manual) workers. This is most notable in the case of authors and journalists, although it is questionable to what extent this is a result of the high earnings of journalists rather than of authors (most of whom are likely to be self-employed). Faring best of all are actors and entertainers, whose earnings are two-thirds higher than the average for all employees. This last group also has a rather wider dispersion of earnings than does other identified groups, so that those in the top 10 per cent of earners (the top decile) earn, on average, nearly four times as much as those in the bottom 10 per cent (the bottom decile). Quite the opposite is the case for archivists, curators and librarians: the highest-earning 10 per cent earn only just over twice the earnings of the lowest-earning 10 per cent, suggesting a much more even distribution of income.

All the occupations for which earnings can be identified are white-collar occupations and occupations with a relatively high status. In this respect, the findings concerning average earnings are not surprising. One of the identified industries, radio and TV, also has rather high earnings – more than 50 per cent higher than the average in the workforce as a whole (Table 3.7). Analysis of the *New Earnings Survey* by cultural industry also shows that earnings in the libraries and museums sector are much lower than elsewhere. They are also much more narrowly distributed than elsewhere. Relative to the other two industries, the libraries and museums sector employs a considerable number of blue-collar (manual) workers, and it is this which contributes to its below-average pay levels. The *New Earnings Survey* shows that male blue-collar workers in the sector earn only two-thirds (65 per cent) of the average for all workers. The libraries and museums sector also has a disproportionate number of women among the white-collar labour force, and these women earn only four-fifths (79 per cent) of the average for all employees. Moreover, given that libraries and museums are largely in the public sector, this might further contribute to the relatively low earnings in the cultural sector recorded in the *New Earnings Survey*.

Earnings data presented so far relate to people who are employees. Data on the income of those who operate on a self-employed basis are

*Table 3.7 Gross weekly earnings of employees in the cultural sector*

| | Both sexes (£s) | As a percentage of all occupations | Bottom decile (£s) | Top decile (£s) | Top decile + bottom decile (ratio) |
|---|---|---|---|---|---|
| **Occupations (SOC)** | | | | | |
| Entertainment and sports managers (176) | 324 | 96 | 191.9 | 576 | 3.0 |
| Authors, journalists, etc (380) | 466 | 139 | 208.2 | 747 | 3.6 |
| Artists, graphic designers, etc (381) | 366 | 109 | 246.2 | 799 | 3.2 |
| Actors, entertainers, etc (384) | 570 | 169 | 245.8 | 924 | 3.8 |
| | | | | | |
| All white–collar occupations | 372 | 110 | 172.7 | 605 | 3.5 |
| All occupations | 336 | 100 | 160.0 | 543 | 3.4 |
| | | | | | |
| **Industries (SIC 92)** | | | | | |
| Publishing (221) | 400 | 119 | 188.0 | 672 | 3.6 |
| Radio and TV (925) | 532 | 158 | 251.7 | 836 | 3.3 |
| Libraries, museums, etc (926) | 279 | 83 | 172.0 | 416 | 2.4 |

Source: New Earnings Survey 1995, Vol A. London: HMSO.
SIC: Standard Industrial Classification. SOC: Standard Occupational Classification.

available only on an ad hoc basis. A number of surveys of particular sub-groups of cultural-sector workers, sometimes confined to particular sectors, have been made, some of which have been described by Towse (1996)[10]. The persistent finding is that the incomes of artists (broadly defined) are lower than for all adult workers or all white-collar workers.

For example, a survey of 1,700 craftspeople carried out in 1992 found that those working full-time earned, on average, under £10,000 if they were men and under £7,000 if they were women. The majority of crafts-people, consequently, relied on income from other sources to supplement their craft production. Some taught, some relied on private incomes such as pensions, investments or savings. Over one third of full-time craftspeo-ple relied on support from others – partners and other family members (Knott, 1994). Similarly, a much smaller survey of visual artists in 1994 found that nearly 30 per cent derived no income from their visual arts activities. The majority earned up to £5,000 from their visual arts activi-ties. Like the full-time craftspeople, a substantial proportion of visual artists relied on their partners for financial support and many were at least partially dependent on state benefits (SAC, 1995).

The unemployment rate among people from the cultural sector is, as has been shown, considerably higher than the national average. Unemployment figures for the cultural sector do not, of course, take account of, for example, "resting" actors currently working as bar-staff, or artists who, for want of commissioned work or the ability to sell their sculp-tures, may also work as painters and decorators. Because such people are categorised under their principal occupations (in this case, non-cultural occupations) no data are available on their earnings as actors or artists.

Under some circumstances, people with low earnings can claim top-up social security benefits. Those living in rented property might be able to claim housing benefit; those with children might be able to claim family credit. Social security statistics show that there were just over 4,000 fami-lies (of which a third were headed by lone parents) where the main earner was in a literary, artistic or sports occupation and which were in receipt of family credit in October 1994 (*Social Security Statistics, 1995*). Also, those who are unemployed might be entitled to social security benefits. If they have been in dependent employment and have satisfied contribution requirements (the equivalent of a full year's contributions in the last completed tax year), they can draw unemployment benefit for 12 months. If they do not, because their contributions are insufficient – and this is quite likely for people who have only short and irregular engagements – or if they have been working on a self-employed basis, they are entitled only to means-tested income support. Theoretically, it is possible for

---

10   The forthcoming National Artists Association's report on the status and conditions of visual artists in the 1990s promises to be the first comprehensive national survey of visual artists' earnings.

certain people to continue their "occupation" while being in receipt of benefits – for example, artists may occupy their enforced leisure by continuing to paint and still be "available for work" as required by the social security or employment authorities[11].

# Volunteers

As well as making use of paid staff, organisations in the cultural sector also rely on the contribution of people working as volunteers. Voluntary labour enables the staffing-up of everyday activities, the bringing in of special skills and the undertaking of exceptional activities, as well as providing general oversight and direction through membership of management committees and boards of trustees. Unfortunately, other than broad aggregates for some types of voluntary work in this sector, very little is known about the extent of voluntary activity in the UK, and few individual organisations provide details in their own reports. As noted above in this chapter, this section therefore draws largely upon one-off studies.

## Use of volunteers

A number of studies point to the importance of volunteering in the cultural sector. For example, one recent survey of the characteristics of the workforce in the museum, gallery and heritage sectors found that volunteers made up 16 per cent of the workforce in local-authority-funded establishments and 47 per cent of the workforce in establishments which were not funded by local authorities. The researchers estimated that, in total, between 25,000 and 30,000 volunteers worked in museums and related organisations in the UK (Scott et al, 1993).

Similarly, a study by PSI estimated that there were 29,000 volunteers working in arts centres, museums and heritage sites (Hutchison and Feist, 1991). Of these, it was estimated that nearly half (13,600) worked at heritage sites, just under 40 per cent (11,400) worked in museums and the remaining 13 per cent (3,700) worked in arts centres.

Eighty per cent of arts centres utilised volunteer labour compared to 41 per cent of museums and 32 per cent of heritage sites. It appeared as if nearly a quarter of independent museums and one in ten arts centres functioned with no paid staff at all. However, in most cases the size of the input made by individual volunteers was small. Over 80 per cent of volun-

---

11   Thus, it is not surprising to find that over half of the visual artists in one survey had been registered as unemployed for an average of 18 months at some point in the last five years (SAC, 1995).

teers in arts centres contributed fewer than five hours per week, while only two per cent contributed more than 20 hours per week.

There is also some evidence that the number of volunteers in the cultural sector is increasing. For example, surveys by British Tourist Authority/EnglishTourist Board (BTA/ETB) found that the number of volunteers in historic properties had risen from 19,000 in 1991 to 20,600 in 1994, and that the number in museums and galleries had risen from 12,500 to 17,200 in the same period (BTA/ETB, 1991; 1995).

A PSI survey of arts festivals in the UK confirms the importance of voluntary labour in the arts and cultural sector. It found that 38 per cent of arts festivals were run entirely by volunteers (Rolfe, 1992). Some 350 festivals were surveyed, and while over half used fewer than 10 volunteers for the duration of the festival, one in twenty employed more than 100. Similarly, while a quarter of festivals used no volunteers in the whole year and half used fewer than five, a quarter used six or more.

Information about volunteer labour in the visual, literary and performing arts and in radio and television is contained in a study commissioned by the ACE (Martin, 1994). It found that in 1994 some 65 per cent of units used volunteers, and those doing so had between two and three volunteers for every paid member of staff. However, over half of those who used volunteers estimated that these met less than 10 per cent of their staffing requirements. Grossing up from this survey is difficult, but based upon the employment information given in the study, and assuming that non-responders were similar to responders, the annual input of volunteers to the sector could be as much as 5 million hours.

## Size of the input

The National Trust (NT), which contributes to the upkeep and display of the built-heritage sector is recognised as one of the organisations in the cultural sector which makes the heaviest use of volunteers. According to the NT's annual report, in 1993 nearly 28,000 people contributed just over 1.6 million unpaid hours to its work and accounted for about one sixth of its total labour input (NT, 1994). However, it is likely that this estimate of the size of the volunteer workforce includes individuals who are working outside what this study defines as the cultural sector (for example, in nature conservation). Using the BTA/ETB's estimates (see above) of the number of volunteers, but the NT's estimates of the hours worked per volunteer (just over 57 hours per year), it can be assumed that volunteers contributed 1.1 million hours of the total labour input in the historic-properties sector (as noted in Chapter 2).

If it is assumed that the amount of time the average volunteer contributes is approximately the same across all cultural activities, it is also

*Table 3.8 Hours worked by volunteers in the cultural sector, converted into full-time equivalents*

| | Number of volunteers | Hours worked per year (millions) | Full-time equivalents | Number of employees (fte) |
|---|---|---|---|---|
| Living arts and media | .. | 5.0 | 3,000 | 25,000 (SIC 92.32–3) |
| Museums and galleries | 16,000 | 0.9 | 600 | 28,400 (SIC 92.51) |
| Historic properties | 20,000 | 1.1 | 700 | |
| Total | | 7.0 | 4,300 | 53,400 |

Sources: information about volunteers cited in text; LFS (employees, not self-employed, full time equivalents (fte) calculated by counting each part-timer as half a full-timer).
(a) According to the ad hoc research quoted in the text.

55

possible to estimate the contribution of volunteer labour in museums and galleries. Here, the total input is just under one million hours per year. The hours worked by volunteers can be converted into "full-time equivalents", as shown in Table 3.8.

In the sectors which do make use of them, and taking account of part-time working by regular employees, volunteers might contribute 7 million hours, or 4,300 full-time-equivalent jobs, the equivalent of a further eight per cent to the paid labour input.

## Summary and conclusions

Even narrowly defined, the cultural sector is not insignificant as an employer. It accounts for nearly two per cent of the labour force and is, thus, as large as retail banking and twice as large as motor manufacturing.

In some respects, the cultural sector is like others: it is not dominated by one sex rather than the other, and it uses full-timers and part-timers much as do other sectors. However, in other respects the cultural sector is very different: it is heavily concentrated in London; it engages a much higher share of highly qualified people than do most other sectors; and a disproportionate number of those working in it work on a self-employed or a temporary basis, and in this sense the incidence of "flexible" or "precarious" employment is high.

That "precarious" is an apposite description of employment in the sector is indicated by the high level of joblessness among some cultural-sector workers. Not only is the unemployment rate for the cultural sector higher than the national rate, but for every two unemployed persons from the sector there is another person who had worked in the sector, who is without a job and wants to work.

Because of the high level of self-employment in the sector, it is difficult to obtain a satisfactory picture of earnings and income from work. There are, however, indications of a wider-than-average dispersion in earnings among employees in some occupations. In so far as unemployment levels for some occupations are high, it cannot be presumed that living standards are always high. Indeed, a considerable number of people from the sector are likely to be living on benefit and a considerable number have to take up non-cultural occupations to support themselves.

However, certain parts of the sector offer sufficient non-pecuniary rewards for a considerable number of people to give their services free of charge. The living arts, museums and historic properties attract a considerable number of volunteers who make a substantial contribution to their operation.

Lastly, the sector should not be regarded as homogeneous. Especially with respect to qualifications and the nature of employment forms, there are considerable differences between different parts of the cultural sector, so that the librarians and curators are, on the whole, highly qualified, and the visual, literary and performing arts sectors display a high incidence of "flexibility" or "precariousness".

# Chapter 4
## Audiences

The audience for cultural activities ranges from those attending events and activities outside the home, to those for predominantly home-based cultural products. It embraces those who attend museums, galleries, theatres, cinema and heritage sites as well as those who read books, listen to the radio and watch television and video. In all of these activities, the distinction between culture and entertainment is blurred – in some cases more than others. However, all provide a source of access to cultural events and activities and each, therefore, contributes to the audience as a whole.

This chapter examines what might be termed the market for both the funded sector and the wider, commercial context in which the former sector also operates. It considers the number of attendances at cultural events and audiences' spending on cultural events and activities. It also examines audience profiles by social group, age, gender and region. It draws together already published data from a variety of sources to create an overview of this market as a whole.

## Attendances

The reliability of information about attendances at cultural events and activities is variable. However, since the second half of the 1980s, the government has encouraged funded organisations to increase access and increase their visitor numbers, and to operate more efficiently. The increasing numbers of museums and galleries charging admission has contributed to the more widespread and accurate reporting of visitor numbers. More recently, attention has been paid to the nature and number of those participating in the arts, as opposed to attending the arts – through amateur activities, volunteering and community involvement (DNH, 1996).

In 1993/94, there were at least 325 million attendances at cultural events and activities (Table 4.1)[1]. Over a third of these were accounted for by cinema visits (113 million). The average person visited the cinema twice a year, with nearly 70 per cent of the population claiming to be cinemagoers (CAA, 1994). Heritage sites attracted 95 million visits and museums, galleries and exhibitions a further 90 million visits, each of these two categories accounting for just under 30 per cent each of total visits[2].

*Table 4.1 Total number of attendances at cultural activities, 1993–94*

|  | *Millions* | *Percentages* |
|---|---|---|
| Cinema | 113 | 34.8 |
| Heritage properties and sites | 95 | 29.2 |
| Museums, galleries and exhibitions | 90 | 27.7 |
| Performing arts (a) | 23 | 8.3 |
| Total (b) | 321 | 100.0 |

Sources: CAA (1994); BTA/ETB (1994b); MGC (1994); SOLT data compiled by Caroline Gardiner, City University; TMA data compiled by Michael Quine, City University.
(a) SOLT and TMA members only.
(b) Not including 0.5 million readers at the three National libraries.

There are no reliable data on attendances at performing arts events: the figure of 23 million in Table 4.1 represents only paid attendances at SOLT and TMA member theatres in 1993 and fails to record attendance at non-member venues[3]. As another measure of attendances at performing arts

1 This includes both the commercial and the supported sectors. Such data do not allow calculations to be made on the level of support per attendance, or other measures of the importance of support. However, such calculations can be made for individual recipients of support: for example, it has been estimated that every paid attendance at the Royal Opera, Covent Garden in 1993/94 was supported by £36 of public funds (*Cultural Trends 22*).
2 Allowance should be made for the estimated nature of these figures. In particular, where museums and galleries allow free admission, audience data are not necessarily accurate.
3 There are two main sources of box-office data for theatres in the UK: the Society of London Theatre Management (SOLT) and the Theatrical Management Association (TMA). For 1993/94, box-office statistics were produced on behalf of both SOLT and TMA by the City University in London. The SOLT survey details activity in some 50 London member theatres, and analyses box office and audience statistics by type of production. TMA produces an equivalent report for regional theatres and a number of performing arts companies. It has a membership of around 250 to 300, which varies slightly from year to year. On average, its membership consists of approximately 100 each of subsidised repertory companies and commercial theatres or touring companies. In addition, members include around 10 to 12 opera or ballet companies, 60 resident manager members (which are receiving houses only, with no in-house productions) and a number of individual and associate business members. The memberships of SOLT and TMA are mutually exclusive, so there is no overlap in the statistics that they produce.

*Table 4.2 People attending performing arts events, 1993/94*

|  | Millions | Percentage of GB adult population |
|---|---|---|
| Plays | 10.8 | 23.8 |
| Classical music | 5.5 | 12.2 |
| Ballet | 3.1 | 6.8 |
| Opera | 3.0 | 6.6 |
| Jazz | 2.8 | 6.2 |
| Contemporary dance | 1.6 | 3.4 |

Source: ACGB (1994).

events, Table 4.2, drawn from the Target Group Index (TGI), provides an estimate of the number of people who claim to attend arts events "nowadays", as opposed to the total number recorded as attending. For 1993/94, TGI data suggest that plays were the most popular type of performing arts events, attracting 11 million people to attend (just under a quarter of the adult population). Opera, jazz and ballet were all equally popular, each being attended by around 3 million people.

The figures in Table 4.2 cannot be added up to give a total number of attendances as they represent overlapping populations: for example, some of the 11 million who said they attended plays may also be part of the 3 million people who claimed to visit the opera. These figures give an indication of the relative popularity of different types of event rather than a total number of attendances, comparable to the data in Table 4.1.

## Consumer and family expenditure

Total consumer expenditure on cultural events and activities is examined in detail in the individual chapters of Part II. Table 4.3 below considers spending on a range of activities including books, recorded music and videos, and identifies at least £5bn consumer expenditure. Books attracted the highest level of consumer spending, at £1.7bn (a third of total expenditure shown). This included expenditure on a wide range of books, from fiction to technical and academic texts. A further £1.4bn was spent on recorded music, and just over £1bn on renting and buying video tapes. In 1993, 73 per cent of the population had access to a video recorder at home (*Social Trends 25*). Theatre box-office figures are again underestimated, with the £330m in Table 4.3 representing only the box office revenues of SOLT and TMA members in 1993/94. However, it is worth noting that even this limited figure is higher than the total cinema box office takings of £320m[4]. Although both heritage sites and museums had high levels of

---

4   However, it should be remembered that the level of expenditure on any one sector depends not only on the number of units or tickets sold, but also on the price charged for each unit or ticket.

*Table 4.3 Total consumer expenditure on cultural activities, 1993–94*

|  | £m | Percentages |
|---|---|---|
| Books | 1,700 | 33.0 |
| Recorded music | 1,400 | 27.1 |
| Video rental and retail | 1,100 | 21.3 |
| Theatre box office (a) | 330 | 6.4 |
| Cinema | 320 | 6.2 |
| Heritage properties and sites | 240 | 4.7 |
| Museums (b) | 67 | 1.3 |
| Total | 5,157 | 100.0 |

Source: LISU (1995); BPI (1994); BVA (1995); SOLT data compiled by Caroline
Gardiner, City University; TMA data compiled by Michael Quine, City University; CAA
(1994); BTA/ETB (1994b); MGC Domus database
(a) SOLT and TMA members only.
(b) MGC registered museums only.

*Table 4.4 Family expenditure on the cultural sector*

|  | Average weekly spend, £.p |
|---|---|
| Television, video and audio equipment (a) | 4.34 |
| Books, newspapers, magazines and periodicals | 4.10 |
| Cinema admissions | 0.25 |
| Theatres, sports events and other entertainments (b) | 3.68 |
| Television and video rental and TV licences | 2.61 |
| Total | 14.98 |

Source: Family Expenditure Survey (1994).
(a) Including repairs but excluding rental.
(b) Excluding gambling.

attendance, many of these were free, accounting for their lower level of
consumer expenditure in Table 4.3.

Household expenditure on a number of areas within the cultural
sector can also be identified: in 1993, some £15 per week was spent on the
cultural sector (Table 4.4)[5].

# Audience profiles

For the purposes of profiling audiences, the population can be considered in terms of four broad social groups:

5   Some of these categories represent an overestimate of the cultural sector as defined
in this study. For example, newspapers, magazines and periodicals, which lie outside the
remit of this sector, are compounded with data for books. Equally, data for theatres, etc,
could not be disaggregated from those for sports and other entertainments.

- AB: higher and intermediate managerial, administrative or professional;
- C1: supervisory or clerical and junior managerial, administrative or professional;
- C2: skilled workers;
- DE: Semi-skilled and unskilled workers, state pensioners or widows, casual or lowest grade workers, or long-term unemployed.

Table 4.5 shows the percentage of each of these groups attending a selection of cultural activities away from the home. It also shows the percentage of the population as a whole who attended these events. In all categories but one (rock and pop concerts), a higher percentage of ABs attended these events than the other social groups. Moreover, the percentage attending decreased with each social group, so that the lowest percentage in all groups was recorded for band DE.

*Table 4.5 Participation in cultural activities outside the home, by social group, 1993/94*

|  | Percentage of each group | | | | |
|  | AB | C1 | C2 | DE | All |
|---|---|---|---|---|---|
| Visit to: | | | | | |
| Cinema | 46 | 39 | 29 | 24 | 33 |
| Historic building | 41 | 29 | 19 | 12 | 23 |
| Theatre | 33 | 24 | 16 | 10 | 19 |
| Museum or gallery | 34 | 23 | 14 | 10 | 19 |
| Exhibition (a) | 24 | 17 | 10 | 8 | 14 |
| Rock or pop concert | 8 | 9 | 8 | 6 | 8 |
| Classical concert or opera | 15 | 9 | 3 | 3 | 7 |

Source: *Social Trends 25.*
(a) May include activities outside the cultural sector, such as trade exhibitions.

The most popular activity for all groups, and for the population as whole, was visiting the cinema. Just under half of all ABs and nearly 40 per cent of C1s claimed to go to the cinema, compared to a national average of 33 per cent. This activity was least popular with DEs, with just under a quarter of this group being cinema-goers.

Historic buildings were markedly more popular with ABs than the other groups, with 41 per cent of this group visiting such attractions (nearly double the national average of 23 per cent). ABs were also five times more likely than DEs to go to classical concerts or the opera, with 15 per cent of this former group attending, compared to 3 per cent of DEs.

The profile of audiences for home-based cultural activities (Table 4.6)

*Table 4.6 Participation in cultural activities in the home, by social group,*
*1993/94*

| | Hours per week | | | | |
|---|---|---|---|---|---|
| | AB | C1 | C2 | DE | All |
| Watch television | 13.5 | 15.4 | 17.5 | 20.2 | 17.1 |
| Listen to the radio | 9.2 | 8.7 | 11.6 | 10.9 | 10.3 |
| Listen to music | 4.3 | 4.0 | 3.4 | 4.4 | 4.0 |
| Read books | 5.1 | 4.3 | 3.2 | 3.4 | 3.8 |

Source: *Social Trends 25.*

contrasts with activities outside the home described in Table 4.5. In 1993 almost all homes in the UK owned a television and most of the population had access to a radio during the day, be it in the home, workplace or car (*Social Trends 25*). Satellite television services were accessible to 12 per cent of the population with a further 3 per cent using cable television services[6]. On average the UK television viewer watched 3.7 hours of television per day in 1993 (ITC, 1994). Approximately 88 per cent of the population listened to some radio each week, for an average of 18 hours per week a head (AIRC, 1994).

The most marked difference in the profile of audiences for home-based cultural activities was in television watching. ABs spent 14 hours a week watching television and DEs, 20 hours – as compared with a national average of 17 hour per week. Radio listening was most popular among C2s, with this group listening for an average of 12 hours per week, two hours more than the national average. Both ABs and C1s listened for fewer hours than the national average, at around 9 hours per week each. Most groups spent around four hours per week listening to recorded music, except for C2s, at three hours per week. Reading books was most popular among ABs, at five hours per week, and least popular among C2s, at three hours per week. The national average was just under 4 hours per week.

Tables 4.7 to 4.10 show the share of the audience for selected cultural activities, according to age group. The data for the cinema come from a different source to that in Table 4.5, and indicate that nearly 70 per cent of the population went to the cinema at least once in 1993 (compared to 33 per cent according to Table 4.5)[7]. According to Table 4.7, those under the age of 15 were the most likely to be cinema attenders, with 93 per cent of this age group ever going to the cinema. This decreased over the age groups, to 53 per cent of those aged 35 and over. Dance, drama and opera

---

6 Although there may be some overlap between those with satellite and cable services, this is unlikely to be significant as both services provide much of the same content.
7 The figures for cinema in Table 4.7 come from the CAVIAR (Cinema and Video Industry Audience Research) conducted by the Cinema Advertising Association. Figures in Table 4.5 are derived from the CSO statistical publication, *Social Trends 25.*

*Table 4.7 Percentage of the population participating in selected
cultural activities, by age*

| | | | | Percentage of the population | | | |
|---|---|---|---|---|---|---|---|
| | under 15 | 15 to 24 | 25 to 34 | 35 to 44 (a) | 45 to 54 | 55 to 64 | 65 and over |
| Cinema, 1993 | 93 | 92 | 83 | 53 | – | – | – |
| Drama, dance and opera, 1991 | .. | 40 | 43 | 48 | 49 | 47 | 34 |
| Music, 1991 (b) | .. | 63 | 48 | 40 | 38 | 35 | 21 |

Sources: CAA (1994); RSGB Omnibus Survey 1991.
(a) Aged 35 and over for cinema attenders.
(b) Including classical, rock, pop, jazz, folk and traditional musics.

were more popular with older age groups, with nearly 50 per cent each of those aged 35 to 44, 45 to 54 and 55 to 64 attending such events. Music (including popular and traditional music as well as classical music) was more popular among the younger age groups, with over 60 per cent of those aged 15 to 24 attending these events in 1991, decreasing to 21 per cent of those aged 65 and over, with a national average of 41 per cent.

Data on book buying and video renting/buying in Table 4.8 show the percentages of the audience for these activities, rather than percentages of the population as a whole, as used in Table 4.7. To make the figures in Table 4.8 more meaningful, therefore, it also includes the percentage of the population as a whole that fall into these age groups. As might be expected, few under the age of 15 bought videos (3 per cent, while making up 19 per cent of the population), but significantly more (22 per cent) rented videos. Indeed, renting videos was popular with all the age groups under the age of 54, in each case representing a higher percentage of all video renters than of the population as a whole. Those over the age of 55

*Table 4.8 Profile of those participating in selected cultural activities, by age,
1993–94*

| | | Percentage of participants | | | | |
|---|---|---|---|---|---|---|
| | under 15 | 15 to 24 | 25 to 34 | 35 to 54 | 55 and over (a) | All/ total |
| Buy videos | 3 | 16 | 28 | 19 | 34 | 100 |
| Rent videos | 22 | 20 | 25 | 27 | 6 | 100 |
| *Percentage of GB population* | 19 | 14 | 15 | 26 | 26 | 100 |
| Buy books | .. | 18 | 22 | 32 | 29 | 100 |
| *Percentage of GB population* | .. | 17 | 19 | 32 | 33 | 100 |

Sources: BVA (1995); BML (1994); LISU (1995).
(a) 44 and over for video buyers.

were significantly less likely to be video renters (at 6 per cent of video renters but over a quarter of the population as a whole). By contrast, video tapes were bought by more people aged over 55 than any other age group, at 34 per cent of all video buyers.

Book buying more closely followed the age profile of the population as a whole, although those aged 25 to 34 were marginally more likely to be book buyers, and those aged 55 and over, marginally less likely.

Television audiences show a strong bias to the older age groups for all terrestrial channels, but especially BBC2 (Table 4.9): nearly half of the audience for this channel was aged 55 and over, although this group makes up only a quarter of the population as a whole. By contrast, this age group contributed only 12 per cent of the audience for satellite and cable services, with those aged under 34 accounting for over half of the audience for these channels.

*Table 4.9 Television and radio audiences, by age, 1993 (Percentages)*

|  | under 15 | 15 to 24 | 25 to 34 | 35 to 54 | 55 and over | Total |
|---|---|---|---|---|---|---|
| Television |  |  |  |  |  |  |
| BBC1 | 22 | 15 | 13 | 13 | 37 | 100 |
| BBC2 | 17 | 13 | 13 | 13 | 45 | 100 |
| Channel 3 | 23 | 15 | 13 | 12 | 37 | 100 |
| Channel 4 | 27 | 17 | 14 | 12 | 31 | 100 |
| Satellite and |  |  |  |  |  |  |
| cable channels | 34 | 21 | 19 | 14 | 12 | 100 |
| Radio | 20 | 23 | 19 | 15 | 24 | 100 |
| *Percentage of GB* |  |  |  |  |  |  |
| *population* | *33* | *15* | *14* | *11* | *26* | *100* |

Sources: AGB Television Services (1994); AIRC (1994).

Household expenditure on the cultural sector also varied according to age (Table 4.10). The amount spent per week on television, video and audio equipment was highest in households where the head was under the age of 30 (at £5.97 per week). Of all age groups, those aged between 30 and 49 spent the most on cinema admissions, on theatre, sports and other entertainments, and television, video rentals and TV licences (at £0.38, £4.62 and £2.95 per week respectively).

Gender differences in audiences can be seen in a number of performing arts events: in 1993/94 more men than women attended music events (at 45 per cent of men compared with 38 per cent of women), while the reverse was true for drama, dance and opera events (at 37 per cent of men and 48 per cent of women). Other events were more closely matched between the genders (*Social Trends 25*). By comparison, 31 per cent of

*Table 4.10 Family expenditure on the cultural sector, by age of head of household, 1993 (£, p)*

|  | Under 30 | 30 to 49 | 50 to 64 | 65 to 74 | 75 and over |
|---|---|---|---|---|---|
| Television, video and audio equipment (a) | 5.97 | 5.90 | 3.87 | 1.89 | 1.08 |
| Books, newspapers, magazines and periodicals | 3.07 | 4.48 | 4.89 | 3.85 | 2.79 |
| Cinema admissions | 0.36 | 0.38 | 0.24 | 0.04 | 0.02 |
| Theatres, sports events and other entertainments (b) | 3.56 | 4.62 | 3.96 | 3.09 | 0.75 |
| Television and video rental and TV licences | 2.34 | 2.95 | 2.69 | 2.28 | 2.01 |
| Total | 15.3 | 18.33 | 15.65 | 11.15 | 6.65 |

Source: Family Expenditure Survey (1994).
(a) Including repairs but excluding rental.
(b) Excluding gambling.

men and 13 per cent of women (and 22 per cent of the population as a whole) attended spectator sports events in 1994/95.

# Regional trends in audiences

The percentage of those resident in particular areas who attend selected cultural events is shown in Table 4.11. It is reasonable to assume that the majority of the events attended were within local areas. A specialist study on arts festivals, for example, estimated that around two-thirds of audiences were local (BAFA, 1995). Attendance at events may depend on the opportunity to do so and, therefore, the level of provision in that area.

Londoners were more likely to attend performing arts and media events, than were people resident elsewhere in Great Britain. For example, over half of the London population went to the cinema, and over a third went to plays, both of which values were higher than the national average (at 45 per cent and 24 per cent respectively).

At museums, Londoners were no more likely to be attenders than those living in Yorkshire and Humberside, with just over a third of the population in each area claiming to be attenders. Interestingly, those living in Yorkshire and Humberside were the most likely to attend exhibitions and galleries, at 15 per cent of the local population, compared to 11 per cent in London and a national average of 10 per cent.

Wales was under-represented, recording below the national average in

*Table 4.11 Profile of audiences for cultural activities by geographic location, 1991*

| | Plays | Cinema | Orchestral music | Museums | Exhibitions/ galleries | Stately homes |
|---|---|---|---|---|---|---|
| | | *Percentage of the population in each area* | | | | |
| **England** | | | | | | |
| London | 35 | 54 | 15 | 35 | 11 | 29 |
| South East | 26 | 42 | 14 | 35 | 9 | 38 |
| South West | 25 | 40 | 13 | 31 | 13 | 36 |
| East Anglia | 22 | 41 | 11 | 34 | 11 | 34 |
| West Midlands | 21 | 43 | 9 | 24 | 5 | 29 |
| East Midlands | 21 | 42 | 11 | 29 | 6 | 38 |
| North West | 23 | 46 | 11 | 29 | 9 | 34 |
| Yorkshire and Humberside | 21 | 46 | 8 | 35 | 15 | 38 |
| North | 19 | 42 | 9 | 34 | 8 | 34 |
| Wales | 18 | 38 | 6 | 26 | 5 | 25 |
| Scotland | 25 | 48 | 8 | 35 | 11 | 25 |
| All Great Britain | 24 | 45 | 11 | 32 | 10 | 33 |

Source: RSGB Omnibus Survey, 1991.

every category, while Scotland recorded above the national average for plays, the cinema, museums and exhibitions.

While Table 4.11 shows how many people attended such events, it does not indicate the number or level of attendances. For example, while showing that over a third of Londoners went to plays, the table gives no indication as to how often these people went to see plays, and whether frequency of attendance was higher in London than elsewhere in the country. Analysis of SOLT and TMA data shows that around half all attendances in member theatres in 1993 were in London, but not all of this audience was resident in London. For example, around one in three tickets for London theatres are sold to overseas tourists.

Overseas tourists form part of the audience for many cultural events, both in London and around the country, although exactly how much of the audience they comprise is not clear. Many visitors cite cultural events as being important in their decision to visit the UK (Table 4.12). Museums were an important attraction, for 60 per cent of overseas visitors as whole and 45 per cent of those who were specifically visiting London. Historic buildings were of more importance than museums for overseas visitors to London, with more than half citing this as an important attraction to the capital. Interestingly, theatres and concerts were less important to visitors

*Table 4.12 Importance of cultural events to overseas visitors, 1993*

| | Percentages | |
| | 'Very or fairly important' in reason for visiting Britain | 'Of importance in encouraging visitors to London' |
|---|---|---|
| Museums | 60 | 45 |
| Historic buildings | .. | 54 |
| Churches and cathedrals | .. | 41 |
| Art galleries | 35 | 28 |
| Theatres | 35 | 23 |
| Concerts | 20 | 14 |
| Festivals | 20 | .. |
| Ballet and opera | 12 | .. |

Sources: Overseas Passenger Survey; Survey of Overseas Visitors to London.

to London (at between 23 and 14 per cent) than to overseas visitors as a whole (each of which being important to over a third of overseas visitors to the UK).

There were also some regional variations in family expenditure on the cultural sector (Table 4.13). In 1993, the highest average weekly spend on television, video and audio equipment was in London (at £5.55), but the average in Scotland was higher than that for all of England (at £5.25 and £4.35 respectively). The same was true for books, newspapers and magazines, with households in Scotland spending an average of £4.40 a week on these items, compared with £4.12 in England.

Regionally, the amount spent on cinema admissions, theatres and other events will vary, not only according to the number of admissions, but also by the ticket price, which will be lower in some areas than in others. The data in the table, therefore, for these categories of activity, are not a direct reflection of the popularity or otherwise of these elements of the cultural sector.

# Summary

Although data on audiences are often partial and come from diverse sources, some conclusions can be drawn. Heritage sites and museums, galleries and exhibitions attract nearly as many people as the cinema. Identifiable consumer expenditure was highest on home-based cultural products, such as books, recorded music and videos, while at least the same amount was spent at the theatre box office as on cinema visits.

In general, it can be said that the audience for cultural events outside the home is predominantly from the higher social groups, while that for

### 4.13 Regional distribution of family expenditure on the cultural sector

| | Average weekly spend, £.p | | | | |
| --- | --- | --- | --- | --- | --- |
| | *Television, video and audio equipment (a)* | *Books, newspapers, magazines and periodicals* | *Cinema admissions* | *Theatres, sports events and other entertainments (b)* | *Television and video rental and TV licences* |
| North | 3.91 | 4.17 | 0.21 | 3.07 | 2.30 |
| Yorkshire & Humberside | 4.08 | 4.09 | 0.23 | 3.66 | 2.65 |
| East Midlands | 3.39 | 3.79 | 0.21 | 2.89 | 2.73 |
| East Anglia | 4.70 | 4.01 | 0.15 | 3.28 | 2.64 |
| Greater London | 5.55 | 4.34 | 0.33 | 4.75 | 2.60 |
| Rest of South East | 5.00 | 4.68 | 0.29 | 3.85 | 2.66 |
| South West | 4.35 | 4.36 | 0.20 | 3.38 | 2.40 |
| West Midlands | 3.03 | 3.27 | 0.25 | 2.78 | 2.67 |
| North West | 4.09 | 3.57 | 0.27 | 3.52 | 2.83 |
| All England | 4.35 | 4.12 | 0.25 | 3.58 | 2.63 |
| Scotland | 5.25 | 4.40 | 0.24 | 5.31 | 2.54 |
| Wales | 3.36 | 3.51 | 0.17 | 2.82 | 2.57 |
| Northern Ireland | 2.07 | 3.55 | 0.11 | 2.61 | 2.11 |
| All UK | 4.34 | 4.10 | 0.24 | 3.68 | 2.61 |

Source: Family Expenditure Survey (1994).
(a) Including repairs but excluding rental.
(b) Excluding gambling.

cultural activities taking place within the home tends to be (but not so markedly) from the lower social groups. The profile of the audience by age varies according to the particular activity and while the younger age groups are better represented in some sectors (such as the cinema), older age groups are better represented in others (such as television viewing). There is a tendency for more women than men to attend certain performing arts events, such as dance and drama, while audiences for musical events tend to be more predominantly male.

Regionally, a percentage of Londoners greater than the national average attend the performing arts, while audiences for museums and the visual arts tend to be more evenly spread geographically. Audiences are also partly made up of overseas visitors, who cite cultural events as an important aspect of their visit to the UK.

# Part II
# Cultural activities

# Chapter 5

# The performing arts

This chapter covers the performing arts, and deals with a wide range of activities, including drama, dance, mime, music and opera. Combined arts, including arts festivals, which might also include elements of the performing arts, are dealt with separately in Chapter 6[1].

Traditionally, the arts-funding bodies, such as the arts councils, have treated these areas of the performing arts as separate categories, and this is reflected in the statistical information they produce. However, the distinctions between these categories of performing arts are not always clear-cut, and other sources of data do not always follow them. For example, performances might combine music, drama and dance. Even in the more traditional of the performing arts, such as ballet, both dance and music are involved.

In general, this chapter examines the performing arts as a whole, and analysis by activity (or groupings of activities) is made only where appropriate. The areas of overlap that exist within activities may make some of the divisions used within these statistics appear rather arbitrary, if not illogical. For example, a ballet or opera company may have a resident orchestra, the activities of which will be represented under dance or opera rather than music. Similarly, performing arts venues will be relevant to all these activities.

Where these categories are considered separately, it is assumed that

---

1   Where an arts festival is dedicated to only one cultural activity, funding for it may appear under the relevant activity. In other cases, festivals and combined arts are accounted for separately.

within each there is a core of activity which is dedicated solely or primarily to that type of activity. To take the example of the ballet company again, it is likely that the operation of the orchestra is understood as being part of the operation of the ballet company. As the orchestra exists solely because of the ballet company, it is reasonable to include funding for this orchestra within the overall support for dance.

This chapter contains the following sections:

- the wider context – commercial activity, and employment in the performing arts;
- sources and nature of support for the performing arts, including business sponsorship and charitable donations;
- the regional dimension – geographical distribution of audiences, venues and companies, employment and funding;
- survey results.

## The wider context

As is the case for many areas of the cultural sector, the supported aspect of the performing arts is contained within, rather than separate from, commercial activity. For example, supported companies may tour to commercial theatres and venues. Supported venues may act as receiving houses for wholly commercial productions. Freelance performers and technicians may work in both sectors. There may be some parts of the supported sector that have no relationship at all with the commercial sector, either financially or professionally, but these will be relatively few and far between.

Some of those who are trained and gain experience in the public sector go on to have commercial successes in other forms of the performing arts: one only need think of the actors who have started their careers in the Royal Shakespeare Company (RSC) or the Royal National Theatre and who have gone on to have successful careers, not only in the commercial theatre, but also in television and on film. This also applies to less high-profile workers in the performing arts, such as technicians and stage designers.

There have also been occasions where productions developed by publicly funded companies have made successful transfers to the commercial market: the RSC's production of *Les Miserables*, which transferred to the West End in 1985 and continues to run more than a decade later, is one obvious example.

However, while the supported sector of this activity is largely identifiable and measurable, the same is not true of the wider commercial sector. Companies and organisations that are wholly commercial have very different obligations with respect to the disclosure of financial information, even when they can be identified. Moreover, it becomes increasingly difficult to identify precisely those areas of activity that relate solely to the performing arts rather than other activities. For example, a large company which owns cinemas, hotels and leisure centres, may employ musicians, dancers and actors on a regular basis, but as a separate activity this would be almost impossible to quantify.

There is also scant information in this wider sector on who attends and participates in the performing arts, how much provision there is in terms of venues and performances, and what the regional distribution of these activities is.

There are, however, certain areas of the wider context that are more clearly defined as dedicated to the performing arts and for which reliable statistical information exists. Statistics on drama, dance and opera are available from the box-office records of theatres and other venues. Data on the music industry, and to a lesser extent, live performed music, are available both from industry sources and from arts funders.

## Drama, dance and music: venues, companies and earnings

It is estimated that there are around 300 professional theatres in the UK (Table 5.1). Some are privately owned, but the majority are owned either by local authorities or by non-profit-making organisations. Most, however, are commercially run and self-financing. Over 40 of these venues have resident theatre companies that are supported by various arts funding bodies.

*Table 5.1 Performing arts venues and companies: selected statistics*

|  | London | Great Britain (a) |
| --- | --- | --- |
| Theatres: all types | 205 | .. |
| Theatres: professional only | 83 | 300 |
| Dance companies | 125 | 220 |
| Musicians (b) | 14,676 | 34,000 |
| Major orchestras | 5 | 17 |

Sources: LAB (1996); Central Office of Information (1995).
(a) Including London.
(b) Members of the Musicians' Union.

To these professional theatres can be added approximately 200 arts centres, where performing arts events may be staged, dedicated concert halls, open air-theatres, and a variety of other buildings such as pubs and village and community centres.

Counting professional theatres only, there are some 83 in London. However, the London Arts Board (LAB) estimates that, if all the other types of theatre venue are counted, there are over 200 such venues in London alone (LAB, 1994). Allowing for some concentration of venues in the capital, this gives some indication of the number of venues there may be across the UK.

There are estimated to be between 200 and 220 professional dance companies in the UK, along with 17 professional orchestras. There is a concentration of this activity in London (as shown in Table 5.1), but the distribution throughout the rest of the UK is not known.

Table 5.2 shows summary information on box-office takings and attendances in UK theatres for 1993 drawn from TMA and SOLT data (see Chapter 4). It shows that for the members of these two organisations, box-office takings were over £329m, with nearly 23,000 paid admissions. This table shows that different types of productions have different earning capacities. For example, in London, drama took 23 per cent of paid attendances, but 17 per cent of the box office. By comparison, opera, with

*Table 5.2 UK theatres: key statistics, 1993*

|  | Box–office takings (£m) | Attendances (thousands) |
|---|---|---|
| **SOLT** | | |
| Drama | 36.3 | 2,615 |
| Dance | 10.1 | 410 |
| Opera | 21.8 | 660 |
| Musicals | 135.2 | 6,860 |
| Children's | 1.2 | 112 |
| Other | 11.2 | 847 |
| Subtotal | 215.8 | 11,504 |
| **TMA** | | |
| Drama | 33.7 | 3,478 |
| Dance | 10.9 | 848 |
| Opera | 14.1 | 889 |
| Musicals | 23.3 | 1,810 |
| Children's | 19.6 | 2,918 |
| Other | 12.2 | 1,383 |
| Subtotal | 113.8 | 11,326 |
| UK totals | 329.6 | 22,830 |

Source: SOLT, Box Office Data Report 1994 compiled by Dr Caroline Gardiner, City University, Department of Arts Policy and Management; TMA, data compiled by Michael Quine, City University, as above.

higher ticket prices, took 6 per cent of the London audiences, but 10 per cent of the box office.

This is not to say, however, that opera is more profitable than drama. These box-office figures are gross, and do not take into account the relative costs of production. Rather, they represent the level of consumer expenditure on each type of production. Moreover, they represent the minimum total consumer spend at the box office, as they do not include all the performing arts venues in the UK.

Information on the earnings of the music industry is more reliable and detailed than on live performed arts. Like the rest of this sector, the music industry embraces funded organisations as well as entirely commercial ones. Industry earnings from the physical sales of recordings and from copyright royalties can thus be earned by funded orchestras, musicians and composers as well as entirely commercial artists such as pop groups and composers working in, for example, broadcasting or film.

Two-thirds of the total consumer expenditure on recorded music (£1.4bn) in 1993 was spent on CDs (BPI, 1994). However, not all the revenues accruing to artists, composers and record companies comes from the physical sale of records. Copyright licensing brings royalties from the public performances, broadcasting and other uses of music subject to copyright. Such royalties also contribute to the invisible overseas earnings of the music industry[2]. In 1993/94, a total of £254m in royalties earnings was redistributed to copyright holders. Of this total, over half went to composers and songwriters, while a further 40 per cent was earned by record companies for the physical sale of records.

The UK music industry also has overseas earnings, the majority of which are "invisible", including: fees from live performances and broadcasts, recording sessions and other work; royalties accruing to composers, artists, publishers and record companies; and earnings from music education and payments to music agents.

British Invisibles (1994) assessed the real balance of payments attributable to the UK music industry, including these invisible earnings. Apart from the trade in musical instruments, all sectors of the music industry had a positive balance on overseas earnings in 1993. This stood at £571m, of which £490m (nearly 90 per cent of the total) was attributed to invisible earnings (Table 5.3).

---

2   There are two principal forms of copyright involved in music. First, copyright exists in the music itself, that is the words and music of a song or the composition of a composer. This copyright can be exercised when the copyright material is either recorded or performed live. Second, a separate copyright exists when a particular artist makes a recording of his/her performance of the musical work. These royalties are collected by the four collecting societies, Mechanical-Copyright Protection Society (MCPS), Performing Rights Society (PRS), Phonographic Performance Limited (PPL) and Video Performance Limited (VPL).

*Table 5.3 Overseas earnings and payments of the UK music industry, 1993 (£m)*

|  | Estimated gross earnings from overseas | Estimated gross payments | Net earnings |
|---|---|---|---|
| **Invisibles** |  |  |  |
| Recording | 368.1 | 145.6 | 222.5 |
| Music publishing | 246.8 | 106.8 | 140.0 |
| Live performance | 100.9 | 46.4 | 54.5 |
| Miscellaneous | 83.3 | 10.0 | 73.3 |
| Total invisibles | 799.1 | 308.8 | 490.3 |
| **Visibles** |  |  |  |
| Recordings | 260.0 | 158.7 | 101.3 |
| Music publishing | 12.8 | 6.8 | 6.0 |
| Musical instruments | 86.0 | 112.6 | (26.6) |
| Total visibles | 358.8 | 278.1 | 80.7 |
| Total | 1,157.9 | 586.9 | 571.0 |

Source: British Invisibles (1994).

## Employment

There are a number of sources of information on employment in the performing arts. This section compares the data in Chapter 3 with other sources of data specifically on employment in the performing arts. It is not possible to create an aggregate total from the different sources considered because they relate to different years, they use different classifications of activity and some sources relate to actual employment while others rely on self-classification of occupations.

Table 5.4 summarises three sources of data relating to employment in the performing arts. The first column shows the results of research carried out by Jackson et al (1994) of the Institute of Manpower Services (IMS) on behalf of the Arts Council of Great Britain (ACGB). That report recognised the difficulty in assessing the size of the labour force in the performing arts, not only because available data are limited, but also because the labour markets themselves are "complex and far from self-contained" (Jackson et al, 1994). They estimated that nearly 60,000 people are employed in dance and drama, including teachers, administrators and those working in associated professions in the UK.

The second column relates to the Labour Force Survey (LFS) of spring 1994. This source identifies some 40,000 working as actors, entertainers, stage managers, producers and directors as their main job, similar to the total drama figure arrived at by the IMS. By comparison, the third column, derived from the 1991 population census, separately identified 54,000 actors. This difference is related to the nature of the data collected:

*Table 5.4 Employment in the performing arts*

| | Institute of Manpower Studies, 1994 | Labour Force Survey, Spring 1994 (a) | Population Census, 1991 (a) |
|---|---|---|---|
| Drama | | | |
|   Actors | 30,000 | .. | .. |
|   Associated professions | 3,000 | .. | .. |
|   Teachers and administrators | 6,000 | .. | .. |
|   Subtotal drama | 39,000 | | |
| Dance | | | |
| Dancers | 2,000 | .. | .. |
|   Associated professions | 1,000 | .. | .. |
|   Teachers and administrators | 16,500 | .. | .. |
|   Subtotal dance | 19,500 | .. | .. |
| Subtotal drama and dance | 58,500 | 40,000 | 54,000 |
| Musicians | .. | 20,000 | 22,000 |
| Total estimate | 58,500 | 60,000 | 76,000 |

Sources: Jackson et al (1994); O'Brien and Feist (1995); Labour Force Survey, Spring 1994.
(a) Includes actors, entertainers, stage managers, producers and directors.

the LFS refers to people's "main jobs", while the census data include people who are not involved in these areas as their main jobs but still describe themselves as belonging to that sector.

Both the LFS and the population census identified roughly the same number of musicians, at 20,000 and 22,000 respectively. It would appear from these classifications that while musicians are represented, people in occupations associated with music are not counted, making this figure the lower limit for employment in music.

# Funding and support for the performing arts

The main sources of funding for the performing arts are:

- European funds;
- central government departments (both directly and through their funding of the arts councils);
- local authorities (including their support of the regional arts boards);
- business sponsorship; and
- grant-making trusts.

In 1993/94, European funding for the performing arts mainly took the form of project funding. It came not only from DGX, the directorate with the specific remit for culture, but also programmes such as the European Regional Development Fund (ERDF) and the European Social Fund (ESF).

Central government support for the performing arts is mainly channelled through the arts councils. The only money for the performing arts that came directly from the DNH in the period 1993/94 was for specific projects such as National Music Day. Support for the performing arts from other central government departments totalled £35m and accounted for just over 7 per cent of the total funding for the performing arts. In England, support for the performing arts is also channelled through the ten regional arts boards (RABs).

Local authorities directly support the performing arts in a number of ways – through owning and running venues, such as theatres, concert halls and other arts venues, promoting performing arts events in their own and other premises, and supporting professional and amateur performing arts organisations through revenue, project and other grants, and sometimes "partnership agreements" with RABs. In those areas without resident orchestras, local authorities are usually responsible for the majority of orchestral performances (ACE/BBC, 1994).

These functions are normally performed by the local authority leisure and recreation departments. However, support for the performing arts can come from other departments. For example, local education authorities fund peripatetic music teachers (Marsh and White, 1995) and make mandatory awards of grants to music students and discretionary grants awards to drama and dance students[3].

Table 5.5 summarises the funding of the performing arts through these various sources in 1993/94. For the arts councils, RABs and business sponsorship, this information is analysed by three categories of performing arts activities – drama, dance and ballet, and music and opera. The figures for each activity represent identifiable funding only: there are likely to be elements of funding in budgets such as development, planning, or touring, which also support the performed arts, but which cannot be disaggregated. These figures should therefore be treated as minimum estimates.

For European funds, central government departments other than the DNH, local authorities and charities, the figures could not be disaggregated and are presented in total. Moreover, the local authority figure is an overestimate, as it includes all expenditure on arts venues (excluding museums and galleries), promotions and grants. It may, therefore, contain some

---

3   A report in 1996 estimated these discretionary awards to be worth at least £7m in 1994/95 (NFER, 1996). These have not been included in the figures here on local authority expenditure.

*Table 5.5 Funding for the performing arts, 1993/94*

| | Drama | Dance and ballet | Music and opera | General performing arts | Total | Percentage down |
|---|---|---|---|---|---|---|
| | | | *£m and percentages* | | | |
| European funding (a) | .. | .. | .. | 27.9 | 27.9 | 5.8 |
| Department of National Heritage | .. | .. | 0.1 | 1.3 | 1.3 | 0.3 |
| Other central government departments (a) | .. | .. | .. | 42.5 | 42.5 | 8.8 |
| Arts Councils (b) | 48.5 | 23.9 | 50.9 | – | 123.3 | 25.5 |
| Regional Arts Boards (b) | 7.7 | 2.0 | 3.2 | 4.7 | 17.5 | 3.6 |
| Local authorities (c) | .. | .. | .. | 222.1 | 222.1 | 45.9 |
| Business sponsorship | 9.2 | 2.7 | 22.6 | – | 34.5 | 7.1 |
| Charities | .. | .. | .. | 14.2 | 14.2 | 2.9 |
| Total | 65.4 | 28.6 | 76.8 | 312.7 | 483.3 | 100.0 |
| Percentage across | 13.5 | 5.9 | 15.9 | 64.7 | 100.0 | – |

Sources: ACGB (1994); ACNI (1994); RABs' Annual Reports, 1993/94; CIPFA (1994); ABSA (1994); PSI survey of grant-making trusts.
(a) Includes cross arts and arts festivals.
(b) Minimum estimates.
(c) All arts spending excluding museums and galleries.

expenditure on areas outside the performing arts, such as the visual arts and literature, although the majority is likely to be on the performing arts. A minimum total of £483m was identified as having been spent on the performing arts by these sources in 1993/94. Nearly half of this funding for the performing arts came from local authorities (at £222m), with the arts councils contributing just over a quarter (at £123m). The overestimate of local authority expenditure not withstanding, local authorities are still a major source of funding for the performing arts.

European funding accounted for 6 per cent of the total, and the majority of this funding came through ERDF and ESF programmes. Central government departments other than the DNH contributed £42m to funding performing arts, just under 9 per cent of the total. Just over 7 per cent of funding for the performing arts came from business sponsorship, with two thirds of this going to music and opera.

Of the total funding in Table 5.5, at least 14 per cent went on drama, 6 per cent on dance and 16 per cent on music. However, nearly 65 per cent of this funding could not be disaggregated into the component art forms, making these percentages less than indicative of the overall breakdown by art form.

In addition to the sources described in Table 5.5, the performing arts are also supported by the broadcast media which create employment through productions and generate earnings through the exploitation of copyright through the broadcast and selling of recordings of programmes. The BBC is also a major supporter of orchestras – at present, it funds the BBC Symphony Orchestra, the BBC Philharmonic Orchestra, the BBC Scottish Symphony Orchestra, and the BBC Concert Orchestra, and (in part) the BBC National Orchestra of Wales and the Ulster Orchestra. While these orchestras are primarily intended to meet broadcasting needs, they also perform live. In 1993/94, the BBC spent £15m on maintaining its in-house orchestras.

## The regional dimension of funding

The high concentration of theatres and other venues in London has already been noted (Table 5.1). So too, has the high share of actors and associated professionals (47 per cent) living in London (LAB, 1996, and Chapter 3). Confirming this concentration, analysis of SOLT and TMA data for 1993 shows that 38 per cent of performances given by member organisations in the UK took place in London, where only 12 per cent of the UK population lives[4]. This, however, represents the residential population and not people who travel to London to work.

This strong regional bias is reflected in the funding of the performing arts. Thus, of ACGB's £99m allocation to the performing arts in 1993/94, just over one third went to four London organisations – the English National Opera, the Royal National Theatre, the Royal Opera and the Royal Ballet[5] (Table 5.6). Equally, when the relative importance of each of the RABs in England is considered, that of London stands out. The London Arts Board (LAB) accounted for over a quarter of RAB spending on the performing arts in 1993/94 – £4.5m out of £17.5m. Only one other RAB has a similar rate of spend – Northern Arts, where per capita expenditure at £0.63 compares with that of LAB at £0.65. Both are almost double the England average of £0.36.

Similarly, London local authorities allocate a far higher level of spending per capita to the performing arts than do authorities elsewhere in the country. The per capita spend in 1993/94 was £8.40 compared to £4.16 in England as a whole. Excluding London authorities, expenditure on the performing arts in the rest of England falls to £2.95. Lastly, the same

---

4   A further 21 per cent took place in the rest of the South East where 19 per cent of the population lives.
5   1993/94, ACGB funding for these organisations was, respectively, £11.7 million, £7.9 million, £7.8 million and £6.6 million. These figures exclude grants to the Birmingham Royal Ballet, which is counted as being based at the Royal Opera House, Covent Garden, for accounting purposes, and to the Royal Shakespeare Company, which had bases in both Stratford-upon-Avon and at the Barbican in London for the 1993/94 season.

*Table 5.6 Share of performing arts funding in London, 1993/94*

|  | Percentages |
|---|---|
| ... of English funding |  |
| ACGB (a) | 34 |
| Regional Arts Board (b) | 26 |
| London share of English population | 14 |
|  |  |
| ... of UK funding |  |
| Local authority (c) | 26 |
| Business sponsorship | 47 |
| London's share of the UK population | 12 |

Sources: ACGB (1994); RABs' Annual Accounts 1993/4; CIPFA (1994); ABSA (1994).
(a) Funding of London-based "national" companies.
(b) London Arts Boards expenditure.
(c) Expenditure on arts venues (excluding museums and galleries), promotions and grants.

picture emerges from ABSA's statistics on business support for the performing arts for 1993/94. Nearly half (47 per cent) went to London organisations and events, and a further 14 per cent to organisations in the rest of the South East. The only other region to receive a substantial share of funding was Scotland (13 per cent). This reflects the importance of the Edinburgh and, to a lesser extent, Glasgow festivals[6].

## Survey results

While existing data allow a picture to be constructed of the wider sector, and levels of support to be identified, they do not describe in any detail the operations of funded organisations. PSI therefore carried out a survey of 155 funded performing arts organisations (including "one-person" operations). This survey examined their incomes and expenditures, levels of employment and financial outturns. While this chapter considers the performing arts alone, Chapter 10 compares this sub-sector to the other areas of the cultural sector examined.

Grossing up the figures produced by the survey suggested a population of between 1,600 and 1,700 performing arts organisations, receiving support or funding as defined in this study (see Appendix for details of sampling and grossing). Table 5.7 shows the breakdown between the component parts of the performing arts sector as indicated by the survey. The majority of performing arts organisations comprise drama companies and theatres.

6   Business support for "national organisations" has not been taken into account in these calculations on regional distribution.

*Table 5.7 Survey results: performing arts organisations by category*

|  | Share of organisations (Percentages) |
|---|---|
| Drama | 54 |
| Dance | 14 |
| Orchestras | 24 |
| Other music | 8 |
| Opera | 1 |
| Total | 100 |

## Overall size and characteristics

The total number of employees in the funded performing arts sector can be estimated at some 25,000 (excluding any self-employed), and the total income of the sector as between £900m and £950m.

Funded performing arts organisations, as suggested above, are dispro-portionately to be found in London (Table 5.8).Over two-thirds (36 per cent) were based in the capital, with a further 23 per cent being located in the rest of the South East of England.

*Table 5.8 Survey results: regional distribution of performing arts organisations*

|  | Share of organisations (Percentages) |
|---|---|
| London | 36 |
| South of England (excluding London) | 23 |
| North of England | 14 |
| Northern Ireland | 10 |
| Wales | 7 |
| Scotland | 6 |
| Midlands | 5 |
| Total | 100 |

Given the large number of performing arts organisations in the sector, they were analysed according to size. Organisations were divided into three bands, according to the size of their annual incomes. They were also divided according to the relative importance of public support to their income[7]. Table 5.9 illustrates how these size bands reflect the estimated total popula-tion of funded performing arts organisations[8]. Although the majority (59

---

7   A further way of banding organisations by number of employees was also attempted, but the chosen bandings proved more productive. In addition, drama organisations were investigated in their own right, but this produced no additional insights.
8   Sample numbers for size, from smallest to largest, were 49, 57 and 49. For importance of support from lowest to highest, they were 47, 55 and 53.

per cent) had incomes of less than £200,000, 15 per cent had an annual income of more than £1m. Taking the whole population of funded organisations, a rather finer breakdown of income could be made. Thus, one in eight had a total income of under £25,000 per year, but one in twelve had a total income in excess of £2m. The median income – the income level which half the organisations were above and half below – was £136,000.

*Table 5.9 Survey results: performing arts organisations by income*

|  | Share of organisations (Percentages) |
| --- | --- |
| **Annual income** | |
| Less than £200,000 | 59 |
| £200,000 to £999,999 | 26 |
| £1,000,000 or more | 15 |
| All | 100 |
| **Public support as percentage of income** | |
| Less than 40 per cent | 49 |
| 40 to 59 per cent | 20 |
| 60 per cent or more | 32 |
| All | 100 |

A substantial share of performing arts organisations had no employees as such (Table 5.10). This does not mean, however, that nobody was working for them – all their workers might have been self-employed, as might be the case with a "one-person" organisation or a "partnership". One organisation surveyed had no employees, but recorded 80 self-employed people as working with it. Similarly, all workers might be volunteers, or a mixture of self-employed people and volunteers. Subject to these caveats, over one in ten performing arts organisations had no employees at all, and half had no more than two. Only a quarter had more than ten employees.

*Table 5.10 Survey results: performing arts organisations by number of employees*

| *Number of employees* | Share of organisations (Percentages) |
| --- | --- |
| None | 11 |
| 1 or 2 | 38 |
| 3 to 10 | 25 |
| 11 to 40 | 12 |
| More than 40 | 13 |
| Total | 100 |

## Income sources

Performing arts organisations obtain income from commercial activities such as charging admission, selling recordings and from catering and merchandising. Over and above this, they can benefit from donations and sponsorships, and from grants from public bodies. On average, income from commercial activities constituted about half of the total income of performing arts organisations (the mean was 49 per cent, and the median was 46 per cent). There is a strong relationship between the importance of commercially generated income and an organisation's size. Commercially generated income tended to be much less important for small organisations and much more important for large organisations (Table 5.11).

*Table 5.11 Survey results: performing arts organisations, by contribution of commercial income to total income and by organisation size (a) (Percentages)*

| Contribution of commercial income to total income | *Annual income* | | | |
|---|---|---|---|---|
| | *Less than £200k* | *£200k to £1,000k* | *£1,000k or more* | *All performing arts organisations* |
| Less than 20 per cent | 29 | 9 | – | 19 |
| 20 to 39 per cent | 29 | 28 | 19 | 28 |
| 40 to 59 per cent | 15 | 23 | 26 | 18 |
| 60 to 79 per cent | 16 | 14 | 7 | 14 |
| 80 per cent or more | 11 | 26 | 48 | 21 |
| Total | 100 | 100 | 100 | 100 |

(a) Size determined by total income.

Income from commercial activities made up less than 40 per cent of total income for well over half (58 per cent) of the smallest organisations (with incomes of less than £200,000), while it made up at least 80 per cent of income for half (48 per cent) of the largest (with incomes of £1m or more). The share of support (public and private) is effectively the reverse of the picture given in Table 5.11. Support is more important to small organisations than large, where importance is measured by share of income.

Table 5.12 shows the percentage of organisations which received support from various sources (although it does not reflect the relative importance of that support to their total income). The largest organisations received the fewest grants from central government, but the most from other than the usual public sources, with 50 per cent getting support from this source. Overall, performing arts organisations were most likely to get sponsorship and donations and least likely to receive funding

*Table 5.12 Survey results: performing arts organisations by source of support (Percentages)*

| | Annual income | | | |
| | Less than £200k | £200k to £1,000k | £1,000k or more | All performing arts organisations |
|---|---|---|---|---|
| Central goverment | 5 | 6 | 1 | 4 |
| Arts councils | 58 | 58 | 46 | 56 |
| RABs | 58 | 47 | 47 | 53 |
| Local authority | 50 | 49 | 67 | 52 |
| Other public sources | 5 | 20 | 50 | 15 |
| Sponsorship and donations | 55 | 66 | 79 | 61 |

directly from central government, reflecting the role of the arms' length agencies such as the arts councils and RABs.

Three forms of support are considered in more detail: from central and local government arts funders (ACGB, SAC, WAC, ACNI and the RABs); from local authorities; and from charities, foundations, sponsors and donors. Arts funders provided, on average, just over a quarter (26 per cent) of the income of performing arts organisations and were more important for smaller organisations. Table 5.13 shows this by looking at two extremes of support.

*Table 5.13 Survey results: share of income of performing arts organisations from arts councils and RABs (Percentages)*

| Arts council and RAB funding as a share of total income | Annual income Less than £200k | £200k to £1,000k | £1,000k or more | All performing arts organisations |
|---|---|---|---|---|
| Less than 5 per cent | 16 | 37 | 62 | 28 |
| 60 per cent or more | 22 | 5 | Less than 1 | 14 |

With respect to direct local government funding, however, the picture is rather different. Local government provided an average of 10 per cent of the income of performing arts organisations. This funding was of equal importance to both large and to small organisations (Table 5.14).

Just over half of performing arts organisations received little or no support from local authorities. However, a quarter received 15 per cent or more of their income from this source. Support in the form of sponsorship, donations or grants from non-public sources tended to go to larger organisations. However, when it went to smaller organisations, it contributed a larger share of total income (Table 5.15).

*Table 5.14 Survey results: share of income of performing arts organisations from local authorities (Percentages)*

| Local authority funding as share of total income | Annual income | | | |
| | Less than £200k | £200k to £1,000k | £1,000k or more | All performing arts organisations |
|---|---|---|---|---|
| Less than 5 per cent | 55 | 53 | 55 | 55 |
| 15 or more per cent | 22 | 31 | 22 | 25 |

*Table 5.15 Survey results: share of income of performing arts organisations from sponsorships (Percentages)*

| Sponsorship funding as share of total income | Annual income | | | |
| | Less than £200k | £200k to £1,000k | £1,000k or more | All performing arts organisations |
|---|---|---|---|---|
| No sponsorship | 45 | 34 | 21 | 39 |
| Less than 5 per cent | 7 | 16 | 53 | 16 |
| 15 per cent or more | 29 | 29 | 2 | 24 |

## Expenditure

Turning to organisations' expenditure, the only item it was possible to identify across the board was staff costs (comprising salaries, national insurance and pension costs). A considerable proportion of organisations had no staff costs at all. This was either because all those working in them were self-employed[9], or because they relied on volunteers. On average, staff costs made up a third of total costs. However, there were considerable differences between organisations, depending on their size and on their reliance on public support (Table 5.16).

Smaller organisations spent a considerably smaller share of their total expenditure on staff than did larger ones. This might reflect their greater reliance on freelances and other self-employed staff members, or the fact that they are more likely to be volunteer organisations. The relationship between staff costs and the importance of public support suggested that more heavily supported organisations are far more labour intensive. The reasons for this cannot be drawn from the survey. It could be that they are higher payers or that they employ people full-time. It could be that their output relies much more upon staff and much less upon, for example, accommodation or equipment. It is not, or not straightforwardly, the case

9  Fees paid to freelance staff may appear under different headings in organisations' accounts, such as direct project costs.

*Table 5.16 Survey results: share of employee costs in total costs by type of performing arts organisation (Percentages)*

|  | *Average* | *Median* |
|---|---|---|
| Annual income | | |
| Less than £200,000 | 26 | 19 |
| £200,000 to £999,999 | 53 | 59 |
| £1,000,000 or more | 49 | 58 |
| | | |
| Public support as percentage of income | | |
| Less than 40 per cent | 28 | 19 |
| 40 to 59 per cent | 35 | 39 |
| 60 per cent or more | 46 | 54 |
| | | |
| All performing arts organisations | 35 | 32 |

accommodation or equipment. It is not, or not straightforwardly, the case that the higher share of expenditure attributable to employed staff in more highly supported organisations is a consequence of less highly supported organisations making greater use of self-employed workers whose fees are not counted in staff costs[10].

## Financial outturn

Although most funded performing arts organisations are non-profit-making, and are registered as charities or friendly societies, this does not mean that they always operate at break-even. In any one year, some generate a surplus and others make a loss. At least two-thirds of organisations broke even, or made a surplus in 1993/94, but for a minority, a substantial share of expenditure in that year was not matched by income. Tables 5.17 and 5.18 consider the gap between income and expenditure measured as a proportion of total expenditure – according to the characteristics of organisations.

Total losses in excess of 5 per cent made in 1993/94 by organisations recording an income can be estimated to amount to rather more than £50m. These losses might be added to losses made in earlier years, so that the total deficit of performing arts organisations is likely to be much

10    11 per cent of performing arts organisations had no employees. Where public support made up under 40 per cent of income, the proportion was 12 per cent, where public support made up between 40 per cent and 60 per cent of income, the proportion was 18 per cent, and where public support made up 60 per cent or more of income, the proportion was 7 per cent.

*Table 5.17 Survey results: financial outturns of performing arts organisations by level of income (Percentages)*

| | Annual income | | | |
| --- | --- | --- | --- | --- |
| Financial balance | Less than £200k | £200k to £1,000k | £1,000k or more | All performing arts organisations |
| Break even | 47 | 42 | 42 | 45 |
| Surplus greater than 5 per cent of income | 19 | 23 | 32 | 22 |
| Loss greater than 5 per cent of income | 34 | 35 | 26 | 33 |
| *Loss greater than 12.5 per cent of income* | *12* | *10* | *16* | *12* |

greater than that incurred in any one year. Large organisations were more likely to make a surplus, but were also more likely to make a large loss.

The extent to which organisations make a surplus or loss, or simply break even, appears to be related to the importance, to them, of public support. However, the relationship is not unidirectional, as is shown in Table 5.18.

*Table 5.18 Survey results: financial outturns of performing arts organisations by importance of public support (Percentages)*

| | Public support as a share of total income | | | |
| --- | --- | --- | --- | --- |
| Financial balance | Less than 40% | 40 to 50% | 60 per cent or more | All performing arts organisations |
| Break even | 33 | 82 | 41 | 45 |
| Surplus greater than 5 per cent of income | 29 | 2 | 24 | 22 |
| Loss greater than 5 per cent of income | 38 | 16 | 35 | 33 |

Organisations for which public support was of middling importance were much more likely to break even than those for which it was of greater or lesser importance. Such organisations were disproportionately in the Midlands or the North of England (45 per cent against a share of 19 per cent for all organisations) and were much more dependent upon local authority support than either less- or more-heavily funded organisations[11].

*Table 5.19 Summary of survey results for performing arts organisations*

| | Amount Median (£000s) | Amount Mean (£000s) | Share of total income (Percentages) Median | Mean |
|---|---|---|---|---|
| Source of income | | | | |
| Central government | – | 1 | – | 1 |
| Arts councils/RABs | 16 | 104 | 15 | 26 |
| Local authorities | 1 | 49 | 2 | 10 |
| Other public sources | – | 14 | – | 2 |
| Sponsorship, etc | 4 | 33 | 2 | 12 |
| Commercial activities | 54 | 202 | 46 | 49 |
| Total income | 136 | 564 | .. | 100 |
| Total expenditure | 131 | 584 | 100 | 105 |
| Surplus/(loss) | – | (20) | – | (5) |

## Summary of survey findings

The financial details of the performing arts sector are summarised in Table 5.19.

The mean average income of organisations is much higher than the median income. This indicates that the sector is made up of a large number of relatively small organisations and a few rather large ones. Other cases where the mean amount of income is considerably larger than the median amount, indicate something similar. For example, there are a large number of organisations receiving relatively small grants from the arts councils and RABs and a few organisations receiving very large grants.

Considering the shares of income made up by various sources, a comparison of means underlines the importance of arts councils and RABs as sources of funding. The difference between the median and the mean share for this, and other funding sources, suggests that they are very important for a few organisations, but considerably less important for the majority. Both local authority and sponsorship funding also stand out in this way.

Income from commercial activities among funded performing arts

---

11   Of performing arts organisations surveyed, 25 per cent received over 15 per cent of their total income from one or more local authorities. Where public support made up under 40 per cent of income, local authorities contributed more than 15 per cent of total income in 5 per cent of cases; where public support made up 60 or more per cent of income, local authorities contributed more than 15 per cent of the total income in 38 per cent of cases, and where public support made up between 40 and 60 per cent of income, local authorities contributed more than 15 per cent of total income in 51 per cent of cases.

organisations was important. Commercial activities provide, on average, half of all income. Moreover, organisations which generate more of their income are more or less balanced by organisations generating less.

The median performing arts organisation breaks even. However, in terms of mean income and expenditure, performing arts organisations make a loss. The figures indicate that the losses are being made on a large scale by a relatively few organisations.

# Chapter 6

# Combined arts and arts festivals

As implied by its title, this chapter deals with activities that combine the various cultural activities defined elsewhere in this report, including the performing arts, the visual arts, and media. Combined arts can take a number of forms, including:

- general arts venues (such as arts centres);
- organisations, companies and individuals which operate across a number of forms, or who specialise in combining art forms within their practice; and
- arts festivals.

There are also service organisations, such as training and marketing companies, which specialise in the arts and operate across all sectors and are therefore, for the purposes of this study, included in the combined arts.

Combined arts do not, by their very nature, have a distinct profile that allows them to be analysed in the same way as more distinct activities. This is mainly because the term "combined arts" has arisen as a funding category used by the arts councils and regional arts boards (RABs) to categorise those organisations that do not correspond to the more traditional definitions of the performing arts, visual arts, and media[1].

---

1   The term "combined arts" was first used as a funding category by the ACGB in their annual report of 1987/88.

Different types of organisations receive grants given under a combined arts budget, such as: arts centres (for example the South Bank Centre, and the Institute for Contemporary Arts, both in London); organisations which produce work across the traditional cultural activity definitions, or provide resources and services across the board to the cultural sector; organisations which usually concentrate on one activity (such as dance troupes or drama companies) but receive such grants for special cross-disciplinary projects; and arts festivals, which may involve the combination of activities[2].

Conversely, organisations which can be considered as combined arts bodies can receive funding under other cultural-sector budgets. For example, a combined arts organisation might receive a number of grants for different projects, each of which concentrated on a particular activity. These grants would then be categorised under the relevant budget headings, although the body in receipt was actually a combined arts organisation. As a result, some of the funding for the bodies identified in the survey as combined arts organisations will be accounted for under other cultural-sector activities included in this report.

The following topics are covered in this chapter:

- the wider context – a detailed profile of audiences and attendances at arts festivals, a profile of arts festivals in the UK, and employment in arts festivals;
- public support for combined arts and arts festivals from Europe, central and local government, arts funding bodies, businesses and grant-making trusts;
- survey results.

## The wider context

The wider context of the combined arts is largely synonymous with that of the other activities described in this report. However, one sub-sector of the combined arts, namely arts festivals, is in itself more distinct and identifiable, and therefore will be focused on in this section.

The British Arts Festival Association (BAFA) estimates that there were almost 400 non-competitive arts festivals in the UK which have some degree of professional arts input, either artistic or organisational in 1995. The BAFA had approximately 50 full members and over 20 affiliate members in that year, which represented most of the leading professional arts festivals which occur on a regular basis. In general, the purpose of such festivals is to:

---

2   Where appropriate, arts festivals that are concerned with only one art form have been included in the relevant chapter rather than in this chapter.

> *stage events and performances of a high standard, concentrated in a relatively short period of time ... in many cases ... the culmination of a year-round programme and includes events that would not otherwise have taken place (Rolfe, 1992).*

There are many different types of arts festival, some of which are almost entirely commercial (such as the Reading music festival, or Glyndebourne Opera), while others receive support from arts funding bodies and local authorities (such as the Edinburgh Festival or the Mayfest in Glasgow). In PSI's study of arts festivals (Rolfe, 1992), the following categories of festival were identified: general arts; mixed music; classical music; jazz; folk; literature; film and other single art forms. Of these, only the first (general arts) comes under the category of combined arts. According to that study, some 40 per cent of all arts festivals fall into this category.

## Audiences for arts festivals

Data on audiences for arts festivals are collected in an annual survey by BAFA[3]. It is not known how many people annually attend arts festivals, but it is possible to profile those who attend certain types of festival (Table 6.1)[4]. The BAFA survey covered 13 festivals in 1994, at least five of which concentrated on classical or traditional music. The sample excluded other sorts of festivals, such as rock and pop festivals and carnivals, which might be expected to have a different audience profile from that described in Table 6.1.

Two-thirds of the respondents to this survey were over the age of 45, compared to just over 45 per cent of the population of Great Britain as a whole. Those aged under 34, while representing 37 per cent of the GB population, made up only 15 per cent of the arts festivals audience.

Analysis of the household incomes of respondents to the survey needs to take into account that over a quarter of the sample were retired from full-time employment. However, nearly a third of respondents reported their annual household income to be in excess of £30,000. When asked to describe their occupation, only one per cent of all respondents described themselves as manual workers (BAFA, 1995).

It is worth noting that two-thirds of the respondents to the BAFA survey were local to the areas where the festivals were based. Of the remaining third, people who travelled to visit a festival, two in ten included an overnight stay in their visit (BAFA, 1995).

---

3  *Arts Festivals 1994: audiences, attitudes and sponsorship*, involved the survey of over 2,000 visitors spanning 13 separate arts festivals held in 1994. It was carried out by the BAFA in association with ABSA.
4  This survey covered both single-art-form festivals and general arts festivals.

*Table 6.1 Profile of audience for arts festivals, 1994*

|  | *Percentages* |
|---|---|
| **Age** | |
| Under 34 | 15 |
| 35 to 44 | 15 |
| 45 to 54 | 23 |
| 55 to 64 | 23 |
| 65 and over | 21 |
| **Gender** | |
| Male | 44 |
| Female | 53 |
| **Household income** | |
| Less than £10,000 | 12 |
| £10,000 to £20,000 | 21 |
| £20,000 to £30,000 | 18 |
| £30,000 to £45,000 | 17 |
| £45,000 or more | 15 |
| Non–respondents | 16 |

Source: BAFA (1995).

## Arts festivals in the UK

The PSI study (Rolfe, 1992) estimated that there were over 500 festivals in the UK in 1991 which lasted for more than one day and contained some level of professional input, either artistic or organisational (higher than the more recent BAFA estimate quoted above)[5]. Nearly two-thirds of these festivals were professionally run. Over half of the respondent festivals were first established in the 1980s, and a further 21 per cent in the 1970s. Only six of the festivals surveyed predated the twentieth century. While this might indicate an increase in activity during the 1970s and 1980s, it may also suggest the potential life span of an arts festival. It may be that just as many arts festivals were established in the decades before, but had ceased to exist by the time the research in question was undertaken in the early 1990s.

However, according to the PSI study, "it is generally agreed that the 1980s were a period of quite remarkable growth for arts festivals." (Rolfe, 1992). These festivals were considered a "second generation" of arts festivals, and were in general concerned with the promotion of new and

---

5   This research involved a postal survey of 527 festivals (which gained 351 replies), including general arts, mixed music, classical music, jazz, folk, literature, film and other single-art-form festivals. It was carried out by PSI on behalf of the Office of Arts and Libraries (now the Department of National Heritage).

contemporary works as opposed to the celebration and performance of a received canon of historical works.

The majority of festivals (over 90 per cent) in 1991 were held annually, usually in the summer months, with July being the most popular month. The most usual length of duration of a festival was 8 to 14 days. Half of all those festivals surveyed also included some non-arts recreational activities aimed at adults. The total income of arts festivals in 1991 was estimated to be £41m, of which the largest share (43 per cent) came from box-office receipts.

## Employment at arts festivals

Some indication of the levels and nature of employment at arts festivals is also available from the 1992 PSI study. Due to the seasonal nature of most of the work, and the temporary employment of artists and performers for the duration of the festival, only 29 per cent of festivals in 1991 mainly employed permanent staff (Rolfe, 1992). Of all staff, including full-time, part-time, temporary and self-employed staff, 62 per cent were paid (Table 6.2). Only one in twenty festivals employed more than 20 full-time or 30 part-time staff on a permanent basis, and these festivals tended to be run by local authorities or attached to arts centres where staff had other duties.

*Table 6.2 Staffing at arts festivals, 1991*

| Type of festival | Percentage employing paid staff |
| --- | --- |
| General arts | 72 |
| Mixed music | 62 |
| Classical | 61 |
| Jazz | 61 |
| Folk | 27 |
| Single art form | 87 |
| All | 62 |

Source: Rolfe (1992).

While 38 per cent of the festivals were run entirely by unpaid staff, 24 per cent made no use of volunteers at all. Half of all festivals used 10 or fewer volunteers, and only 9 festivals reported using more than 50 volunteers during the year. Those that did have volunteers used them for administration, publicity and stewarding work.

Arts festivals also provide employment for artists through the commissioning of new works: in 1991, 42 per cent of general arts festivals commissioned new work.

# Support for combined arts and arts festivals

Funding for combined arts and arts festivals can be identified from arts-funding bodies, business sponsorship and charities. It is not possible to disaggregate funding for combined arts and arts festivals from the data available on European funding and local authority expenditure. Central government funding for these activities is mainly channelled through the arts councils. However, it is clear from the PSI survey of arts festivals that local authorities may provide funding and also run arts festivals themselves.

Table 6.3 summarises the support for combined arts and arts festivals from the four arts councils, the RABs, business sponsorship and grant-making trusts. As it excludes European and local government funding, the total of over £70m in the table represents a minimum estimate.

*Table 6.3 Support for combined arts and arts festivals, 1993/94*

|  | £m (a) | Percentage |
|---|---|---|
| Arts councils |  |  |
|   ACGB | 28.6 | 40.5 |
|   SAC | 4.1 | 5.8 |
|   ACW | 2.3 | 3.2 |
|   ACNI | 1.5 | 2.1 |
| Regional arts boards | 10.8 | 15.3 |
| Business sponsorship | 13.1 | 18.5 |
| Charities | 10.2 | 14.5 |
| Total | 70.6 | 100.0 |

Sources: ACGB (1994); ACNI (1994); Regional arts boards' annual Reports, 1993/94; ABSA, 1994; PSI survey of charities.
(a) Minimum estimates.

The totals given for the arts councils and more especially the RABs in Table 6.3 should also be treated as minimum estimates. Not all the RABs separately identify funding for combined arts and arts festivals, so estimates have been made from their schedules of grant recipients. Even where combined arts and arts festivals are identified, it is likely there will also be expenditure under budgets for other, more particular, activities going to arts festivals and combined arts organisations. As much as half of identifiable support for combined arts and arts festivals (£36m) came from the four arts councils.

*Table 6.4 Arts festivals in the UK: income, 1991*

|  | £m | Percentage |
|---|---|---|
| Box–office receipts | 17.6 | 43.3 |
| Business sponsorship | 6.8 | 16.7 |
| Local authorities | 5.0 | 12.3 |
| Regional arts boards | 2.0 | 4.9 |
| Other (a) | 9.2 | 22.7 |
| Total | 40.6 | 100.0 |

Source: Rolfe (1992).
(a) Including national arts councils, friends' associations, donations and other earned income.

PSI's 1992 study provides an indication of the significance of support for arts festivals (Table 6.4). It represented 57 per cent of the total income of those surveyed, and included grants from arts bodies, sponsorship and donations. Grants from local authorities and RABs accounted for about 17 per cent of the total income of responding festivals (approximately £7m). However, funding from the national arts councils was not separately identified, and is included in the sizeable contribution of "other" sources in this table.

Three-quarters of responding festivals claimed to have received business sponsorship in 1991. In 1993/94, business sponsorship for combined arts and arts festivals accounted for 18 per cent of total support (at £13m) and, according to the Association for Business Sponsorship of the Arts (ABSA) statistics, combined arts and arts festivals attracted nearly 20 per cent of all business sponsorship of the arts in that year. This made combined arts second only to the performing arts, in the receipt of such support (ABSA, 1994).

In 1991, the main sources of sponsorship in financial terms were large companies with a local presence, but in terms of the number of companies involved, the majority of sponsors were small local businesses, who often gave support in kind, such as the production of free publicity material (Rolfe, 1992).

Other sources of unearned income include friends' associations and other charitable donations. In 1991, just over a quarter of responding festivals received income from friends' associations, while nearly half received income from other sources. The median amount received was £50. Another area of revenue is the sale of branded merchandise and other goods associated with the festival (Rolfe, 1992).

## The regional dimension to support for combined arts and arts festivals

The PSI study of arts festivals suggested that a quarter of festivals in 1991 took place in London and the South and South East of England. In 1993/94, business sponsorship of combined arts and arts festivals was also concentrated in London (at 20 per cent), with Scotland second (at 10 per cent)[6].

However, the number of festivals in any one location is not necessarily an indication of regional impact, as festivals can vary widely in the scale and scope of the activities they provide. Moreover, festivals serve a wider constituency than the local population, with a proportion of the performers (and other employees) and audience travelling to the festivals.

### *Edinburgh Festivals Study*

As global information on arts festivals is scarce, the following paragraphs summarise a study of an individual festival. As the largest arts festival in the UK, the Edinburgh Festival (which actually consists of nine separate festivals) is one of the best documented[7]. The two main festivals are the Edinburgh International Festival and the Edinburgh Fringe Festival. In 1993/94, these two festivals combined attracted £1.9m in public funding, £0.9m in sponsorship and donations and £2m in earned income (SAC, 1995).

A study of the impact of all nine Edinburgh festivals was conducted over 1991 and 1992[8] and aimed to identify the economic activity in the region that would not exist without them. It estimated that visitors spent £44m on festival-related activities (such as tickets, programmes, and merchandise and refreshments available at festival venues) and a further £9m on non-festival related activities (such as accommodation, travel and food). It also estimated that nearly 6,500 people were directly involved in organising and participating in the festivals. A large number of these can be assumed to be unpaid, or paid from any profits accruing from their particular event. The number of permanent paid jobs identified was only 54.

---

6   Nearly 30 per cent of business sponsorship for combined arts and festivals went to national and umbrella agencies, again making regional comparisons difficult.
7   The nine Edinburgh festivals are: the International Festival; the Fringe Festival; the Military Tattoo; the Jazz Festival; the Film Festival; the Folk Festival; the Science Festival; the Book Festival and the Children's Festival.
8   This study was undertaken by the Scottish Tourist Board in conjunction with Lothian and Edinburgh Enterprise Ltd, City of Edinburgh District Council and Lothian Regional Council.

*Table 6.5 Survey results: all combined arts organisations by category*

|  | Share of organisations (Percentages) |
|---|---|
| Arts festivals | 11 |
| Combined and cross arts | 76 |
| Service organisations | 14 |
| Total | 100 |

# Survey results

To examine the nature of funded organisations in more detail, PSI carried out a survey of 96 organisations (including "one-person" operations) in the combined arts, festivals and services sectors. Comparisons between the results given below and the rest of the supported cultural sector can be found in Chapter 10.

Grossing up the figures from the survey for this particular area of activity suggested a population of nearly 1,600 organisations and individuals receiving support as defined in this study (see Appendix). Table 6.5 shows the breakdown between the component parts of the sector in the survey.

## Overall size and characteristics

On the basis of the survey, the total number of employees in the combined arts and festivals sector can be estimated as some 17,000 (to which, perhaps, another 34,000 self-employed can be added)[9] and the total income of the sector as between £500m and £550m. Half the funded, combined-arts and festival organisations surveyed were in Southern England, and a further quarter were located in the North of England (Table 6.6).

Given that relatively few of the organisations surveyed provided consultancy or specialist services, these were not examined in their own right. Furthermore, the small number of festivals in the sample, and the heavy overlap between combined arts organisations and festival organisations, made it appropriate to combine these two categories for purposes of analysis. Thus, in this section, results are shown for the sector as a whole, but where appropriate, particular findings with respect to combined arts and festival organisations are also described[10].

---

9   Calculated according to the ratio of self-employed to employed people in the cultural sector suggested by the LFS.

10   Sample numbers were: combined and cross arts organisations, 68; arts festivals, 12; service organisations, 16.

*Table 6.6 Survey results: regional distribution of all combined arts organisations*

|  | Share of organisations (Percentages) |
|---|---|
| South of England (excluding London) | 30 |
| North of England | 24 |
| London | 18 |
| Scotland | 10 |
| Midlands | 9 |
| Wales | 6 |
| Northern Ireland | 3 |
| Total | 100 |

A third of organisations in the sector had an income of under £50,000 per year, while a further third had an income of £250,000 or more (Table 6.7). Only one in twenty of the latter group were service organisations, whereas such organisations represented a fifth of those with an income below £250,000. Nearly 10 per cent of respondent organisations had incomes in excess of £1m in the survey year.

*Table 6.7 Survey results: all combined arts organisations by income*

| Annual income | Percentages |
|---|---|
| Less than £25,000 | 18 |
| £25,000 to £49,999 | 19 |
| £50,000 to £99,999 | 8 |
| £100,000 to £249,999 | 23 |
| £250,000 to £999,999 | 24 |
| £1,000,000 or more | 9 |
| Total | 100 |

As many as one in ten organisations had no employees as such, although some relied on self-employed workers or volunteers (Table 6.8). Very few organisations had more than a hundred employees. Again, many of the smallest respondent organisations were service organisations.

## Income sources

Combined arts and festivals organisations generated income from commercial activities such as charging admissions, merchandising and catering. On average, income from such commercial activities constituted

*Table 6.8 Survey results: all combined arts organisations by number of employees*

| Number of employees | Share of organisations (Percentages) |
|---|---|
| None | 10 |
| 1 or 2 | 28 |
| 3 to 10 | 28 |
| 11 to 40 | 27 |
| More than 40 | 7 |
| Total | 100 |

some 40 per cent of the sector's income (Table 6.9). Almost one in five of the sector received less than a tenth of their income from this source, although a further fifth gained at least two-thirds from admissions, merchandising or catering. The share of support, however is effectively the reverse of the picture in Table 6.9.

*Table 6.9 Survey results: all combined arts organisations by contribution of commercial income to total income*

| Share of total income | Percentage of organisations |
|---|---|
| Less than 20 per cent | 28 |
| 20 to 39 per cent | 22 |
| 40 to 59 per cent | 25 |
| 60 to 79 per cent | 15 |
| 80 per cent or more | 10 |

Table 6.10 shows the percentage of organisations which received support from different sources. The vast majority received funding from arts funders (arts councils and RABs) and from local authorities (at 91 per cent and 79 per cent of organisations respectively). Just under half of all organisations received sponsorship and donations.

The following paragraphs consider various forms of support in more detail – central and local government arts funders (ACGB, SAC, WAC, ACNI and the RABs), local authorities; and charities, foundations, sponsorships and donations

Arts funders provided, on average, 21 per cent of the income of organisations in the sector (Table 6.11). One in twelve organisations received at least half of their income from one or more dedicated arts funders.

Local government provided, on average, just over a quarter of the

*Table 6.10 Survey results: combined arts organisations by source of support*

| Share of total income | Percentage of organisations |
|---|---|
| Central goverment | 5 |
| Arts councils and RABs | 91 |
| Local authority | 79 |
| Other public sources | 28 |
| Sponsorship and donations | 45 |

*Table 6.11 Survey results: share of income of combined arts organisations from arts councils and RABs*

| Share of total income | Percentage of organisations |
|---|---|
| Less than 5 per cent | 29 |
| 5 to 19 per cent | 28 |
| 20 to 39 per cent | 19 |
| 40 per cent or more | 25 |

income of combined arts, festivals and services organisations (Table 6.12). It was the source of at least 50 per cent of income for one in five organisations.

*Table 6.12 Survey results: share of income of combined arts organisations from local authorities*

| Share of total income | Percentage of organisations |
|---|---|
| Less than 5 per cent | 30 |
| 5 to 14 per cent | 14 |
| 15 to 29 per cent | 17 |
| 30 to 50 per cent | 21 |
| 50 per cent or more | 18 |

Support in the form of sponsorship, donations or grants from non-public sources was received by nearly half the organisations, and made up an average of one twelfth of their income (Table 6.13). For nearly one-tenth of the sector, such support provided at least a third of their total income.

*Table 6.13 Survey results: share of income of combined arts organisations from sponsorships*

| Share of total income | Percentage of organisations |
|---|---|
| No sponsorship | 55 |
| Some, but less than 5 per cent | 12 |
| 15 per cent or more | 15 |

## Expenditure

Staff costs (including wages, national insurance and pension costs) made up an average of 40 per cent of expenditures across all organisations, including the 10 per cent with no employees. For half the organisations in the sector, wages and related costs made up less than a third of total costs, but for one in twelve all expenditure was accounted for by staff costs.

## Financial outturn

Although most funded combined-arts, festival and service organisations are non-profit-making, (being registered as charities or friendly societies), this does not mean that they always operate at break even. In any one year, some generate a surplus and others make a loss. In 1993/94 approximately half broke even and just under one in five made a surplus. Table 6.14 considers this income gap – the difference between income and expenditure measured as a proportion of total expenditure.

*Table 6.14 Survey results: financial outturns of all combined arts organisations*

| | Percentage of organisations |
|---|---|
| Break even | 47 |
| Surplus greater than 5 per cent of income | 18 |
| *Surplus greater than 12.5 per cent of income* | 7 |
| Loss greater than 5 per cent of income | 35 |
| *Loss greater than 12.5 per cent of income* | 20 |

A third of organisations made a loss in the survey year – and one in five made a substantial loss. Total losses made in 1993/94 by organisations recording an income gap in excess of 5 per cent amounted to nearly £13m.

*Table 6.15 Summary of survey results for combined arts organisations*

|  | Median amount (£000s) | Mean amount (£000s) | Share of total income (percentages) Median | Mean |
|---|---|---|---|---|
| **Source of income** |  |  |  |  |
| Central government | – | 7 | – | 2 |
| Arts councils/RABs | 10 | 38 | 17 | 21 |
| Local authorities | 14 | 66 | 21 | 26 |
| Other public sources | – | 15 | – | 3 |
| Sponsorship, etc | – | 18 | – | 8 |
| Commercial activities | 25 | 192 | 39 | 40 |
| Total income | 111 | 336 | .. | 100 |
| Total expenditure | 125 | 311 | 100 | 113 |
| Surplus/(loss) | – | 25 | – | (13) |

These losses might well be in addition to losses made in earlier years. Consequently, the total accumulated deficit of any one organisation might well be much greater than that incurred in any one year.

## Summary of survey findings

The financial details of the combined-arts, festivals and services sector are summarised in Table 6.15. The mean average income of organisations is much higher than the median income, indicating that this sector is made up of a large number of relatively small organisations and a few rather large ones. Similarly, many organisations receive little, if any, support from the major arts funding bodies – the arts councils and RABs – and local authorities. A few, however, receive relatively substantial grants from at least one of these funders. This kind of support tends not to be concentrated on a small number of organisations, but is spread relatively evenly across the sector.

The "bottom line" of Table 6.15 reflects the existence of the losses described earlier. On average, organisations in the sector made losses (although nearly half broke even), leaving deficits to be covered in the future, either out of increased activity or out of increased support.

# Chapter 7

# Museums, galleries and the visual arts

This chapter covers a group of related cultural activities, namely:

- museums and galleries;
- collections;
- the visual arts;
- crafts; and
- the art trade.

Although these categories overlap, data exist for discrete activities which are defined in this section.

In keeping with the definition of museums adopted by the Museums' Association, the term "museums and galleries" is used to refer to: "an institution which collects, documents, preserves, exhibits and interprets material evidence and associated information for the public benefit" (MGC, 1995).The term "collections" is used here to refer to national and specialist university library collections[1].

The term, "visual arts" is used by arts-funding bodies, such as the arts councils and the regional arts boards (RABs) to refer to various contemporary, visual arts practices. These include temporary and touring exhibitions, fine art photography, some aspects of film and video, installation, live art and education initiatives such as artists in residence, but may

---

1   The national and special university library collections, funded through central government, are included here because of the way they are funded. In general, however, libraries are outside the remit of this study.
2   Film and video arts are also funded under separate media budgets (see Chapter 8).

also include crafts[2]. The Crafts Council (CC), the main funding body for crafts in the UK, defines craft as characterised by the technical competencies of the maker and by a specific range of materials. Its understanding of craft requires:

> *the dominant impact of an individual maker at all stages of production; a sense of innovation; design content; aesthetic content; technical competence. Broadly the Crafts Council is particularly concerned with certain materials, for example, glass, fibre, wood, clay. (CC, 1986)*

The art trade, including the antiques trade, is distinguished from the majority of activities considered here by virtue of being an essentially commercial activity. The trade itself is defined by the items it handles. The Standard International Trade Classification 896 identifies these as pictures, prints, sculpture, postage stamps, museum items and antiques. In practice, auction houses and dealers deal in both these and other items, such as decorative arts, photographs, textiles and carpets, rare books and wine.

All these categories overlap. For example, some galleries which do not have permanent exhibitions nevertheless use the word "museum" in their title. Commercial galleries may display works produced by practising artists or craftspeople in receipt of grant funding. Subsidised galleries may generate income from sales of work. Works by the same artist may be simultaneously shown, and for sale, in both public and commercial galleries working together for their and the artist's mutual advantage. Private galleries, dealers and auction houses provide important sources of acquisition for other museums, galleries and collections, some of which will be in the public sector. The newsletter *art aktuell*, between 1971 and 1985, traced how exhibitions in public galleries across the world contributed to the market value of artists' work (see Lauf, 1990), and it is reasonable to assume that, in the UK in the 1990s, contemporary art prices are affected by exhibitions in public galleries, and by prestigious visual arts awards and media events such as the Turner Prize.

This chapter examines museums and galleries, collections, the visual arts, crafts and the art trade, referring to individual activities or combinations of activities as appropriate. The chapter is divided into three sections which consider the wider context, sources of funding and the results of the PSI survey.

## The wider context

This section considers various aspects of the sector as a whole:

- detailed audience statistics – visitors to museums and galleries, national library readers, and buyers from the art trade;
- the number of museums and galleries, libraries, and art trade establishments;
- production and outputs – the earned income of museums and galleries, the turnover, sales and earnings of the art trade, and employment.

## Visitors to museums and galleries, national library readers and buyers from the art trade

The reliability of information on visits and visitors to museums and galleries is variable. Since the second half of the 1980s, there has been an increasing interest in museum and gallery visitors in the UK – the number of visitors, the nature of their experience and the evaluation of the exhibitions they see – and the numbers of people using the national libraries.

It is estimated that during 1993 there were 60 million visits to 1,544 museums and 19 million visits to 245 art galleries (BTA/ETB, 1994c). Of those visits, 25 per cent were by overseas visitors and 32 per cent by children. A further 11 million visits were made to 209 properties which the tourist boards do not include in their classification of museums and galleries, but which the Museums & Galleries Commission (MGC) counts as registered museums. They comprise historic properties, visitor centres and steam railways. There are no data which provide an accurate breakdown of visits to contemporary visual arts or crafts exhibitions and events.

In 1993/94 over half a million readers visited the national libraries – the British Library, the National Library of Scotland and the National Library of Wales. In addition, the British Library's Document Supply Centre at Boston Spa and the National Library of Scotland satisfied about 3.5 million requests for material from the UK and abroad (see British Library, 1994; National Library of Scotland, 1994; and National Library of Wales, 1994).

In comparison with data about visitors to museums and galleries, statistics produced by the art trade focus on buyers and people attending specialist fairs. In 1993, for example, 17,000 people attended the Grosvenor House Fair and 37,000 the Olympia Fine Art and Antiques Fair. Research commissioned by the organisers of the latter suggests that as many as 69 per cent of visitors buy from that event[3].The most comprehensive information about buyers derives from the membership surveys of two dealers' associations, the British Antique Dealers' Association (BADA) and Society of London Art Dealers (SLAD)[4].This is presented in

---

3   Research commissioned from NOP Research by P&O Events.
4   BADA's survey is based on its membership of 400; SLAD's on its membership of 100.

*Table 7.1 Types of art trade buyer, 1993/94 (Percentages)*

| | BADA London, South East and Southern England | Elsewhere | SLAD |
|---|---|---|---|
| Private collectors: | | | |
| First–time | 24 | 23 | }55 |
| Established | 41 | 48 | |
| Corporate collectors | 2 | – | 7 |
| Investors | 1 | – | .. |
| Other dealers | 21 | 26 | 14 |
| 'Interior design' trade | 7 | 2 | .. |
| Museums, galleries | 4 | 1 | 20 |
| Sales via auctions | .. | .. | 4 |
| All buyers | 100 | 100 | 100 |

Sources: BADA (1994); SLAD (1994).
BADA: British Antique Dealers' Association.
SLAD: Society of London Art Dealers.

Table 7. 1. Private collectors and other dealers dominate their markets. Both associations found that in 1993/94, nearly 50 per cent of their buyers were from overseas.

## The number of museums and galleries and collections, and art trade establishments

The Department of National Heritage (DNH) estimates that there are over 2,000 museums in Britain, across both the public and private sectors (DNH, 1995). In 1993, these included some 800 local authority museums, about 300 university museums and about 30 museums directly funded by the DNH itself, the Ministry of Defence (MoD) the Welsh Office (WO) the Scottish Office (SO) Education Department, and the Department of Education Northern Ireland (DENI). *The Guide to Military Museums* (1994) estimates that there are 219 military museums[5]. The Association of Independent Museums estimates that there are 1,500 independent museums[6] – museums in the private sector which function outside the frameworks of central and local governments. Both types of museum are included in the DNH's total. Only 1,600 of both independent and public museums, however, met the standards of ownership and collection management necessary to ensure registration with the MGC in 1993/94.

5  Reference supplied by the MoD.
6  Reference supplied by the Association of Independent Museums.

In addition to museums, there are the three national libraries – funded by the DNH, SO and WO. There is no audit of the number of visual arts organisations or craft outlets in the country, although the CC (1994) estimated that there were over 3,000 commercial craft fairs in 1993/94.

In 1993 about 7,500 art trade establishments could be identified, including auction houses, antiques dealers, arts dealers, picture framers, dealers in stamps and coins and second-hand furniture shops. The majority (95 per cent) comprised dealer establishments and the remainder, auction houses (London First, 1995).

## Earned income of museums and galleries and the national collections

The majority of independent museums, which by definition receive little or no public subsidy, depend on revenue generation for their survival. In recent years, museums and galleries in receipt of central government funding have been encouraged to supplement their grants with income from other sources, in particular self-generated income from admissions, trading activities (including bookshops, publications and catering) sponsorship and donations. Many museums and galleries have set up trading companies specifically to generate such income. Examples of these include V&A Enterprises (Victoria and Albert Museum), the British Museum Company and the Natural History Trading Company (Natural History Museum).

There are no data on the earnings of independent museums, and those which exist on the earnings of funded museums and galleries in the UK are far from comprehensive. However, two sources provide some estimates. The MGC's Digest of Museum Statistics (DOMUS), estimates the turnover of registered museums to be some £287m, of which 23 per cent (£67m) is earned income[7]. The DNH's annual report publishes details of the self-engendered income – income from trading, sponsorship and other public sector sources – of those museums and galleries it supports. In 1993/94 these museums and galleries generated income of over £75m (38 per cent of their total incomes).

Only half of all museums charged admission in 1993/94 (BTA/ETB, 1994b) and of those, half charged under £1. Furthermore, the majority of visual arts venues do not charge. The national libraries generated nearly £30m from "major priced activities", including document supply, publishing and sales (see British Library, 1994, National Library of Scotland, 1994 and National Library of Wales, 1994).

---

7   This is likely to be an underestimate, particularly on the part of university and local authority museums and galleries (MDA, 1996).

Data from the CC about sales generated directly by its own shops, and estimated sales by craft businesses at events organised by the CC, indicate sales of £3.3m in 1993/94. Based on research carried out in 1993, the CC also estimated that the combined turnover of craftspeople working in England, Scotland and Wales was £400m (Knott, 1994).

## Turnover and sales of auction houses and dealers

Dealers are not obliged to disclose financial information and, in some cases, it is difficult to identify precisely if their trade relates exclusively to the fine arts, antiques or other types of stock[8]. Information about the art trade is, consequently, based on a combination of statistics and estimates.

The turnover of the art trade in 1993/94 is estimated to have been between £1.7bn and £2bn (DTI, 1994). However, it had fluctuated widely in previous years. Following a period of rapid growth in the late 1980s, with turnover rising to £3.1bn in 1989, the art trade experienced a short-lived but severe recession. In 1992 turnover fell to £1.6bn, and 25 per cent of businesses operating in 1990 had closed by 1994 (DTI, 1994).

In 1993/94, almost 85 per cent of art-trade establishments reported a turnover of under £250,000, with 30 per cent generating less than £50,000. Fewer than 3 per cent had turnovers which exceeded £1m. This reflects an uneven distribution of sales within the sector. The four leading auction houses – Christie's, Sotheby's, Phillips and Bonhams – together accounted for sales of £627m (40 per cent of total sales). Dealers accounted for 52 per cent of sales. This disparity is largely due to the type of business handled. Few dealers command a sizable or international market or carry as stock goods with a very high value. Auctioneers, by definition, have a wider market, are better capitalised, take goods on consignment, and are better placed to deal with "high end" goods (London First, 1995).

In 1993 the value of art trade exports was £1.2bn and the value of imports £1.1bn. Pictures, collages, prints, sculptures and museum items represented about 70 per cent of the art trade's turnover. They showed a positive balance of £67m, 47 per cent of the total balance for the art trade shown in Table 7.2. A considerable share of the international trade reflects not so much a change in the UK's permanent stock of the goods auctioned, but of goods being brought into the country solely for auction to be purchased by a foreign buyer and re-exported. The large positive balance for antiques, however, also represents a high foreign demand for this element of UK culture, the satisfaction of which the art trade is able to help meet[9].

---

8   Sotheby's Holdings, Inc, the parent company of Sotheby's worldwide auction, finance and real estate operations, does not publish separate accounts for its UK auction sales.
9   Antiques, in particular, showed a very substantial positive trade balance in 1993, 1994 and 1995.

*Table 7.2 Imports and exports of works of art, antiques, stamps and museums items, 1993 (£m)*

|  | Exports | Imports | Balance |
|---|---|---|---|
| Pictures | 696 | 661 | 35 |
| Prints | 17 | 17 | – |
| Sculptures | 78 | 68 | 10 |
| Postage stamps | 31 | 21 | 10 |
| Museums items | 46 | 24 | 22 |
| Antiques | 352 | 287 | 65 |
| Total | 1,220 | 1,078 | 142 |

Source: DTI (1994).

## Employment in the arts trade and museums and galleries

The major sources of information about employment in the visual arts, crafts, museums galleries and arts trade are discussed in Chapter 3 on employment in the cultural sector. Table 7.3 compares those figures with data from other sources.

*Table 7.3 Employment in museums, galleries, collections, visual arts, crafts and the art trade*

|  | Numbers |
|---|---|
| **Museums and galleries** | |
| Labour Force Survey, Spring 1994 (UK) | 38,000 |
| Population Census, 1991 (GB) (a) | 6,500 |
| MTI, 1992 (UK) | 40,000 |
| DOMUS, 1993/4 (UK) | 12,236 |
| BTA/ETB, 1993 (UK) | 15,500 |
| **Visual arts** | |
| Labour Force Survey, Spring 1994 (UK) | 98,000 |
| Population Census, 1991 (GB) (a) | 93,200 |
| **Crafts** | |
| Population Census, 1991 (GB) (a) | 15,500 |
| Crafts Council, 1992 (GB) | 25,000 |
| **Art trade** | |
| London First, 1993 (GB) | 21,000 |

*Sources:* O'Brien and Feist *(1996);* BTA / ETB *(1994b);* London First (1995); Scott, et al (1993).
(a) By occupational groups.

The sources presented in Table 7. 3 show considerable variations as to the number of people estimated to be employed in the sectors covered in this chapter. The sources cannot be aggregated, because they relate to different years, different geographical remits, have been collected in different ways, refer to different classifications of activity, are not presented in uniform format (such as full-time equivalents), and refer to both employment and self-classification of occupations.

The MTI report (Scott et al, 1993) estimate is based on two surveys: one of 106 local authorities; and one of 944 individual museums. Its total is very close to that of the Labour Force Survey (LFS) which is based on industrial classifications. The BTA/ETB (1994b) data refer to a survey of 1,800 museums and galleries; whereas the DOMUS data, which show fewer people employed, are based on a survey of 1,400 registered museums. The 1991 Population Census (O'Brien and Feist, 1995) identified 6,500 archivists and curators by cultural occupation – a number which could not be further disaggregated.

There are no comprehensive estimates of the number of visual artists or craftspeople currently practising in the UK. The LFS (1994) aggregates artists and designers (identified through occupational classifications). Its definition is the same as that of the 1991 census, and the two sources closely agree. The 1991 Census (O'Brien and Feist, 1995) aggregates artists, commercial artists and graphic designers in Great Britain, identified by occupational categories. The same source also estimates that there were 15,500 self-employed craftspeople on the basis of four occupational groups – weavers, knitters, cabinet makers and glass product and ceramic makers. However, the CC estimates that there are 25,000 craftspeople (Knott, 1994)[10]. Two factors are likely to explain this discrepancy. First, the Standard Occupational Classifications used by the Census do not include all the craft-sector activities used by the CC and may have included some craftspeople under other cultural occupational unit groups. Secondly, the definitions of the population of craftspeople used were different (O'Brien and Feist, 1995). The CC included 4,500 craftspeople who worked for fewer than ten hours per week.

Estimates of the number of people employed in the art trade in 1993 are provided by London First (1995)[11]. It estimated that the majority of employees in the art trade (18,000 or 86 per cent of the total) were employed by dealers. The remainder (3,000) worked for auction houses, with nearly two-thirds of those employed by the four leading houses, Christie's, Sotheby's, Phillips and Bonhams.

## Sources of funding

Apart from the revenue generated through commercial activities, support

---

10  The Crafts Occupational Standards Board (1993) estimates that there are as many as 227,000 craftspeople. However, they include those employed in such activities as stone masonry, saddlery, rural crafts, soft furnishings and upholstery, flower arranging, sugar crafts and taxidermy which are outside the remit of this report.
11  See also DTI (1994).

*Table 7.4 Sources of funding for museums and galleries, collections, visual arts, crafts and the art trade (£m and percentages)*

| | Visual arts | Crafts | Museums and galleries, and collections | Art trade | Spend not disagg-regated | Total | Percentage down |
|---|---|---|---|---|---|---|---|
| European funding | 0.1 | – | – | – | 12.6 | 12.7 | *2.1* |
| DNH (a) | – | – | 286.0 | – | – | 286.0 | *46.2* |
| SO, WO, DENI (b) | – | – | 57.6 | – | – | 57.6 | *9.3* |
| Other central government departments (c) | 7.6 | 0.5 | 37.5 | 0.1 | – | 45.7 | *7.4* |
| Arts councils and Crafts Council (d)(e) | 7.4 | 3.9 | – | – | – | 11.3 | *1.8* |
| National Heritage Memorial Fund (f) | – | – | 5.4 | – | – | 5.4 | *0.9* |
| MGC (g) | – | – | 5.5 | – | – | 5.5 | *0.9* |
| RABs (d)(h) | 6.3 | – | – | – | – | 6.3 | *1.0* |
| National and area museum councils | – | – | 6.3 | – | – | 6.3 | *1.0* |
| Local authorities (j) | – | – | 159.1 | – | – | 159.1 | *25.7* |
| Business sponsorship | 3.1 | – | 9.0 | – | – | 12.1 | *2.0* |
| Charities | – | – | – | – | 10.9 | 10.9 | *1.8* |
| Total | 24.5 | 4.4 | 566.4 | 0.1 | 23.5 | 618.9 | *100.0* |
| *Percentage across* | *4.0* | *0.7* | *91.5* | *\** | *3.8* | *100.0* | *–* |

Sources: DNH (1995); individual government departments; ACGB (1994); ACNI (1994); CC (1994); RABs, annual reports, 1993/94; AMCs, annual reports (1993/94); MGC (1994); NHMF (1994); ABSA (1994); CIPFA (1994); DoE data on local authority museums and galleries; PSI survey of charities.

(a) Includes spending on Royal Armouries, government indemnity, MTI, MGIF and grants.

(b) Includes non–formula spending on museums and galleries and specialised research collections.

(c) The figure under "art trade" refers to DTI spending on trade fairs, etc.

(d) This is a conservative estimate and does not include additional funding through combined or cross arts.

(e) Excluding expenditure on administration and overhead costs for the arts councils (but included for the Crafts Council).

(f) Refers to grants for paintings, works of art and other museum and library objects only.

(g) Excluding grants to the AMCs, accounted for below, and on administration and overheads.

(h) Visual arts includes crafts.

(j) Includes museum and gallery and other visual arts spend. Combines data from DoE and Section 48 schemes for England, CIPFA for Wales, SO and DENI.

for the sector considered in this chapter is largely channelled through:

- European funds;
- central government departments (directly or through their funding of arts councils, the CC, and MGC);
- local authorities (including their support of RABs);
- business sponsorship;
- grant-making trusts and foundations.

Museums and galleries, collections, visual arts, crafts and the art trade together received support to the value of £620m during 1993/94. The majority of this funding went to museums and galleries which, as Table 7.4 shows, accounted for over 90 per cent of the total identified.

## European funding

About 2 per cent of the total funding to the sector identified in Table 7.4 came from the European Commission. Very little of this was from DGX, the directorate of the European Commission which directly funds cultural activities, or its Kaleidoscope programme which supports innovatory artistic and cultural events. The majority came through the structural funds and took the form of capital funds for museum and gallery developments, and arts training for young people. Structural fund grants to the sector totalled £12.6m in 1993/94.

## Central government funding

Several central government departments fund museums and galleries and the national libraries directly. The DNH, SO, WO and DENI's funding of museums and galleries, as shown in Table 7.4, includes funding of the government's art collection, the Museums and Galleries Improvement Fund, the MTI and grants to organisations other than the directly funded national and non-national collections. The government indemnity scheme is available to meet claims on works loaned for public display. The costs of operating the scheme for non-national museums fall to the MGC. The four government departments' support for museums and galleries accounts for £216m. The DNH, SO and WO provided £79m to national libraries; the DNH contributed a further £37m for the new British Library building, St Pancras, the Royal Geographical Society and the Royal National Institute for the Blind Libraries, the Library and Information Council and the Royal Commission on Historical Manuscripts. In total, the DNH, SO, WO and DENI provide about half the total funding shown in Table 7. 4.

Other government departments from which museums and galleries also receive support include: the Ministry of Agriculture, Fisheries and Food, which funds the Royal Botanical Gardens, Kew (the national botanical reference collections); the Foreign & Commonwealth Office, which supports the Commonwealth Institute; and the MoD, which directly supports six devolved institutions and, indirectly, provides for a further 70 non-devolved museums through grants and the provision of staff or services. The Department for Education (subsequently the Department for Education and Employment) indirectly funded museums and galleries and specialised research collections in the humanities in institutions of higher education, but the extent of this support cannot be identified. The Department also provides direct grants for collections or specialised research collections in the form of non-formula funding through the Higher Education Funding Councils[12].

As part of their support to museums and galleries and collections, the DNH, SO, WO and DENI above provided nearly £40m solely intended for acquisitions (excluding the government's own art collection)[13]. As Table 7.5 shows, a substantial part of this was for the national libraries. Individual museums and galleries receive this support through grant-aid and purchase grants available from the MGC. They also benefit through the private sector support provided by the National Art Collections Fund (NACF). The national libraries' total expenditure on acquisitions in 1993/94 was about £15m. Further support for museums and galleries and collections is provided through National Heritage Memorial Fund (NHMF).

Objects are also acquired by museums and galleries on behalf of the nation through the Acceptance in Lieu (AIL) scheme, administered by the MGC on behalf of the DNH. This allows the Commissioners of the Inland Revenue to accept objects, land and buildings in lieu of capital transfer and inheritance taxes. The scheme covers only items which are considered important to the national heritage. In 1993/94 this represented £3m for which the DNH reimbursed the Inland Revenue for tax forgone. As noted in Chapter 2, the DNH budget for AIL is £2m. When the value of acceptances exceeds this figure, access may be sought through the Public Expenditure Reserve. (In 1994/95 and 1995/96 the figures were £6m and £9m respectively).

Potential sellers of works of art deemed to be of national importance

---

12  Non-formula funding is provided for museums, galleries and collections of national importance in institutions of higher education over and above that provided through the institutions' grant (formula funding).

13  From 1993/94 museums and galleries funded by DNH were able to decide on the proportion of their grant aid to be allocated to purchases. Estimates as to libraries' acquisitions is based on their spend.

*Table 7.5 Assistance towards purchase and acquisition of objects by museums and galleries, 1993/94 (£m)*

| | |
|---|---|
| National and non–national museums' allocations for purchases from grant in aid | |
| DNH (a) | 8.9 |
| Scottish Office | 3.2 |
| Welsh Office | 1.5 |
| Northern Ireland Office | 0.5 |
| Subtotal | 14.1 |
| | |
| National libraries' spend on acquisitions, including allocations from grant aid | 15.1 |
| | |
| Other purchase grants | |
| MGC/V&A Purchase Grants and grants for the Preservation of Industrial and Scientific Material | 1.7 |
| National Heritage Memorial Fund (b) | 4.4 |
| Subtotal | 6.1 |
| | |
| Tax concessions | |
| AIL | 3.0 |
| Private treaty sales | 1.7 |
| Subtotal | 4.7 |
| | |
| Private sector support | |
| National Arts Collections Fund | 2.5 |
| | |
| Total | 42.5 |

Sources: MGC (1994).
(a) From 1993/94, DNH allocations towards purchases have been decided by recipients. Funds from other central government departments are allocated according to tripartite division between runnings costs, building and purchases.
(b) Excludes £1.7 towards private treaty sales, accounted for below.

are also able to take advantage of a reduction in what would otherwise be due under capital taxes. The concession is available if the owner is ready to negotiate a sale by private treaty (PTS) directly to an appropriate public collection, instead of selling the work on the open market. The incentive to the seller is that in these circumstances, the Treasury is willing to reduce the notional tax by an amount which averages around 25 per cent. This incentive, or sweetener, is known technically as a "douceur"[14]. No data are

---

14    For both AIL and PTS this is not so much a reduction of tax liability, as a computation of a proportion of the notional tax which would have been paid on an open-market sale. This is added to the agreed valuation net of open-market sale tax, to give the tax settlement figure (AIL) or the price paid to the vendor (PTS). For AIL on land and buildings, the douceur is 10 per cent, for AIL on chattels it is 25 per cent, and for PTS it is flexible and at the discretion of the institutions negotiating the purchase.

available on the value of such transactions. However, the NHMF's *Annual Report 1993/94* records grants of £1.7m made towards private treaty purchases in that year. However, as noted in Chapter 2, this would have only represented a fraction of the total value of Private Treaty Sales for that year, since not all would have been assisted by the NHMF.

A small share of central government expenditure on the visual arts and crafts is distributed by the four arts councils, the CC and the RABs. This support is often directed towards "individual artists in the production of exciting and innovative work" (LAB, 1994). This is provided in two ways: directly, by giving grants to artists, and indirectly, through the support of galleries and other agencies, workshops, studio spaces and training provision, which support and promote artists' work. The support of individual artists' work is also often a stated objective of those galleries and other promoters (see, for example, Whitechapel Art Gallery, 1994). While the MGC provides grants directly to museums, it also redistributes a small share of central government expenditure on museums and galleries to the English regional area museum services, which in turn give grants to museums and galleries. Elsewhere in the UK, local museums and galleries are supported through the Scottish Museums Council, the Northern Ireland Museums Council and the Council of Museums in Wales, each of which are funded through their respective Secretaries of State, while the British Library distributed some £1.5m on grants for external research and the dissemination of research findings in 1993/94.

Support for the visual arts by central government departments other than the DNH, SO, WO and DENI is made on the premise that the visual arts contribute to other activities. For example, the Home Office, through its Central Drugs Unit, prison and probation services, funds the visual arts to provide people in its care with social and vocational skills. The Department of the Environment funds the visual arts to contribute to urban regeneration; the Department of Employment, vocational training; the Health Department, for the "psychological" benefits of the visual arts, and the DTI, to encourage enterprise.

Although the art trade received only a small amount of direct financial support from the DTI, as shown in Table 7.4, it benefits from minimal government legislation and a supportive framework regarding taxation. Until 1995, and unlike in other European countries, no VAT was levied on imported pre–1973 works of art. After 1995, and as a step toward meeting EU requirements, a reduced rate of 2.5 per cent was imposed, with a minimum of 5.0 per cent (still lower than the standard rate of 17.5 per cent prevailing in the UK) due to apply in 1999[15]. Moreover, the art trade is not liable, in the sums settled at auction, to make provision for royalty payments on the work of living artists or, within 70 years of death, their

---

15   The 7th VAT Directive is due to be reviewed by the EC during 1999.

estates. This advantage may be removed by a proposal to generalise across Europe this so-called *droit de suite*, which already applies, theoretically, in 11 of the 15 member states. The attempts to establish a level playing field in Europe have been fiercely resisted by the art trade which fears losing ground to non-EU centres, such as New York, where neither VAT nor *droit de suite* apply. The extent of advantage given by current derogations, and their worth, has not however been quantified[16].

## Support by local authorities

Local authorities own and run museums and galleries, and support professional and non-professional art organisations through project, revenue and other grants. They also contribute to RABs and Section 48 schemes (see Chapter 2)[17]. The majority of that funding is provided by regional, metropolitan authorities for their own museums and art galleries. Local authority funding represents over a quarter of the total sum identified in Table 7.4. This, however, is not fully representative of local authorities' total spend, as other departments not included in these statistics also contribute to this sector. A PSI study on public art (Selwood, 1995) observes, for example, that planning departments and those concerned with environmental, economic and technical matters are more likely to be involved, if not responsible for, the financing of public art than those concerned with the arts, recreation and leisure. Other funds for the visual arts may be available through education, libraries, social services, and other departments.

In 1984, the Arts Council of Great Britain (ACGB) in an attempt to create a more equitable distribution of arts funding, introduced a ten-year development strategy, commonly known as *The Glory of the Garden*. Its intention was to encourage local authorities to increase their funding of museums and galleries through a sliding scale of partnership funding. It proposed that the ACGB would withdraw its funding and the local authorities would increase theirs[18].

---

16 However, their importance to the art trade is demonstrated by the campaign by the British Art Market Federation (established in 1996) for their perpetuation.

17 Local authority support for museums and galleries, visual arts and crafts has been identified through several sources. Data for English museums and galleries derive from the DoE. These DoE statistics are collected retrospectively from all local authorities in England. They describe a total expenditure of £113.4m. CIPFA sources have been used for local authority spending in Wales. Other data derive from the Scottish Office, Scottish Local Government Statistics, DENI and Section 48 schemes.

18 A summary of ACE's assessment of that strategy is due to be published in 1996.

## Business sponsorship, trusts and foundations

Combined funding for museums, visual arts and sculpture, photography and craft as recorded by the Association for Business Sponsorship of the Arts (ABSA, 1994) represented £12m, less than 20 per cent of total business sponsorship for all arts and cultural activities in 1993/94 and only 2 per cent of subsidy to the museums and galleries, and visual arts sector.

PSI's survey of grant-giving trusts and foundations found that they provided nearly £11m to the sector, nearly as much as business sponsors. This included £2m from the Wolfson Foundation and Wolfson Family Charitable Trust to match DNH funding through the Museums and Galleries Improvement Fund and £2.5m from the NACF (referred to above).

## Regional dimension

The funding of London's visual arts, crafts and museums and galleries shows a strong regional bias. In 1993/94 it received 70 per cent of the funding allocated to the ACGB's visual arts revenue clients, over 70 per cent of UK business sponsorship for museums, the visual arts and sculpture, photography and craft. Because the DNH has responsibility for the national museums in England and for the British Library, it is not surprising that nearly 90 per cent of the DNH direct funding of museums and over 90 per cent of its funding of libraries is spent on institutions in London. Of all the RABs, the London Arts Board spent the most on visual arts – £1.4m out of a total of £6.3m (nearly 25 per cent) in 1993/94. Given the presence of the national and non-national museums, funded by

*Table 7.6 Share of visual arts, crafts and museums and gallery funding going to organisations based in London, 1993/94 (percentages)*

| | |
|---|---|
| Share of English funding | |
| ACGB revenue clients | 70 |
| RAB | 22 |
| DNH spending on national and non–national museums (a) | 86 |
| London's share of the English population | 14 |
| Share of UK funding | |
| Local authority (b) | 3 |
| Business sponsorship | 71 |
| London's share of the UK population | 12 |

Sources: ACGB (1994); RAB annual reports, 1993/94; DNH (1995); CIPFA (1994); ABSA (1994).
a) Excludes Royal Armouries.
b) Excludes Section 48 schemes.

central government, London's local authorities spend relatively less on museums and galleries than those in regional, metropolitan areas.

# Survey results

PSI conducted a survey of funded organisations in this part of the cultural sector, to examine in more detail their incomes and expenditures, regional distribution and levels of employment[19].

The survey covered 72 organisations (including "one-person" operations) in the visual arts, crafts, museums and galleries sectors. Grossing-up these figures suggested a population of between 850 and 900 organisations receiving support or funding as defined in this study. Museums and galleries represented 62 per cent of respondents, and visual arts and crafts, 38 per cent.

## Overall size and characteristics

On the basis of the survey, the total number of employees in the museums and galleries, crafts and visual arts sector can be estimated as some 22,000 (to which could be added perhaps 7,000 self-employed)[20] and the total income of the sector as between £700m and £750m.

*Table 7.7 Survey results: regional distribution of funded organisations (percentages)*

| | All organisations | of which, museums and galleries |
|---|---|---|
| London | 26 | 5 |
| South of England (excluding London) | 34 | 51 |
| North of England | 15 | 16 |
| Northern Ireland | * | * |
| Wales | 3 | 1 |
| Scotland | 18 | 26 |
| Midlands | 5 | * |
| Total | 100 | 100 |

19  Comparisons between this part of the survey and other areas of the cultural sector, as well as with the wider cultural sector and parts of the UK economy as a whole, can be found in Chapter 10.
20  Calculated according to the ratio of self-employed to employed people in the cultural sector suggested by the LFS.

*Table 7.8 Survey results: share of funded organisations by size of income (percentages)*

| Annual income | Museums and galleries | All organisations |
|---|---|---|
| Less than £30,000 | 34 | 21 |
| £30,000 to £49,999 | 7 | 20 |
| £50,000 to £99,999 | 25 | 28 |
| £100,000 to £249,999 | 17 | 13 |
| £250,000 or more | 19 | 17 |
| Total | 100 | 100 |

Funded museums and galleries, crafts and visual arts organisations as noted above, are disproportionately to be found in London. Table 7.7 shows the geographical distribution of organisations suggested by the survey.

Given the relatively few visual arts and crafts organisations and individuals surveyed, it was not possible to examine these in their own right. Thus, in the analysis which follows, results are shown for the sector as a whole, and where appropriate for museums and galleries by themselves[21].

Four in ten organisations in the sector had an income of under £50,000 per year, and, as Table 7.8 shows, the difference between the figures for the whole sector and for museums and galleries on their own was small.

Only 6 per cent of organisations had an income in excess of £1m (all but four of which were museums or galleries) and two per cent an income in excess of £10m.

A substantial share of organisations in the sector had no paid employees. This was as true for museums and galleries as it was for all organisations: nearly one in five museums operated only with volunteers or by using only self-employed people. However, museums tended to be larger than visual arts organisations, since one third of museums had 10

*Table 7.9 Survey results: funded organisations by number of employees (percentages)*

| Number of employees | All organisations | of which, museums and galleries |
|---|---|---|
| None | 15 | 18 |
| 1 or 2 | 26 | 32 |
| 3 to 10 | 31 | 14 |
| 11 to 40 | 22 | 28 |
| More than 40 | 6 | 9 |
| Total | 100 | 100 |

21 Sample numbers were: museums and galleries, 52; visual arts, 17; crafts, 3.

employees, and one in twelve had 100 or more employees (see Table 7.9).

## Income sources

Museums and galleries and visual arts organisations generate income from commercial activities such as charging admissions, merchandising, catering and selling original works. Over and above this, they benefit from donations and sponsorships, and grants from public bodies. On average, income from commercial activities constituted about half the sector's total income (49 per cent), and a slightly higher share (55 per cent) where museums and galleries were considered alone (Table 7.10). More than a third of organisations in the sector gained at least three-quarters of their income from commercial activities, but for a quarter this constituted less than a fifth of total income. However, when considering the share of support organisations receive from different sources, the picture is effectively reversed.

*Table 7.10 Survey results: funded organisations by contribution of commercial income to total income (percentages)*

|  | Museums and galleries | All organisations |
|---|---|---|
| Less than 20 per cent | 16 | 25 |
| 20 to 39 per cent | 16 | 15 |
| 40 to 59 per cent | 27 | 26 |
| 60 to 79 per cent | 4 | 3 |
| 80 per cent or more | 39 | 33 |
| Total | 100 | 100 |

Table 7.11 shows the percentage of organisations receiving funding from different sources. More than half of all organisations received funding from the arts councils and RABs, but this drops to a quarter when considering museums and galleries alone. However, nearly two-thirds of this group received funding from what might be termed collections funders

*Table 7.11 Survey results: funded organisations by source of support (percentages)*

|  | Museums and galleries | All organisations |
|---|---|---|
| Central goverment | 4 | 4 |
| Arts councils & RABs | 26 | 54 |
| Collections funders | 64 | 42 |
| Local authority | 42 | 55 |
| Other public | 26 | 19 |
| Sponsorships and donations | 74 | 65 |

*Table 7.12 Survey results: share of income of funded organisations from arts councils and RABs (percentages)*

| Share of total income | Museums and galleries | All organisations |
|---|---|---|
| Less than 5 per cent | 83 | 55 |
| 30 to 59 per cent | 5 | 15 |
| 60 per cent or more | 6 | 5 |

(such as the MGC, NHMF and area museum services), compared with just over 40 per cent of all organisations.

Four forms of support can be considered in more detail – from: central and local government arts funders (ACGB, the Scottish, Welsh and Northern Ireland arts councils and the RABs); local authorities; collections funders; and charities, foundations, sponsorships and donations. Arts funders provided, on average, 13 per cent of the income of organisations in the sector and 8 per cent of the income of museums and galleries. Table 7.12 shows this by looking at two extremes of support. Collections funders (as defined above) provided, on average, about 5 per cent of the organisations' income (Table 7.13). They were, not surprisingly, important for museums and galleries considered alone, which drew an average of 7 per cent of income from them. Over two-thirds of museums and galleries received support from this source, but collections funders provided more than one tenth of total income for fewer than one in five museums and galleries.

*Table 7.13 Survey results: share of income of funded organisations from collections funders (percentages)*

| Share of total income | Museums and galleries | All organisations |
|---|---|---|
| None | 36 | 42 |
| More than 10 per cent | 18 | 13 |

Local government provided an average of 16 per cent of the income of organisations in the sector and slightly less (14 per cent) of museums and galleries alone. Just over half of museums and galleries and visual arts organisations in the sector received little or no support from local authorities (Table 7.14). However, a third derived a substantial share of their

*Table 7.14 Survey results: share of income of funded organisations from local authorities (percentages)*

| Share of total income | Museums and galleries | All organisations |
|---|---|---|
| Less than 5 per cent | 60 | 53 |
| 15 per cent or more | 27 | 34 |

*Table 7.15 Survey results: share of income of funded organisations from sponsor-ships (percentages)*

| Share of total income | Museums and galleries | All organisations |
|---|---|---|
| No sponsorship | 31 | 38 |
| Less than 5 per cent | 30 | 24 |
| 15 or more per cent | 9 | 19 |

income from this source.

Support in the form of sponsorship, donations or grants from non-public sources is more frequently received by visual arts organisations than by museums and galleries and it is also more important to such organisations (Table 7.15).

## Expenditure

Turning to organisations' expenditure, the only item the survey was able to identify across the board was staff costs (including wages, national insurance and pension costs). A not inconsiderable proportion of organisations – one in four of all organisations in the sector and nearly a third of museums and galleries – had no staff costs at all, either because all those working in them were self-employed or because they relied on volunteers. On average, staff costs made up nearly half (47 per cent) of total expenditure, but a rather lower share (42 per cent) for museums and galleries. In as many as a fifth of all organisations, and an eighth of all museums and galleries, staff costs appeared to be the only major costs incurred.

## Financial outturn

Although most museums and galleries and visual arts organisations are non-profit-making, this does not mean that they always operate at break even. In any one year, some generate a surplus and others make a loss. The survey suggests that, while, on average, organisations broke even, for a minority, a substantial share of expenditure in 1993/94 (more than 5 per cent) was not matched by income. Table 7.16 considers this income gap – the difference between income and expenditure measured as a proportion of total expenditure.

Total losses made in 1993/94 by organisations recording an income gap in excess of 5 per cent amounted to rather more than £35m. These represent only those losses that occurred in the survey year and may be added to losses incurred in previous years, contributing to a much larger accumulated deficit.

*Table 7.16 Survey results: financial outturns of funded organisations (percentages)*

| Financial balance | Museums and galleries | All organisations |
|---|---|---|
| Break even | 29 | 35 |
| Surplus greater than 5 per cent of income | 41 | 31 |
| *Surplus greater than 12.5 per cent of income* | *29* | *23* |
| Loss greater than 5 per cent of income | 3 | 28 |
| *Loss greater than 12.5 per cent of income* | *14* | *1* |

## Summary of survey results

The financial details of the museums and galleries and visual arts sector are summarised in Table 7.17. The mean, or average income of organisations was much higher than the median income, suggesting that the sector is made up of a large number of relatively small organisations and a few rather large ones. This holds true for both museums and galleries and other visual arts organisations. Similarly, many organisations received little if any support from most of the funding bodies, but a few received quite substantial grants from at least one of these. The very uneven distribution of arts council, RAB, local authority support and sponsorship is clear from the final two columns of Table 7.17.

*Table 7.17 Summary of survey results for museums and galleries, collections, visual arts and crafts organisations*

| | Median amount (£000s) | Mean amount (£000s) | Share of total income (percentages) | |
|---|---|---|---|---|
| | | | Median | Mean |
| Source of income | | | | |
| Collections funders | – | 5 | – | 5 |
| Arts councils & RABs | 2 | 13 | * | 13 |
| Direct central government | – | 10 | – | 4 |
| Local authorities | 1 | 29 | 3 | 16 |
| Sponsorship, etc | 1 | 47 | 2 | 10 |
| Commercial activities | 28 | 255 | 44 | 49 |
| Total income | 77 | 821 | .. | 100 |
| | | | | |
| Total expenditure | 77 | 810 | 99 | 99 |
| Surplus | 1 | 12 | 1 | 1 |

# Chapter 8
## The media industries

This chapter is concerned with two types of media industry that fall within the cultural sector. The first covers what is termed the moving image industry, which includes film, video and multimedia, and, in the wider context, television and radio. The second covers the writing and publishing of books, and literary journals and magazines. Although in many respects, these two industries conventionally operated separately and distinctly, they are increasingly converging as they develop into a hybrid sector, where multimedia technology collapses the boundaries between the printed word and the moving image[1].

The following topics are considered in this chapter:

- the wider context – audiences and consumer expenditure, the UK film and video industries, television and radio broadcasting, writing, the UK publishing industry, employment in the media industries;
- public support for the media, from central and local government, arts funding bodies, business and grant-making trusts;
- regional trends in media resources and funding;
- survey results.

---

1 Certain areas of the multimedia industry are outside the areas of interest of this study, such as computer games and purely educational products.

# The wider context

The wider context includes all the moving image and broadcast industries, including television and radio. It also includes the production, retailing and consumption of all types of books. The lack of comparable statistics from the various sub-sectors of the media industries makes it difficult to assess the size of the sector as a whole. This section examines discrete data on individual sub-sectors.

## Audiences

In 1993, 113 million people went to the cinema in the UK, contributing to a total box-office take of £319m. The average person visited the cinema twice a year, with nearly 70 per cent of the population claiming to be cinema-goers (CAA, 1994). In the same year, 73 per cent of the population had access to a video recorder in the home (*Social Trends 25*). In 1993/94, £1.1bn was spent on buying and renting video tapes, with video retail accounting for nearly 60 per cent of this expenditure (BVA, 1995)[2].

Consumers spent a total of £1.7m on books (LISU, 1995), with 84 per cent of the population buying at least one book per year (BML, 1995). Over half of this expenditure was on general non-fiction books. By comparison, more than half of the 550 million books borrowed from UK public libraries were adult fiction books.

## Production and output

The production and output of the media industry can best be understood in terms of, respectively, the activities of the film industry and of UK broadcasters, and of writers and publishers. In 1993, the UK film and television industry made net overseas earnings of £93m[3].

### *UK film production*

Film production activity in the UK ranges from purely domestic film-making to the location and studio shooting of Hollywood films (Table 8.1). Films are produced by dedicated film production companies and by television companies, and there is a close relationship between the two in terms of an overlapping pool of specialised staff.

---

2   The consumer market on video rental and retail covers a wider range of programming than cinema exhibition, since it includes films, television programmes, sport and fitness, children's videos and education.

3   *The Times*, 6 October 1994, page 26.

*Table 8.1 Feature film production in the UK, 1993*

|  | Number of films | Total budget (£m) | Average budget (£m) |
|---|---|---|---|
| UK productions | 32 | 42.3 | 1.3 |
| UK co–productions | 27 | 62.7 | 2.3 |
| American films | 10 | 115.4 | 11.4 |
| All films | 69 | 220.4 | 3.2 |

Source: BFI (1994).

In 1993, 69 films were made in the UK, with a total production budget of £220m. Budgets for UK films and UK co-production with other non-UK companies (at an average of £1.3m and £2.3m respectively) were much lower than the average budget for the 10 US productions made in the UK, at £11m.

One major problem for British film producers is that, in general, they are under-capitalised and thus have to raise money on a film-by-film basis. As a result, it often becomes necessary to sell distribution rights in advance to distributors, who then have the opportunity to exploit the long-term potential of any film. This means that even if successful, films funded in this way benefit exhibitors and distributors before the producer realises any profit (Advisory Committee on Film Finance, 1996). Under-capitalisation also means that producers are unable to spread their risk across a number of projects. It is estimated that only one or two in every ten films are successful. The US film industry, unlike the UK, is dominated by companies that are able to cushion those risks. These US companies are vertically integrated in that they control major parts of the exhibition and distribution chains and feed the profits from these parts of the industry into production costs (KPMG, 1992).

Film production by television companies is often difficult to disaggregate from their broadcasting production. The BBC currently has a special unit within its drama department to oversee a three-year programme of film production which will be investing approximately £5m a year to produce up to 30 films. Of these, five films a year will be co-financed by the BBC which will have full cinema and video releases before being shown on BBC television. The BBC has also converted a number of films from television drama to cinema releases (such as *The Snapper* and *Truly Madly Deeply*). In the past four years, ten films have gone through this process (National Heritage Committee, 1995).

Channel Four established its *Film on Four* strand with the intention of producing original British feature films and making them available for theatrical release before broadcasting them on television. Between 1982 and the end of 1993, Channel Four spent 6 per cent of its total programme budget on original feature films (National Heritage Committee, 1995). A few of these films are entirely financed by Channel Four, but most involve a number of financial partners.

The satellite television broadcaster BSkyB has also become an important source of finance for the British film industry in recent years. In 1994, it backed 40 of the 89 films made in the UK or by UK production companies. It invested £13m, most of which was dedicated to commercial and larger-budget areas of production: only five of the 40 films it supported in 1994 had budgets of £2m or less (National Heritage Committee, 1995).

## *The UK broadcasting industry*

There are three types of television and radio broadcasting in the UK:

- public service broadcasting of television and radio, provided by the BBC and funded by the licence fee and central government grant-in-aid;
- commercial television (provided by Channels 3 and 4) and radio, funded by advertising revenue;
- satellite and cable television, financed by subscription and advertising revenues.

The BBC, for operational and funding purposes, is split into two broadcasting divisions: BBC Home Service and BBC World Service. The BBC Home Service (BBC Television and BBC Radio) is almost entirely financed by the collection of the compulsory licence fee, levied on every household (or equivalent) with a television. It provides two television channels (BBC1, a general interest channel, and BBC2, a minority interest channel), five national radio stations and a network of regional radio and television services. The BBC World Service is funded by the Foreign and Commonwealth Office (FCO), and broadcasts to a global audience in English and 40 other languages through both radio and television services (see Table 8.2 below for levels of funding).

By contrast with public service broadcasting, independent broadcasting is provided by a number of different broadcasters at both national and local levels. There are two independent television channels, Channel 3 (also known as ITV), a general interest channel and Channel 4 with more minority-interest programming. Channel 3 is provided by a network of 15 regionally based companies, each licensed by the Independent Television Commission (ITC) to supply programmes in 14 geographic locations[4], while Channel 4 broadcasts nationally.

---

4   There are two licences for the London area, one providing weekday output, the other covering the weekend. There is also a national licence for early morning programming, currently held by GMTV.

In Wales, the fourth television channel is provided by S4C, which is uniquely funded by both central government, through the Department of National Heritage (DNH), and advertising revenues. It broadcast 1,699 hours of Welsh-language programming in that year, a quarter of its total broadcasting output.

A growing number of television services are also available from companies broadcasting via cable and satellite transmission systems, which are also regulated by the ITC. The largest cable and satellite operator in the UK is BSkyB, which provides a number of its own entertainment, news, films and sport channels as well as offering other channels produced by other broadcasters, such as CNN International and MTV.

Independent radio broadcasting in the UK is regulated by the Radio Authority (RA). There are three national independent radio services – Classic FM, Virgin 1215 and Talk Radio UK. In 1993 there were also some 130 local independent radio services.

Table 8.2 summarises the income sources of broadcasters in the UK, which totalled £5bn in 1993. The BBC accounted for just over 40 per cent of these revenues (£2.2bn), including both public funds and revenues generated from their commercial enterprises. Independent terrestrial television broadcasters earned 45 per cent of total revenues (£2.3bn).

*Table 8.2 Income to UK broadcasters, 1993–94 (£m and percentages)*

| | Central government grant | Licence fee | Advertising | Programme sales and other income | Total | Percentage down |
|---|---|---|---|---|---|---|
| BBC Home Service | – | 1,683.0 | – | 296.4 | 1,979.4 | *38.3* |
| BBC World Service | 175.7 | – | – | 10.3 | 186.0 | *3.6* |
| Independent terrestrial television (including S4C) | 58.0 | – | 1,796.0 | 498.0 | 2,352.0 | *45.5* |
| Satellite television (a) | – | – | .. | .. | 471.0 | *9.1* |
| Independent radio | – | – | 178.5 | .. | 178.5 | *3.5* |
| Total | 233.7 | 1,683.0 | 1,974.5 | 804.7 | 5,166.9 | *100.0* |
| *Percentage across* | *4.5* | *32.6* | *38.2* | *15.6* | *100.0* | *–* |

Sources: ITC (1994); BBC (1994); Advertising Association (1995).
(a) Total, which could not be disaggregated, includes advertising revenues, sponsorship and subscription income. Excludes services broadcasting wholly outside the UK.

## The UK publishing industry

It is estimated that UK publishers sold some 649 million books in 1993, with a retail value of £2.7bn, including both domestic and export sales

*Table 8.3 UK publishers' sales, 1993 (a)*

|  | £m | Percentage |
|---|---|---|
| Consumer | 1,845 | 68.4 |
| School | 209 | 7.7 |
| Academic/professional | 645 | 23.9 |
| Total | 2,699 | 100.0 |

Source: The Publishers Association (1994).
(a) At retail value and including exports.

(Table 8.3). This total was made up of three categories of books: general books aimed at the consumer market, school textbooks and academic/professional books. The total sales of consumer books (at £1.8bn), made up nearly 70 per cent of the total market.

The Publishers Association had 180 trade members in 1995. Nearly 84,000 new titles were published in the UK in 1993 (Table 8.4), almost a third of which were academic and professional books. Over a quarter were general non-fiction, with adult fiction accounting for just under 10 per cent. Average cover prices for these new titles ranged from £43.00 for scientific, technical and medical books to £5.50 for children's books[5].

*Table 8.4 New book titles and editions published, 1993*

|  | Number | Percentage | Average cover price (£) |
|---|---|---|---|
| Fiction | 8,022 | 9.6 | 8.70 |
| School text books | 2,880 | 3.4 | 11.97 |
| Childrens' books | 7,030 | 8.4 | 5.49 |
| Scientific/technical/medical | 16,931 | 20.2 | 43.02 |
| Adacemic/professional | 27,264 | 32.5 | 28.29 |
| General non–fiction | 21,653 | 25.8 | 19.06 |
| Total | 83,780 | 100.0 | .. |

Source: BML (1994).

## Employment in the media industries

Employment in the moving image industries is provided by film productions, film studios, television and radio broadcasters and other smaller media organisations. Performers and technicians are often employed on a project basis although more permanent employment can be provided by the film studios and broadcasters.

---

5   There is no index of cover prices of all books in print, only of these new titles.

The Association of Cinematograph, Television and Allied Technicians (ACTT ) reports that its membership has changed since the 1950s, from being primarily employee-based, to being primarily freelance-based, with a large proportion of those under-employed or unemployed (National Heritage Committee, 1995). According to ACTT, it is likely that those employed by the film industry are also engaged in economic activity in other sectors, as increased casualisation forces them to look for means of support outside the film industry. Part of this move towards casualisation can be seen in the BBC's adoption of Producer Choice in 1993, which allows BBC producers to buy in resources from the external market, with the BBC retaining on a permanent basis only those resources for which there is a regular and sustained demand from programme makers (BBC, 1992).

Employment in the media industries is summarised in Table 8.5. The British Screen Advisory Council estimated that a total of 155,000 people were working in television and film in 1993[6], the equivalent of 98,000 full-time jobs. The Labour Force Survey (LFS) estimated a smaller number of people working in the film and broadcasting industries, at 92,000.

*Table 8.5 Estimates of employment within the media industries (numbers)*

| | |
|---|---|
| Media | |
| Employment committee estimates: | |
| film and television 1994 (a) | 98,000 |
| Labour Force Survey: | |
| Film and broadcasting industries | 92,000 |
| | |
| Publishing | |
| Census 1991 | |
| Printing and publishing of books (industry) | 20,200 |
| Labour Force Survey | |
| Authors (occupation) | 53,000 |
| Publishing of books and music (industry) | 38,000 |

Sources: O'Brien and Feist (1995); LFS Spring 1994; HoC Employment Committee (1994).

Employment in literature can be divided into that of authors and that of those in the publishing industry, although there is associated employment in printing and distribution. The LFS estimates 38,000 people working in book and music publishing and 53,000 authors including technical writers

---

6   This estimate includes: those employed directly by film and television companies; "talent"; infrastructure such as laboratories, studios and facilities; distribution, production hardware; exhibition; video; professionals such as lawyers and accountants working in media industries; schools and training. These estimates have been criticised on the grounds that some of the data were at least five years old, and that they did not take into account the mobile nature of this workforce (HoC Employment Committee, 1994).

(of manuals, etc), but excludes journalists. Looking at industries rather than occupations, the 1991 population census also identified 20,200 people working in the printing and publishing of books. Self-employment among authors is very high: according to the LFS, half work for themselves.

## Support for the media industries

Excluding public service broadcasting, which was dealt with above, support for the media industries comes from four broad sources:

- European funding;
- central government;
- arts funding bodies and dedicated media funding bodies;
- business and charities.

*Table 8.6 Support for the media industries, 1993/94*

|  | Moving image arts (£m) | Percentage | Literature £m | Percentage |
|---|---|---|---|---|
| European funding | 4.24 | 7.6 | 1.40 | 9.3 |
| Department of National Heritage | 9.92 | 17.9 | 5.73 | 38.0 |
| Scottish Office | 1.05 | 1.9 | 0.05 | 0.3 |
| Welsh Office | – | – | – | – |
| Northern Ireland Office | 0.03 | 0.1 | – | – |
| Other central government departments | 4.40 | 7.9 | 1.40 | 9.3 |
| British Film Institute (a) | 27.55 | 49.7 | | |
| Arts councils (b) | 0.86 | 1.5 | 3.98 | 26.4 |
| Regional arts boards (b) | 2.04 | 3.7 | 1.54 | 10.2 |
| Business sponsorship | 4.73 | 8.5 | 0.54 | 3.6 |
| Charities | 0.65 | 1.2 | 0.44 | 2.9 |
| Total | 55.48 | 100.0 | 15.08 | 100.0 |

Sources: ACGB (1994); ACNI (1994); Regional arts boards' Annual Reports, 1993/94; ABSA (1994); PSI survey of charities.
(a) Including expenditure on their own activities and grants given to other bodies and individuals.
(b) Minimum estimates.

Total support for the media industries (excluding public service broadcasting) in 1993/94 is summarised in Table 8.6. Support for the moving image industry totalled £55m and for literature £15m[7].

---

7   This section refers to "literature" rather than writing and publishing, etc, as this support is focused narrowly on only those aspects of writing and publishing that are classified by funders as being "literature".

European support for the moving image industry included funding from the MEDIA (*Measures pour Encourager le Developpement de l'Industrie de Production Audio Visuelle*) programme. MEDIA comprises 20 projects supporting various aspects of the film and television industries. Its main concerns are: the training of individuals; improving conditions of film production; the distribution and exhibition of films; contributing to the creation of a "second market" (largely concerned with the preservation and use of archive material); and stimulating financial investments. In 1993, the UK received £0.8m in grants from the MEDIA programme, with a further £3.6m awarded as loans. European Union support for literature (totalling £1.4m in 1993/94) mainly went for translations.

Central government support for the moving image arts was mainly devolved through a number of grant-making organisations, including general arts funders – the Arts Council of Great Britain (ACGB), the Arts Council of Northern Ireland (ACNI) and the regional arts boards (RABs) – and the specific moving image organisation, the British Film Institute (BFI). Other DNH support for the moving image industry (which totalled £10m) went to educational and promotional organisations such as the National Film and Television School and the British Film Commission (BFC). The DNH also supported British Screen Finance (BSF), a private body which makes loans to film makers, and also channels grants to UK film makers from the European Co-production Fund, part of the MEDIA programme. BSF made loans of £4.3m for the production of around 20 feature films in 1994.

In Scotland and Northern Ireland, central government funding for the moving image industries mainly went to the Scottish and Northern Ireland Film Councils respectively, which provided resources, loans and grants to film-makers in their respective countries. The Welsh Film Council, which was first established in 1993, is funded by the Arts Council of Wales.

Central government support for literature totalled £7m, the greatest part of which was accounted for by the DNH's support of the Public Lending Right scheme (PLR), which received £5m from the DNH in 1993/94. PLR pays authors for each time one of their books is borrowed from a public library[8]. In 1993/94, PLR re-distributed £4.3m to authors (at the rate of 2 pence per loan).

The majority of central government support for the moving image arts was devolved to the BFI, which received £15m from the DNH in 1993/94. It spent a total of £27.5m, of which around £3m was redistributed to other bodies (including the RABs). The remainder of its expenditure went on providing resources for film-makers and preserving the moving-image heritage of the UK.

---

8  Local authority expenditure on public libraries totalled £797m in 1993/94. This is not included in Table 8.6 because it falls outside the remit of this report.

The arts councils spent relatively little in support of the moving-image industries (£0.9m, only 2 per cent of the total). In contrast, they spent £4m in support of literary activities – providing over a quarter of the total funding for literature. This funding went to a wide range of recipients, including: writers; literary development workers; publishers and small presses; literary magazines and periodicals; translations; and literary events such as festivals and prizes.

As mentioned in Chapter 2, film-making companies also benefit from special corporate tax provisions.

The moving-image industries received £4.7m from business sponsorship, nearly double the amount spent on the media industries by the arts councils and RABs combined. As this funding was identified through a survey of arts organisations, it can be assumed that this sponsorship was for arts-based media projects, rather than the sponsorship of commercial activities, such as commercial television programmes.

# Regional dimension of funding for the media industries

Within the media industries, there is a concentration of resources and activity in London, which took the largest share of cinema audiences (at just over a quarter of the UK total) and accounts for 20 per cent of cinema screens in the UK. More particularly, 41 per cent each of those employed in the film industry and in radio and television live in London[9].

Equally, although funding for media industries was mainly distributed by national bodies and is therefore difficult to allocate regionally, more than a quarter (£8m) of BFI's total expenditure went on its operations at the National Film Theatre and the Museum of the Moving Image, both based at the South Bank Centre in London.

In contrast, nearly half of the expenditure of the English RABs on the moving-image industry was concentrated in the North of England (with Northern Arts and North West Arts between them accounting for 45 per cent of spending on the media). Such expenditure in the regions may have an impact on the locality concerned. Location shooting generates local expenditure and possibly employment for as long as it lasts. In addition, a more lasting effect may be achieved from the tourism generated by popular films and television programmes and the spending that comes with it. The British Tourist Authority produces a Movie Map which is designed to encourage tourism through the promotion of 70 television and film locations spanning the past sixty years.

---

9   Although this is not necessarily an indication of where the employment is located as some of these people may travel outside London to work on, for example, location shooting.

While there is a dearth of industry-wide statistics, the extent of the local impact of these temporary and more permanent activities can be seen from a study of the moving image industry in Liverpool (Blanc Media, 1993)[10]. That report estimated that in 1992/93, over £31m was spent locally on "moving image development and production", supporting the equivalent of 468 full-time jobs. Liverpool-based production companies accounted for £24m of this expenditure. In addition, film and television production companies based outside Liverpool used the city for location shooting, with a local expenditure of £6m. Community-based and developmental activities, including training and exhibition, created local expenditure of £0.8m, of which the majority came from public sources.

## Survey results

As noted in previous chapters, existing data do not describe in any detail the situation of funded organisations. Accordingly, PSI carried out a survey of these, which included media organisations. However, the random sampling of funded organisations produced relatively few cases, from either the moving image or the literature sectors (see Appendix). Even combined, the total number of cases were too few to permit analysis analogous to that undertaken for the other sectors considered in this study[11]. Consequently, only rather general characteristics of the aggregate of media and literature organisations can be presented, and these are described in the following text, rather than being presented as tables.

The survey suggested the existence of rather fewer than under 400 funded organisations and individuals in the sector, with about half concerned with film and video, and half with literature. Between half and two-thirds of the organisations in the sectors together were to be found in Southern England, including London.

Total income of organisations and individuals is estimated at between £50m and £60m. However, it appeared as if half of all organisations had an income of under £70,000 per year, and a quarter an income of less than £35,000. There were, however, a few very large organisations in the survey, with incomes of over £500,000.

All the organisations had at least one employee. About one in five were one-employee organisations and half had no more than three people working for them. Altogether, there appeared to be rather over 3,000

---

10   This study included the feature film industry, independent production for network television, advertising and commercials production, popular music, video production, corporate and non-broadcast production and arts, community and developmental work. It can be assumed that these sectors are closely interdependent, with shared resources such as studios, post-production facilities and employees.

11   Returns were received from 9 literature and 10 media organisations.

people employed in the sector. There are likely to be at least the same amount who are self-employed.

## Income and expenditure

Income from commercial activities comprises just over half of the total income of individual film and video and literature organisations. Almost all organisations received money from one of the arts councils or from an RAB. On average, these sources provided about a fifth of total income. Only a few were directly funded by the BFI or one of the smaller dedicated media funders mentioned above, and, in most cases, this was by only a small amount. Well over three-quarters enjoyed some local authority support, but on average local authorities contributed little over one tenth of an organisation's income. Lastly, about half received sponsorship from the business sector, from charities or foundations, or from private individuals. For most, the relative importance of such assistance was small, but for a few it was more significant.

About half of the expenditure incurred by organisations in the sector was accounted for by the cost of wages and salaries.

The majority of organisations in the sector broke even. However, about a quarter made a loss and a few made a large loss (representing 12.5 per cent or more of total income). Equally, about one in five made a surplus.

# Chapter 9
## The built heritage

For the purposes of this chapter, the built heritage embraces the human-made historic environment – historic buildings, ancient monuments and archaeological sites, historic gardens and designed landscapes, battle-fields, industrial buildings and historic wrecks. As far as possible, items of historic industrial equipment are excluded, as are sites of historic interest with no built element.

The data in this chapter come from several sources:

- central government funded agencies including Historic Scotland (HS), the Historic Royal Palaces Agency (HRPA) and Cadw: Welsh Historic Monuments (other sources of data include English Heritage (EH), a Non-Departmental Public Body (NDPB), and the Environment Service, Northern Ireland);
- the charities, the National Trust (NT) and the National Trust for Scotland (NTS); and
- many other smaller trusts and charitable organisations.

Aspects of the built heritage overlap with those of the visual arts, crafts and museums and galleries (see Chapter 7). For example, statues and sundials can, like buildings, be listed for special protection. Two-thirds of the historic properties identified by British Tourist Authority/ English Tourist Board Research Services (BTA/ETB, 1993) include museums, exhibitions or collections of fine paintings or furniture. About 136 EH properties have collections of which 16, including Kenwood, Osborne and

Marble Hill, are among those museums registered with the Museums & Galleries Commission (MGC).

Varying amounts of information are available about different aspects of the built heritage. Certain categories of the built heritage, for example, receive more funding, have a more highly developed infrastructure and are better represented in existing sources of data than others. This chapter is divided into three sections which consider the wider context, sources of funding and the results of the PSI survey.

# The wider context

This section considers various aspects of the built heritage: details of visits to historic properties and sites; numbers of historic properties and sites; and their earned income and employment.

## Visits to historic properties and sites

During 1993 in the UK there were 68 million visits to historic properties for which visitor numbers were known (BTA/ETB, 1994b)[1]. Of these visits, just over a third (34 per cent) were by overseas visitors, and nearly a quarter (23 per cent) were by children. The total number of visits to historic properties increases to 79 million if churches are included. An additional 16 million visits were made to gardens (excluding municipal gardens and urban parks, and gardens open for National Garden Scheme).

The majority of visits were to properties in private hands, including those owned by the NT, and other trusts and religious bodies. In 1993, these accounted for nearly 60 per cent of visits to historic houses and private monuments, and over 80 per cent of visits to gardens. Visits to properties in government ownership accounted for nearly 30 per cent of visits to historic houses and less than 10 per cent of visits to gardens. The remaining visits were to properties owned by local authorities (BTA/ETB, 1994c)[2].

In 1993/94, there were nearly 12 million visits to the historic properties managed by the HRPA, Cadw, HS and EH (Table 9.1). A further 12 million people visited historic properties owned by the two National Trusts.

Government statistics on day visits in Great Britain suggest that 22 million GB residents visited stately homes, castles and ancient monuments, cathedrals and churches in 1991/92 (accounting for over 2 per cent of all

---

1   This includes properties for which visitor numbers had been estimated for that year or in previous years.
2   These statistics refer to properties with a minimum of 10,000 visits in 1993. These properties accounted for 50 per cent of attractions supplying visitor statistics to the source cited, and over 90 per cent of visits to such attractions.

*Table 9.1 Visitors to historic properties in Great Britain, 1993/94*

|  | Number of visits (millions) | Number of historic properties (a) |
|---|---|---|
| English Heritage | 4.9 | 406 |
| Historic Scotland | 2.4 | 334 |
| Historic Royal Palaces | 3.1 | 5 |
| Cadw | 1.3 | 131 |
| Subtotal | 11.7 | 876 |
| National Trust (b) | 10.5 | 234 |
| National Trust Scotland | 1.9 | 53 |
| Subtotal | 12.4 | 287 |
| Total | 24.1 | 1,163 |

Sources: EH, HRPA, HS, Cadw, NT and NTS annual reports, 1993/94
(a) In the cases of the NT and NTS, the number of visits refers to charging properties only.
(b) Includes Northern Ireland.

day trips). Most of these were by people from family groups (OPCS, 1993)[3].

According to other research carried out in 1991, a third of the adult population claimed to go to stately homes "nowadays" (ACGB, 1991). Nearly 50 per cent of people in higher or intermediate managerial administrative or professional occupations visited stately homes. This compared with less than 25 per cent of either manual workers or lowest-grade workers and pensioners.

In addition to the number of visits to historic buildings and sites which can be quantified, there are innumerable visits to, or instances of appreciation of, other historic buildings which do not primarily function as attractions. Depending on their social and economic function (as banks, hotels, pubs, town halls, shopping arcades, etc), such properties may be more or less accessible to the public. They nevertheless contribute to the fabric of historic cities, towns and villages. Appreciation of them is encouraged and assisted by various forms of interpretation including heritage centres (permanent exhibitions which show the evolution of the community), guided walks, and "town trails" – usually brochures or maps. These facilities also serve to attract tourists: it was estimated that in 1993 there were 966 town trails in 613 towns or suburbs, guided walks in at least 142 towns and cities, and 60 heritage centres in England (BTA/ETB, 1993).

---

3   Collected by the addition of a questionnaire to the annual General Household Survey.

## The number of historic properties and sites

Information about the number of historic properties and sites in the UK comes from a variety of sources. They are conventionally described in two ways: either by what BTA/ETB refer to as "classified architectural resources" or by the number of historic buildings and gardens open to the public.

Classified architectural resources are those that have been identified, as described below, for protection. They include listed buildings, scheduled ancient monuments, conservation areas, registered parks and gardens and designed landscapes, historic battlefields and wrecks.

Statutory controls exist to protect historic monuments and buildings where this is deemed to be in the wider public interest. The Secretaries of State for the National Heritage, Wales, and Scotland, and the Environment Service, Northern Ireland, are responsible for listing buildings of special architectural or historic significance[4], including ecclesiastical buildings in use and inhabited buildings. This is to ensure that particular care is taken about decisions affecting their future[5]. As Table 9. 2 shows, in 1993 there were about 540,000 entries in the listings for the UK. Given that a listing can comprise more than one structure, the 443,470 entries in England are estimated to have afforded protection for some 500,000 individual buildings (DNH, 1994).

The relevant Secretaries of State are also responsible for compiling and maintaining a schedule of ancient monuments – buildings and monuments other than those covered by listing and often located in rural areas. By the end of 1993/94 there were about 18,000 scheduled ancient monuments in the UK. Again, given that the schedule entries cover several buildings, the 13,800 monuments scheduled in the England are estimated to represent about 20,000 individual monuments (DNH, 1994)[6].

---

4   The Environment Service (Northern Ireland) was taken over by the agency, the Environment and Heritage Service, in 1996.
5   For a description of the different systems of listing used in England, Wales, Scotland and Northern Ireland see *Cultural Trends 26*.
   Annual targets are set for the numbers of listed buildings, scheduled monuments and conservation areas. In England, for example, between December 1992 and 1993, over 3,000 buildings were added to the listings, over 400 new conservation areas identified and nearly 450 ancient monuments scheduled (BTA/ETB, 1994a). These numbers have to be considered against the demolition of such buildings. In 1993 in England, listed building consent was given for the demolition of 64 buildings, and the Ancient Monuments Society received notification of applications to demolish 284 listed buildings.
6   EH is committed to scheduling 45,000 monuments by the year 2003, thereby completing between 70 and 80 per cent of the overall national programme. This required EH to make 1,800 scheduling recommendations to DNH per year. See Public Accounts Committee report *Protecting and Managing England's Heritage Property, 1992/93*.

*Table 9.2 Number of classified architectural resources in the UK, 1993–94*

| | England | Scotland | Wales | Northern Ireland | Total | Percentage down |
|---|---|---|---|---|---|---|
| Listed buildings | 443,470 | 40,000 | 16,088 | 8,399 | 507,957 | *94.7* |
| Scheduled ancient monuments | 13,740 | 395 | 2,748 | 1,080 | 17,963 | *3.3* |
| Conservation areas | 7,947 | 574 | 424 | 45 | 8,990 | *1.7* |
| Historic wrecks (a) | 33 | 4 | 4 | 100 | 141 | * |
| Battlefields | 41 | – | – | – | 41 | * |
| Registered parks and gardens (b) | 1,246 | 275 | 55 | – | 1,576 | *0.3* |
| Total | 466,477 | 41,248 | 19,319 | 9,624 | 536,668 | *100.0* |
| *Percentage across* | *86.9* | *7.7* | *3.6* | *1.8* | *100.0* | – |

Sources: BTA/ETB (1994a); EH (1994); DNH (1994); SO (1996); WO (1995); DNH/WO (1996); HS; Cadw; and Environment and Heritage Service, Northern Ireland.
(a) Historic wrecks are overstated for Northern Ireland as they represent those located.
(b) Those for Scotland include historic gardens and designed landscapes. At the time of writing, registers of parks and gardens were being prepared for Wales and for Northern Ireland. The figures given only represent Gwent.

Local planning authorities are required by law to designate areas – as distinct from individual buildings – of special architectural or historic interest as "conservation areas". The intention is to preserve and enhance the character or appearance of such areas. In 1993/94, there were nearly 9,000 conservation areas in the UK[7].

By the end of 1993/94, there were about 1,600 registered parks and gardens and designed landscapes, and 41 battlefields (EH).

BTA/ETB (1994b) calculate that in 1993 there were about 1,500 historic properties (including 12 historic wrecks) open to the public in the UK, for which the number of visits were known or had been estimated. The same source identified nearly 360 gardens (excluding those open jointly with historic houses) and about 3,000 Anglican churches which are listed as Grade 1 buildings.

The number of historic properties in the UK rises to over 2,000, if properties for which visitor numbers are not known or estimated are included. The same source identifies over 1,960 historic buildings and monuments open to the public in England (BTA/ETB, 1993). This figure does not include cathedrals, listed churches, historic buildings open as a consequence of their economic or social function, or the 200 historic houses which open only by appointment (BTA/ETB, 1993). Excluding gardens included in the National Garden Scheme, municipal parks and urban gardens, there are about 245 gardens regularly open to the public

---

7  For the most recent survey of conservation areas in England see Pearce et al, 1990.

in England, in addition to the 775 open jointly with historic houses (BTA/ETB, 1993).

## The earned income of historic properties and heritage sites

Since the second half of the 1980s, when the concept of the "heritage industry" was introduced[8] there has been an increasing critical interest in the built heritage as a form of economic enterprise. The report by the House of Commons Select Committee on National Heritage, *Our Heritage, Preserving it, Prospering from it* (1994) pointed to the returns which investment in the heritage brings in terms of tourism[9]. The advent of Charter Mark awards and the National Audit Office's report *Protecting and Managing England's Heritage Property* (1992) have encouraged historic properties in the public sector to become more economically efficient, and to improve their facilities and their service to the public.

There are no comprehensive data about the earnings of the built heritage sector, not least because the private owners of historic properties are not obliged to disclose financial information. It is, however, estimated that historic properties in Britain attracted about £240m in revenue from visitors in 1993, of which £192m (80 per cent) would have been accounted for by properties in England (BTA/ETB, 1994a).

The built heritage can generate income in three ways: through admissions, membership subscriptions, and services including retail, catering, renting and the hire of facilities. Historic properties are increasingly being promoted as venues for conferences and product launches, film and television locations, receptions and corporate entertainment, and as hotels and other forms of accommodation (Hudson, 1993).

Historic properties in the public sector tend not to charge admission. Of the 1,960 historic properties in England for which visitors are not counted, as many as 40 per cent admit visitors free. These tend to be in areas where there is a high density of publicly owned properties. In Greater Manchester, for example, admission to 70 per cent of properties is free (BTA/ETB, 1993). Moreover, over 80 per cent of HS's properties, and over 70 per cent of Cadw's properties do not charge. However, charges are made at the majority of historic houses and gardens for which it is feasible to charge admission for the sole purpose of sightseeing. This reflects the high percentage of properties in private hands. In 1993, most historic houses and gardens in the UK charged on average just over £2.00 per admission (BTA/ETB, 1994b).

However, admissions do not attract the total income required for the

---

8 See Wright, P (1985) and Hewison, R (1987).
9 See also SAVE Britain's Heritage (1983) *Preserve and Prosper*, cited in BTA/ETB(1994a).

private sector. The Historic Houses Association (HHA), which represents the interests of private sector owners and guardians of historic properties, noted that some of its members found opening their buildings to the public uneconomic and were concerned about the extent to which commercial activities might destroy the very heritage they were endeavouring to preserve (HHA, 1994)[10]. Of the HHA's 1,400 members, less than a quarter regularly opened their properties to the public in 1993/94. Many were making increasing efforts to use their properties for functions and private, corporate entertainment.

Visitors to historic properties may be offered a range of facilities including guided tours and other forms of interpretation, catering, museums, gardens and parks. Sixty-five per cent of historic properties in England have collections or exhibitions, nearly 40 per cent have gardens, 35 per cent provide guided tours, and over 30 per cent provide "teas" (BTA/ETB, 1993). In recent years, special events such as historical re-enactments, concerts and festivals have also contributed to the income generated by historic properties and heritage sites. BTA/ETB (1993) estimate that more than a quarter of all historic properties in England organised such events in 1993/94. EH claims to run what may be the country's largest programme of special events and open-air music. In 1993 it staged 224 historic displays and 67 concerts, which drew a combined attendance of 450,000.

*Table 9.3 Earned income of historic properties through admissions, memberships and services, 1993/94 (£m and percentages)*

|  | *EH* | *HS* | *Cadw* | *HRPA* | *Subtotal* | *NT* | *NTS* | *Subtotal* | *Total* |
|---|---|---|---|---|---|---|---|---|---|
| Admissions | 6.6 | 4.6 | 1.6 | 13.9 | 26.7 | 7.0 | 1.1 | 8.1 | 34.8 |
| Services | 4.1 | 1.7 | 0.9 | 6.9 | 13.6 | 22.8 | 1.0 | 23.8 | 37.4 |
| Membership | 2.9 | – | 0.2 | – | 3.1 | 40.7 | 3.3 | 44.0 | 47.1 |
| Total | 13.6 | 6.3 | 2.7 | 20.8 | 43.4 | 70.5 | 5.4 | 75.9 | 119.3 |
| *As a percentage of total income* | *11.9* | *17.6* | *19.7* | *75.6* | *22.6* | *77.8* | *40.4* | *73.0* | *34.6* |

Sources: EH, HS, Cadw, HRPA, NT, NTS annual reports 1993/94.

Table 9. 3 provides a breakdown of the £120m earned income of bodies which manage the built heritage in the public, private and voluntary sectors, and illustrates the main differences between them. EH, HS and Cadw earned less than 15 per cent of their total turnovers, whereas HRPA is expected to generate the majority of its operating income. The two National Trusts earned substantial parts of their income (the NT itself,

---

10   A survey of 147 properties showed that each adult visit costs historic houses, on average, £1.74 per hour (HHA, 1994).

some 80 per cent). Overall, over a quarter of the income of the public bodies came from admissions, whereas less than 10 per cent of the National Trusts' income was generated in this way. Conversely, nearly half the National Trusts' income came from membership subscriptions, as against less than five per cent of that of the public bodies.

Research carried out in 1991/92 suggests that the 22 million day trips to stately homes, castles and ancient monuments, cathedrals and churches by British residents generated £216m expenditure on travel, admission, food, drinks, purchases, etc. A further 13 million visits to historic ships and steam railways, formal and historic gardens, generated an £85m spend (OPCS, 1993).

As well as examining the revenue generated by historic properties, their economic performance can also be assessed in terms of the effect of listing on their capital value. Since 1991 the Royal Institution of Chartered Surveyors (RICS) has instigated various studies into the effect of listing. The Investment Property Database shows that, over the long term, listed commercial buildings held in the portfolios of investing institutions out-performed those that were not listed. A 1995 update sponsored by RICS and EH found that listed office buildings moved in value in much the same way as all office buildings. Given that the listed buildings held in investing institutions portfolios are not typical of listed buildings, since they possess more commercial assets, subsequent research was sponsored by RICS, EH and DNH. It found that the capital value of commercial properties was reduced by listing in so far as listing limits future changes to the building. In other words, listing or conservation-area status may provide benefits to society but impose a cost on the owner who may be prevented from altering or developing the property[11].

## Employment in built heritage

The major sources of information about employment in the built heritage sector are discussed in Chapter 3 on employment in the cultural sector, and summarised here in Table 9. 4. The data shown in the table cannot be aggregated because they relate to different years, different geographical remits, have been gathered in different ways, are not presented in uniform format (such as full-time equivalents) and refer to both industrial and occupational classifications.

---

11 See Scanlon et al (1994). Report undertaken by the Property Research Unit, University of Cambridge on behalf of English Heritage, the Department of National Heritage and the Royal Institution of Chartered Surveyors. Cited from Creigh-Tyte, S (forthcoming) "The Development of British Policy on Built Heritage Preservation" in M Hutter, et al (eds) *Economic Perspectives of Cultural Heritage* London: Macmillan.

*Table 9.4 Employment in the built heritage sector, 1993–94 (Numbers)*

| Source | Area | Number employed | FTE | Volunteers |
|---|---|---|---|---|
| ETB, NITB, et al | UK | 20,400 | 9,300 | |
| EH | England | 1,568 | .. | .. |
| HRPA (a) | England | 525 | .. | .. |
| HS | Scotland | .. | 690 | .. |
| Cadw | Wales | 256 | .. | .. |
| Subtotal | | 22,749 | 690 | .. |
| | | | | |
| NT | England, Wales and Northern Ireland | 2,972 | .. | 28,000 |
| NTS | Scotland | 350 | .. | |
| Subtotal | | 3,322 | .. | 28,000 |
| | | | | |
| Total | | 26,071 | .. | .. |

Sources: BTA/ETB (1994a); EH, HRPA, HS, Cadw, NT annual reports, 1993/94; NTS.
(a) Of those HRPA employees listed, 89 are casual/seasonal.

Employment in the built heritage sector cannot be separately assessed through the population census or Labour Force Survey, because the classifications used in these surveys are too broad. As a result, the figures in Table 7. 4 on employment in museums and galleries include the heritage sector as well.

BTA/ETB (1994b) estimate that nearly 20,500 people were employed in the heritage sector in 1993, a number which represents as few as 9,300 full-time equivalents. A survey of employment in the sector for the previous year found that about one third of those employed had full-time permanent jobs; over 40 per cent had part-time seasonal employment, and less than 30 per cent were part-time permanent or full-time seasonal employees (see BTA/ETB, 1994a). The four public sector bodies – EH, Cadw, HS and HRPA – employed nearly 2,500 people in 1993/94. In the same year, the two National Trusts employed over 3,300 people and depended on slightly fewer numbers of volunteers.

# Sources of funding

Apart from the revenue which the built heritage earns through commercial activities, support for this sector is largely channelled through:

- European funds;
- central government departments (directly or through their funding of executive agencies and other bodies);

*Table 9.5 Sources of funding for the built heritage, 1993/94*

|                        | *£m*  | *Percentages* |
|------------------------|-------|---------------|
| European funding       | 37.0  | 10.4          |
| DNH (a)                | 94.1  | 26.4          |
| SO (b)                 | 40.7  | 11.4          |
| WO (c)                 | 15.3  | 4.3           |
| NIO                    | 3.5   | 1.0           |
| English Heritage       | 115.9 | 32.5          |
| DoE/ DE (d)            | 13.4  | 3.8           |
| Local authorities (e)  | 33.0  | 9.3           |
| Charities              | 2.5   | 0.7           |
| Business sponsorship   | 1.0   | 0.3           |
| Total                  | 356.5 | 100.0         |

Sources: DNH, SO and WO annual reports, 1993/94; DOE NI; CIPFA, Planning and
Development Statistics, 1993/94 and 1994/95; Scottish Office, Scottish Local
Government Statistics; PSI survey of charities.
(a) Includes support to NHMF, RCHME and other bodies which subsequently redistribute some funds as grants.
(b) Including Historic Scotland. The Agency's expenditure forms a section within the
Scottish Office.
(c) Including Cadw. The Agency's expenditure forms a section within the Welsh Office.
(d) DoE funding comprises: £1.3m to voluntary organisations,
and £10.7m through urban programme, including £8.5m through English Partnerships.
Department of Employment funding includes project funding channelled through
TECs, LECs and the Training and Enterprise Agency, Northern Ireland.
(e) Figures for England, Wales and Scotland. Figures for England and Wales are based on
estimates made from 1994/95 CIPFA figures for conservation of historic buildings only.

- local authorities; and
- grant-making trusts and foundations, and business sponsorship.

The built heritage received a total of over £355m from these sources in
1993/94, as shown in Table 9. 5.

## European funding

Over 10 per cent of the total funding to the sector identified in Table 9. 5
comes from the European Commission (EC). The built heritage receives
funds through DGX, the directorate of the EC which directly funds cultural
activities. From 1991, before the current Raphaël programme was established to support movable and non-movable heritage, the conservation
and promotion of the EC's architectural heritage was funded through pilot
projects which changed theme annually. The amount of financial assistance provided varied from 5 to 25 per cent of the total cost of the funded

projects. The theme for 1993 was conservation of gardens of historic interest, and six gardens in the UK benefited through this scheme, by a total of £300,000. The EC also provides financial help for the training of architects, craftspeople and conservationists. However, the vast majority of EC funding to the built heritage sector is channelled through structural funds rather than DGX. The built heritage benefits through support directed towards the development of tourism and improvements to the built environment, often in the form of refurbishment of existing buildings.

## Central government funding

Several central government departments fund the built heritage. The DNH, SO, WO and the Northern Ireland Office (NIO) combined provide three-quarters of the support to the built heritage shown in Table 9. 5.

As mentioned above, the DNH, SO and WO support agencies and NDPBs with statutory roles relating to the recording and conservation of the built heritage. These include EH, HS, Cadw and the Royal Commissions for Historical Monuments. As noted above, the NIO's agency – the Environment and Heritage Service – was established in 1996. The DNH supports two other "next steps" agencies – the Royal Parks Agency and the HRPA – and funds various other bodies including the National Heritage Memorial Fund and the Redundant Church Fund (subsequently, the Churches Conservation Trust), both directly and through the Heritage Grant Fund.

EH, HS and Cadw and the Royal Commissions for England and Wales not only work towards the conservation of the built heritage but, together with the National Heritage Memorial Fund and the Environment Service Northern Ireland, they also redistribute over £60m in grants to other

*Table 9.6 Value of grants distributed by dedicated heritage bodies, 1993/94*

| Source of funding | Redistributing body | Value of grants (£m) | Percentage down |
|---|---|---|---|
| DNH | EH | 40.5 | 64.5 |
| | RCHME | 0.5 | 0.8 |
| | NHMF (a) | 2.8 | 4.5 |
| WO | Cadw | 4.4 | 7.1 |
| | RCHMW | 0.1 | 0.2 |
| SO (b) | HS | 11.9 | 18.9 |
| NIO | – | 2.6 | 4.1 |
| Total | | 62.8 | 100.0 |

Sources: DNH,WO, SO and NIO annual reports and accounts, 1993/94.
(a) Grants for buildings and associated contents, industrial heritage, and transport and maritime heritage.
b) RCHMS does not make grants, except with respect to their own programme of aerial photographic survey and their lead role with respect to local authority sites and monuments' records.

*Table 9.7 Breakdown of grant expenditure by type of recipient, 1993/94*
*(£m and percentages)*

| Source of funding | Historic buildings and monuments | Local authorities | Churches and cathedrals | Other | Total | Percentage down |
|---|---|---|---|---|---|---|
| EH | 9.6 | 7.4 | 12.3 | 11.2 | 40.5 | *68.1* |
| Cadw | 1.6 | 0.4 | 0.5 | 1.9 | 4.4 | *7.5* |
| HS | 11.4 | 0.4 | .. | 0.1 | 11.9 | *20.0* |
| NIO (a) | 1.2 | 0.6 | 0.4 | 0.4 | 2.6 | *4.4* |
| Total | 23.8 | 8.8 | 13.1 | 13.7 | 59.4 | *100.0* |
| *Percentage across* | *40.1* | *14.8* | *22.1* | *23.0* | *100.0* | *–* |

Sources: EH, Cadw, HS and NIO annual reports, 1993/94.
(a) "Other" includes grants given to NT and for archaeology.

bodies (see Table 9. 6).

The private sector, which EH estimated spent up to £200m on listed dwellings in 1992, has responsibility for the majority of heritage properties in the UK. It receives some funds from central government. As Table 9. 7 shows, 40 per cent of the amount distributed in grants by EH, HS, Cadw and the Environment Service, Northern Ireland in 1993/94 was dedicated to historic buildings and monuments, which include those in private hands. Almost a quarter can be identified as having gone to ecclesiastical buildings. The majority of funding earmarked for local authorities to conserve the built heritage passed through EH, and was dedicated to its conservation area partnerships. EH estimates that its grants generate an average of 40 per cent in additional partnership funding (although their contribution to specific projects ranges from 10 to 100 per cent) and that its support to conservation areas raises a further £2.50 from various sources for every £1 of its own spend. Cadw expects to raise rather more.

Other central government departments support the built heritage, largely as a result of their other functions. The Ministry of Defence, for example, is responsible for the conservation of 700 listed buildings on its land. The Ministry of Transport builds trunk road by-passes which serve to divert traffic from historic buildings: in 1993 it opened 13 such roads, each costing £0.5m or more (BTA/ETB, 1994a). The Department of the Environment (DoE), which was responsible for the built environment prior to the establishment of the DNH, provides over £1.3m in grants to voluntary bodies involved in the built heritage. English Partnerships, the urban regeneration agency sponsored by the DoE, approved £8.5m investment in the restoration, refurbishment and conversion of listed buildings for commercial, leisure and residential purposes in 1993/94 (in the context of the urban programme, see Chapter 2). Such investments may in turn spawn subsequent spending.

The built heritage also benefits from a supportive framework regarding taxation. The Register of Conditionally Exempt Works of Art (for which the Inland Revenue sustained tax losses of £60m in 1993/94) and Private Treaty Sales, are discussed in Chapter 2 on the funding of the cultural sector, and in Chapter 7 in relation to the art trade. The built heritage sector also benefits through zero-rated VAT for alterations to listed buildings. A briefing by HHA, EH and the NT estimated that the value of the total non-recoverable VAT on repairs to historic buildings in 1993/94 was £64m.

## Local authority funding

Local authorities in England, Wales and Scotland spent at least £33m on conserving the built heritage in 1993 (see Chapter 2), a sum which includes grants from other funding bodies, such as EH. This spend, which has already been accounted for in Table 9. 6, includes staff and overhead costs, and grants to outside bodies. Data on spending by district councils in Northern Ireland on the conservation of the built heritage are not identifiable.

## Grant-making trusts and business sponsorship

In 1993/94, business sponsorship provided £1m for heritage (ABSA, 1994). Business support for heritage is less developed than that for the arts. The government first funded the Business Sponsorship Incentive Scheme (subsequently relaunched as the Pairing Scheme) in 1984, but it was only in 1995/96 that the DNH launched a pilot Heritage Pairing Scheme. Some corporate sponsorship can be identified through the NT and NTS. Businesses do, however, contribute to the built heritage in other ways, not least through the revitalisation of city centres through their involvement in town-centre management, and their investment in listed buildings[12].

# Regional dimension

England has nearly 90 per cent of the listed buildings and conservation areas in the UK, and nearly 80 per cent of the scheduled monuments in GB (see Table 9. 2). As Table 9.8 shows, within England itself, the largest concentrations of classified architectural resources and historic properties

---

12   *The Times*, 22 April, 1996.

*Table 9.8 Distribution of historic properties in the English tourist regions*
*(Percentages)*

| Tourist region | Listed buildings June 1988 | Conservation areas Dec 1993 | Scheduled monuments Dec 1993 | Historical properties open 1993 | EH grants 1993/94 |
|---|---|---|---|---|---|
| Cumbria | 2.0 | 1.2 | 3.9 | 4.9 | 2.0 |
| Northumbria | 0.3 | 3.0 | 6.2 | 5.3 | 5.1 |
| North West | 5.6 | 7.5 | 2.4 | 5.4 | 7.7 |
| Yorkshire | 8.7 | 8.4 | 9.1 | 8.4 | 7.8 |
| Heart of England | 12.7 | 10.7 | 10.6 | 11.8 | 11.6 |
| East Midlands | 7.2 | 10.3 | 7.4 | 7.9 | 13.3 |
| East Anglia | 15.8 | 13.5 | 9.5 | 13.4 | 15.6 |
| London (a) | 3.6 | 10.1 | 1.2 | 7.9 | 8.6 |
| West Country | 17.5 | 11.5 | 28.2 | 12.8 | 15.1 |
| Southern | 12.2 | 12.7 | 14.2 | 12.8 | 7.3 |
| South East | 11.4 | 11.2 | 7.2 | 11.3 | 5.9 |
| All England | 100.0 | 100.0 | 100.0 | 100.0 | 100.0 |

Sources: BTA/ETB (1993, 1994a, and 1995b).
(a) For London, EH estimate that the number of listed buildings represent 8 per cent of all those in England.

open to the public are located in four out of the eleven tourist regions: the Heart of England, East Anglia, the West Country and the Southern region. They jointly account for nearly 60 per cent of listed buildings, nearly 50 per cent of conservation areas and over 60 per cent of scheduled ancient monuments. These regions also have over half of all historic properties open to the public.

England also has the vast majority (over 90 per cent) of historic buildings open to the public (BTA/ETB, 1993), and accounted for a similar share of visits to historic properties in the UK (Scotland has fewer than 10 per cent of all visits; Wales fewer than 5 per cent, and Northern Ireland, fewer than 1 per cent). As Table 9. 8 shows, nearly 20 per cent of all visits to historic properties in England are made in London. The Heart of England, East Anglia, the West Country and the Southern region jointly accounted for 45 per cent of visits.

Not surprisingly, England receives the bulk of central government funding for the built heritage. The four regions identified above accounted for about half of EH's grant spend in 1993/94. Furthermore, the majority of the DNH's £56m expenditure on the Royal Parks, the HRPA, the Occupied Royal Palaces and other historic buildings, in 1993/94, was dedicated to properties in London.

# Survey results

In Chapters 5 to 9, cultural activities have been examined on the basis of their income and expenditure for the financial year under consideration. Arts organisations, with the exceptions of those dedicated to collections, are essentially concerned with the presentation of temporary manifestations – performances or seasons of activity. These tend to be programmed with respect to organisations' annual budgets or three-year funding agreements. However, organisations concerned with the conservation and promotion of the built heritage function in a different way. Their focus is on permanent manifestations and conservation projects which may take several years to realise.

As a result, when PSI surveyed the built heritage sector to assess the situation of funded organisations, it did so in a slightly different way from the rest of the cultural sector. The finances of the built heritage were examined in the context of organisations' assets and liabilities – not merely accumulated deficits considered with regard to, for example, the producing theatres. The NT, for example, draws on its tangible assets – properties, plant and equipment, and investments, and current assets, stocks, debtors and working cash balance. Similarly, the Architectural Heritage Fund (AHF), which operates as a national "revolving fund", or pool of capital, for the preservation of historic buildings, redistributes funds received from DNH, SO and WO to provide short-term loans at a low interest rate for building preservation trusts and other charities for the acquisition and repair of buildings. At the end of 1993/94, AHF's portfolio comprised 39 loans with a contract value of £4m with further commitment on offers valued at £3.7m.

The survey covered all 204 preservation trusts, made up of County Historic Church Trusts and building preservation trusts, as listed by the Association of Preservation Trusts (APT). While not being representative of the heritage sector as a whole, these nevertheless illustrate the workings of a group of dedicated built heritage organisations (see Appendix).

As noted above, these preservation trusts are substantially different from the other organisations considered in this study in so far as their activities relate primarily to "capital" rather than "revenue". They restore properties with the assistance of special loans and grants, and in the case of building preservation trusts, they might also, during restoration, own the properties in question. Of those preservation trusts that responded to the survey, 83 per cent were building preservation trusts, and 17 per cent were church trusts (as compared with 85 per cent and 15 per cent respectively of the population as a whole)[13].

---

13  Sample numbers were: building preservation trusts, 103; church preservation trusts, 21.

## Overall size and characteristics

The survey indicated a total turnover of about £15m for these trusts as a whole for 1993/94. However, as suggested above, these trusts are better measured by their asset values, although church preservation trusts, since they do not own churches in the way that building preservation trusts can own properties, have much smaller assets. Table 9.9 shows the distribution of trusts according to their assets.

*Table 9.9 Survey results: assets of preservation trusts (Percentages)*

|  | All trusts | Buildings trusts only |
|---|---|---|
| Less than £25,000 | 19 | 21 |
| £25,000 to £99,999 | 17 | 15 |
| £100,000 to £249,999 | 25 | 21 |
| £250,000 to £499,999 | 21 | 20 |
| £500,000 or more | 18 | 22 |
| Total | 100 | 100 |

The value of total assets held by trusts is estimated to be between £30m and £35m, of which the assets of building preservation trusts would account for between £25m and £30m. Assets in the form of buildings owned by preservation trusts made up about £11m of the total assets.

Data on employment in trusts are deceptive: the survey suggested total employees of some 250 to 300 (excluding any self-employed). The relatively small number employed in trusts reflects both their heavy reliance upon volunteers, and the fact that when they engage in restoration they employ outside contractors rather than their own staff. Two-thirds of trusts had no employees at all, and only 4 per cent had more than five.

Trusts are to be found disproportionately in the South of England (Table 9.10). Including London, this area accounted for more than half of all preservation trusts.

*Table 9.10 Survey results: regional distribution of preservation trusts*

|  | Share of organisations (percentages) |
|---|---|
| London | 6 |
| South of England (excluding London) | 45 |
| North of England | 15 |
| Northern Ireland | 1 |
| Wales | 4 |
| Scotland | 12 |
| Midlands | 17 |
| Total | 100 |

## Income sources

Preservation trusts are able to obtain income from commercial activities including the hire and letting of properties and a small amount of commercial trading. A very important source of income is interest payments on accumulated capital (Table 9.11). Indeed, the average contribution of interest to commercial income among preservation trusts was 77 per cent. Over half – 53 per cent – of all trusts drew all their commercial income from this source. On average, income from commercial activities constituted half – 49 per cent – of trusts' income. Nearly one in five trusts, and all building preservation trusts, raised all their current income from commercial activities, investments in particular.

*Table 9.11 Survey results: preservation trusts by contribution of commercial income to total income (Percentages)*

| Share of total income | All commercial income | of which, interest |
|---|---|---|
| Less than 20 per cent | 30 | 48 |
| 20 to 39 per cent | 16 | 10 |
| 40 to 59 per cent | 13 | 14 |
| 60 to 79 per cent | 11 | 9 |
| 80 per cent or more | 30 | 19 |
| Total | 100 | 100 |

Dedicated heritage funders, such as EH, HS and Cadw, did not appear to be a prominent source of current income to preservation trusts. Fewer than one in ten identified such funding and these funders contributed little over 2 per cent of total income (Table 9.12).

*Table 9.12 Survey results: preservation trusts, by source of support*

| | Percentage |
|---|---|
| Heritage funders | 7 |
| Other central government | 12 |
| Local authority | 33 |
| Sponsorships and donations | 62 |

The two most important sources of support for preservation trusts were local authorities and private sponsorships and donations. Two-thirds received little or no local authority grants at all (as Table 9.12 shows) but, for 10 per cent, local authority money provided half or more of all income (Table 9.13).

*Table 9.13 Survey results: share of income of preservation trusts from local authorities*

| Share of total income | Percentage |
|---|---|
| Less than 5 per cent | 70 |
| 15 per cent or more | 22 |

Support in the form of sponsorship, donations or grants from non-public sources contributed, on average, between a quarter and a third – 30 per cent – of total income, far more than in any other sector. However, it was uneven in its impact, as Table 9.14 shows. Many organisations received no, or little, support from this source, while a few received a lot.

*Table 9.14 Survey results: share of income of preservation trusts from sponsorships*

| Share of total income | Percentage |
|---|---|
| Less than 5 per cent | 47 |
| 15 to 49 per cent | 17 |
| 50 per cent or more | 30 |

## Sources of capital

Building trusts finance their activities to a considerable extent by employing a "revolving fund" which they draw on to purchase buildings and then to restore them. On completion of restoration, buildings are usually sold on, and the proceeds are reinvested. Church trusts do not buy property, but rather make grants towards their restoration. Both types of preservation trust draw capital from the AHF and, thus, ultimately from the DNH. AHF capital can be supplemented by bequests and endowments from other public and private sources. In addition, to meet shorter-term needs, building preservation trusts can take loans, normally at a reduced rate of interest or on otherwise favourable terms, from public sources, such as the AHF or the local authority for the area in which they are operating, or from private sources such as wealthy benefactors. About a third of the building trusts had such loans, and although the accounts of individual trusts were by no means always sufficiently detailed as to permit a breakdown of loans by source, loans totalling some £4m, split almost equally between public and private sources, were identifiable.

## Summary of survey findings

The financial details of the preservation trusts are summarised in Table

*Table 9.15 Summary of survey results for preservation trusts*

| | Median amount (£000s) | Mean amount (£000s) | Share of total income (percentages) | |
|---|---|---|---|---|
| | | | Median | Mean |
| Source of income | | | | |
| Heritage funders | – | 2 | – | 2 |
| Other central government | – | 8 | – | 6 |
| Local authorities | – | 13 | – | 12 |
| Sponsorship, etc | 3 | 19 | 11 | 30 |
| Interest received | 5 | 19 | 27 | 37 |
| Other commercial income | – | 9 | – | 12 |
| Total income | 23 | 87 | .. | 100 |

9.15. The relatively small size of the average trust is illustrated by the table. So, too, is the importance of sponsorship and the relative unimportance of heritage funders in meeting running costs. Interest on accumulated capital is, by contrast, highly important, contributing a third of current income to the average trust. The principal contribution of heritage funders is towards capital costs, through the AHF, which provides the finance to purchase and preserve historic buildings.

# Part III
# Conclusions

# Chapter 10
## Summary and conclusions

The cultural sector as a whole is clearly important. It is a major employer, responsible for nearly 2 per cent of the workforce or as many jobs as the retail banking industry and between half and twice as many again as the motor manufacturing industry. It attracts foreign visitors, who spend money in the UK and bring in foreign exchange and, in so far as it is engages directly in international trade, it also runs a positive balance. It provides entertainment, education and leisure to a large proportion of the population and, thereby, makes a substantial contribution to the quality of national life. Table 10.1 summarises this, using indicators referred to in the preceding chapters.

Considering the sector as a whole, this study has come up with what some people might regard as rather remarkable findings about the audience for cultural activities. Thus, although cinemas were the cultural venues most heavily visited, historic properties and museums and galleries each attracted almost as many visitors. Equally, theatre box-office receipts were at least as high as those of cinemas, and historic properties generated from their visitors three-quarters as much as did cinemas. Thus, in many respects, it could be said that what might be regarded as "high" cultural activities (those which tend to receive support) are almost as popular as "popular" (mainly commercial) culture. What is more, "culture" is also as popular as many other popular pastimes: total attendances at London theatres in 1993/94 were at least as high as total attendances at Premier League football matches that season; twice as many people visit museums and galleries as go to bingo halls; and the British

*Table 10.1 Indicators of the importance of the cultural sector, 1993/94*

| | |
|---|---|
| Number of people working in sector | nearly 0.5million |
| Trade surplus of: | |
| Art trade | £67m |
| Films and television | £93m |
| Music performance royalties | £254m |
| Percentage of visitors giving the following attractions | |
| as a fairly or very important reason for visiting Britain | |
| Museums | 60 |
| Galleries | 35 |
| Theatres | 35 |
| Percentage of population visiting: | |
| Cinema | 33 |
| Historic buildings | 23 |
| Theatre | 19 |
| Museum or gallery | 19 |

Sources: see individual chapters.

Museum recorded more than twice the number of visitors in 1993 as did the Alton Towers theme park (*Social Trends 25*).

# The importance of support

Despite these indications of popularity, this study took as its premise that many aspects of the cultural sector would be unlikely to exist, either on their current scale or in their current form, without the support of the state, of business and of private individuals who contribute financially or in kind. Markets, it was argued, tend to "under-produce" cultural activities, or at least certain kinds of cultural activities. Support of nearly £1.7bn per year was identified, directed not only to assisting with running costs, but also with facilitating capital projects. Some 90 per cent of this support came from government – European, central or local. By far the largest single contributor to the part of the cultural sector on which this study concentrates was the Department of National Heritage (and its Scottish, Welsh and Northern Ireland counterparts) which gave support worth £0.9bn in 1993/94.

The sum of £0.9bn might look large, but it is only 2 per cent of expenditure on health and only 4 per cent of expenditure on defence in that year. More appropriately, however, it can also be compared to the level of

*Table 10.2 Public support for selected industries and services, 1993/94*

|  | £m |
|---|---|
| Support for the cultural sector |  |
| Department of National Heritage | 870 |
| Local authorities | 372 |
|  |  |
| Support for other sectors |  |
| Department of Transport support for: |  |
| London Transport | 861 |
| British Rail | 1,432 |
| Local authority support for bus services | 295 |
|  |  |
| DTI support for nuclear electricity | 726 |

Sources: Transport Statistics 1995; DTI, Annual Report, 1994.

support given by the state to other industries and services. Table 10.2 illustrates this.

Department of National Heritage (DNH) support for the cultural sector is of the same scale as government support for London Transport, and DNH support together with local authority support is equal to only half of total public support for rail, underground and bus transport. Public transport and nuclear electricity are industries or services subject to market failure, and support for them is justified in much the same economic terms as it is for the cultural sector. Transport services are classic "public goods", and nuclear electricity production involves investment risks which individuals and institutions are seldom willing to underwrite in their entirety.

## Characteristics of the supported sector

This study has investigated the supported cultural sector in some detail, by reference to published data sources and the reports of various funders and through a survey of organisations and individuals. This suggested that, in 1993/94, there were some 5,000 cultural-sector organisations and individuals in receipt of support from government, business, trusts and foundations and individuals. This excludes non-cultural organisations in receipt of grants for arts and heritage projects, and heritage properties managed directly by the government, its various agencies and the independent conservation bodies, the National Trust and the National Trust for Scotland.

The turnover of the funded cultural sector was estimated to be well over £2bn in 1993/94, of which nearly half was accounted for by the

*Table 10.3 Supported organisations by activity: summary characteristics*

| Activity | Approximate number of units | Turnover (£m) | Workforce Employees | Self-employed | Commercial income as a share of total income |
|---|---|---|---|---|---|
| Performing arts | 1,600 to 1,700 | 900 to 950 | 25,000 | 50,000 | Half |
| Combined arts | 1,500 to 1,600 | 500 to 550 | 17,000 | 34,000 | 40 per cent |
| Museums, galleries, collections, visual arts and crafts | 850 to 900 | 700 to 750 | 22,000 | 7,000 | Half |
| Media | c. 400 | 60 to 70 | 3,000 | 6,000 | Half |
| Heritage trusts | up to 200 | c. 15 | 250 to 300 | .. | Half |
| Total (approximate) | 4,500 to 4,800 | c. 2,250 | 67,000 | 97,000 | Nearly half |

Source: PSI survey.

performing arts. Total employment in funded organisations was estimated at 67,000, but this excluded self-employed workers and volunteers. Given that the rate of self-employment in the cultural sector is something like one in three, and that in the performing arts, the visual arts and crafts, literature and the media, the self-employment rate is much higher, it might be safe to assume that the total number of people with jobs in the funded cultural sector might be in excess of 160,000. This suggests that the funded cultural sector represents about one quarter of overall cultural sector employment.

Summary findings from the survey are contained in Table 10.3.

Supported organisations varied substantially in size, but the majority were small. A third had a total turnover of under £50,000 and half had a turnover of under £100,000. Only one in ten turned over more than £1m. Large and small organisations were to be found in each of the areas of activity, indicative of the existence of very small specialist or local museums and very large national museums and single musicians and complete symphony orchestras among the supported population.

One of the unexpected findings of the survey was the importance of income from commercial sources. On average, and with the exception of combined arts organisations and festivals, funded organisations generated half their income from a mixture of admissions, merchandising and cater-ing. Although some cultural organisations were entirely, or almost entirely, dependent on support, most were able to generate at least some income from market activities. In this respect, public funding is often "matched" by income generated from charging and selling to visitors and other customers.

Put against this, there was also evidence from the survey that a substan-tial share of funded organisations were operating at a deficit. Approximately a third of funded organisations in the performing arts, combined arts and festivals, and the museums, galleries and visual arts sectors ran a deficit in the survey year, and their deficits, together, were in the order of £100m – three-quarters of the total value of grants given out by the Arts Council of Great Britain (ACGB) in that year. Whether more intense commercial activity, or whether additional support would clear these deficits is unclear. On the one hand, the new lottery "stabilisation programme" is intended to assist organisations in deficit as a consequence of "severe difficulties not of their own making" (ACE, 1996b). There has also been some discussion of whether funders should cease support of some of the more chronically indebted organisations – especially orchestras and theatres – in order to target shrinking resources more effectively (see, for example, ACE/BBC, 1994). The offsetting £100m, made by the quarter of organisations which made a surplus, might buoy these individual organisations' reserves, but no mechanism exists for its redistribution within the supported sector.

In terms of sources of support, over 90 per cent of identified support came from the state, either supra-national, national or local, and the remainder came from the private and voluntary sources. The initial analysis, and subsequent calculation of overall levels of support, indicated that particular sources were more important for particular areas of activity than others. The findings of the survey were consistent with this, indicating for example, that the arts councils were of especial importance for the combined arts, collections funders for museums and galleries, and local authorities for the built heritage. The study revealed, for perhaps the first time, that a considerable volume of support comes from sources not dedicated to the sector – particularly the European structural funds and a whole raft of what have been termed "other government departments". These sources are well known to individual organisations which have benefited from them, and to those who advise cultural organisations on how to seek funding. That they are not widely promoted might be because not all funders, fearing they might be accused of wasting resources on "non-essential activities", wish the scale of their involvement in "promoting culture" to be made widely known. Moreover, significant as it is – equivalent to nearly 40 per cent of that provided by the DNH – such support also suffers, from the point of view of many organisations, a fundamental deficiency. It is almost all one-off or "project" funding, and so does little to enhance the long-term viability of the recipient.

Non-state support, unlike state support, tends to be concentrated on particular areas of activity – for example, business support goes largely to the performing arts, combined arts and festivals, and support from trusts and foundations goes largely to museums, galleries and collections. It may be that funding the performing arts is more attractive to the corporate sector since it provides opportunities for client entertainment and better press coverage than funding other areas of activity, such as crafts. Whether the present balance of such support might change remains to be seen. Any change would require the interests of sponsors to be widened, so that support for new areas of activity might also be seen as enhancing their profiles or the causes they choose to promote. Equally, it would require encouragement and advice being given to organisations to assist them in the presentation of themselves and what they do and to endow them with the confidence to approach these new sources of support. Indeed, the government already supports the Pairing Scheme and Business in the Arts (both administered by the Association for Business Sponsorship of the Arts) which are intended to increase business support for the cultural sector both in cash and "in kind", and which might also be encouraged to promote greater diversification in the targeting of such support.

## The regional dimension

Focusing on the funded cultural sector emphasised an issue which has long been at the centre of the debate about public support for the arts, namely the heavy concentration of activity and resources on London. Data on audiences and visits do not make this very clear. The proportion of the resident population going to the cinema, theatre, concerts or museums is rather higher in London that in most, or all, other regions of the country, but the share of funded organisations is severely disproportionate to the capital's, or even its hinterland's, share of the population. Table 10.4, which draws from the survey, shows this.

*Table 10.4  Share of supported organisations in Greater London, compared with resident population*

|  | Percentages |
|---|---|
| Share of supported organisations |  |
|   Performing arts | 36 |
| Combined arts | 18 |
|   Museums, galleries, collections, |  |
|     visual arts and crafts | 26 |
|   Heritage trusts | 6 |
| All supported organisations | 25 |
| London's Share of UK population (residents) | 12 |

Sources: see individual chapters.

*Table 10.5 Share of support from selected bodies received by London–based organisations, 1993/94*

|  | Percentages |
|---|---|
| ACGB for performing arts "nationals" (a) | 34 |
| BFI for South Bank Centre operations | 30 |
| DNH for museums (a) | 86 |
| Business sponsorship: |  |
| Performing arts | 47 |
| Museums and galleries, visual arts and crafts | 71 |
| London's share of: |  |
| UK population | 12 |
| England population | 14 |

Sources: see individual chapters.
(a) England is the base population used for the ACGB and the DNH.

Not surprisingly, the allocation of funds between regions shows a similar picture. Data from funders do not always permit a full regional breakdown, but a summary of the survey of supported organisations leaves a very clear impression (Table 10.5).

Although some interesting exceptions were found in the course of the study – for example, a disproportionately high expenditure per head by the Northern Arts Board, a much higher level of attendance at exhibitions in Yorkshire and Humberside, and, across the board, higher-than-average levels of spending per head and attendances in Scotland – the role of London as the centre of supported culture cannot be disputed. Over 80 per cent of all visits to museums and galleries in the UK in 1993 were to museums and galleries in London. London has the majority of national museums and an estimated 70 per cent of the UK's galleries. Over a quarter of all professional theatres are sited in London, and nearly 40 per cent of professional theatre performances take place in the capital.

Of course, centralisation could be argued to have its advantages. Alongside the preponderance of organisations in London, there is a preponderance of people engaged in producing and distributing culture. For example, the capital is the residence of nearly half of professional actors and musicians, and the East End has (according to the London Arts Board) the reputation of being home to the largest concentration of visual artists in Europe. It might be that the achievement of a certain "critical mass" of professionals, institutions and organisations is necessary to realise a degree of excellence. Moreover, this level of excellence, if realised, might have secondary benefits. It might draw tourists who also benefit other parts of the economy. It might also promote secondary industries – there is little doubt, for example, that the art trade benefits from the large number of museums and galleries in London. If this is the case, the funding practices, policies or strategies of the bodies which support the cultural sector have a rationale.

On the other hand, the concentration of support on London may also have its disadvantages, and reflect an element of élitism. Thus, even if the data on audiences referred to above show few differences in visits and attendances across the country outside London, they do not of themselves permit anything to be said about the quality of that which was visited or attended. Although, per capita, attendances at cultural events by people living in the regions differ little from those by people resident in London, it might be that the culture available in London has higher levels of inputs and infrastructure. If there is a quality difference, it also follows that, although certain elements of cultural provision tour the country or are transferred from London venues to other parts of the country (and vice versa), often the only way in which people from outside the region can benefit from London's cultural opportunities is at an additional cost in terms of time and money. Moreover, it is they, and not only Londoners and the residents of the home counties, who pay the taxes which provide the resources for central government to spend on supporting the cultural sector, and who absorb the tax relief given to the business enterprises which engage in its sponsorship. However, it is Londoners and residents of the home counties who have quicker and cheaper access to the product of support.

The debates about the regional dimension of economic policy in general, and cultural policy in particular, are not new. In the 1950s and 1960s, when economic policy makers were discussing the ways in which disparities in well-being between the different regions of the UK could best be solved, there was much debate about the relative merits of trying to "take the jobs to the people or the people to the jobs". Interventionists, then, tended to favour the former solution. The same discussion informed cultural policy making. Thus, it was the aspiration of the Arts Council's first chairman, the distinguished economist Maynard Keynes, that it "decentralise and disperse the dramatic and musical and artistic life of this country" (cited in ACGB, 1984). However, for many years, it appeared that the politics of support were that the "authorities" were acting on a responsibility for a "national" culture which, by default if nothing else, was to be found in the capital. It was not until the mid-1980s that the Arts Council publicly embraced an attempt to reverse its previous practices, acknowledging the need to establish "regional centres of excellence" (see ACGB, 1984). However, the extent to which it has realised its aims is limited, as a recent report of the National Heritage Committee suggests (National Heritage Committee, 1996), and as a continued discussion of the persistence of "two artistic nations" (ACGB, 1984) testifies. Certainly, this study has made clear that a programme of taking "culture to the people", rather than requiring the people to travel to culture, still has a long way to progress.

# The future

This study has been motivated by an interest in improving awareness of what the cultural sector is, what it does, and how it is paid for. It has done so by mapping the situation as it stood in 1993/94, the year before the National Lottery started to come on stream and the year for which the most up-to-date information was available. However, structures and resources are in permanent flux, in the cultural sector as elsewhere. Two changes are of particular importance, one quantitative, one qualitative.

The quantitative change is in the diminution of resources made available to the sector from central government, both directly, in terms of allocations to bodies such as the arts councils, and indirectly through restraints on local government spending. For example, virtually all of ACGB's (and subsequently ACE's) clients have received stand-still funding since 1992/93, representing a cut in real terms (ACE, 1996a).These cutbacks can have profound repercussions, resulting in the closure or partial closure of organisations, and restricting the opportunities people have to attend or visit venues. For example, a number of leading supported regional theatres closed for extended periods during 1995 due to financial difficulties (see *Cultural Trends 22*). Financial restrictions might also cause organisations to place greater emphasis on charging, which might discourage attendance, or reduce accessibility. Consequently, cultural activities might become more élitist. Alternatively, they might become more popular if cultural provision becomes market-led – meeting the tastes of paying customers. This could mean abandoning artistic pretensions, but could also imply the abandonment of creativity or the ability to preserve and interpret cultural artefacts, tangible and intangible.

The qualitative change is marked by the National Lottery, a new source of funding for the sector. The allocation of Lottery funding for the arts and built heritage is substantial. About £400m was awarded in 1995 by the arts, heritage and millennium distributing bodies, which represents nearly half of the DNH's (and its equivalents') expenditure on the cultural sector in 1993/94. This first tranche of Lottery funding, however, supported only capital projects including the acquisition of equipment. While welcomed by the cultural sector, it was thus criticised for failing to assist organisations to meet their running costs (ACE, 1996a). This may ultimately result in new buildings standing empty or instruments unplayed.

Quite apart from the question of whether the existence of Lottery funds permits the Treasury to beat down the DNH's allocation of government spending, the advent of this new source of support raises several other questions. First, it is to be asked whether the pilot "stabilisation programme", referred to above, will, by meeting certain costs, effectively "support good management, not ... bail out bad" (ACE, 1996b), if indeed it will provide a one-off boost, rather than a further crutch to recipient organisations. Second, it is to be asked whether the prospect of Lottery funding is extending organisations' horizons or encouraging inflows of support from elsewhere. By the same token, it may be that the requirement to obtain matching funds merely diverts the resources of businesses and foundations from the type of organisation and activity they normally sponsor, to those deemed worthy by the Lottery boards. Lastly, it is to be asked whether Lottery funding can help counter the bias of support towards the capital – a charge on which, in its first year at least, the Arts Council of England's Lottery board proved as guilty as other national funders in the past (Fitzherbert et al, 1996).

Because of the major changes described above, there is good reason, after an appropriate delay, to repeat this study. Such a review would look again at what is considered culture, at who enjoys it, how it is supported, and to answer the question of whether, in the course of the 1990s, culture has become more of a commodity, subject to market pressures, or whether the sector has been able to retain, albeit in a changing fashion, its special characteristic of producing a product which is worthy of support.

# Bibliography

ABSA (1994) *Business Sponsorship for the Arts: a national research survey 1993/94.* London: Association for Business Sponsorship of the Arts

ACE/BBC (1994) *BBC/Arts Council Review of National Orchestra Provision.* London: Arts Council of England/British Broadcasting Corporation

ACE (1996a) *Annual Report and Accounts 1995/6.* London: Arts Council of England

ACE (1996b) *New Lottery Programmes: consultative document.* London: Arts Council of England

ACGB (1984) *The Glory of the Garden.* London: Arts Council of Great Britain

ACGB (1985) *A Great British Success Story.* London: Arts Council of Great Britain

ACGB (1989) *Better Business for the Arts.* London: Arts Council of Great Britain

ACGB (1991) *Extracts from 1991 RSCG Omnibus Survey.* London: Arts Council of Great Britain

ACGB (June 1993) "EC support for culture almost 500 million ECU per year claims report", *International Update.* London: Arts Council of Great Britain

ACGB (1994) *Annual Report and Accounts 1993/94.* London: Arts Council of Great Britain

ACNI (1994) *Annual Report and Accounts 1993/94.* Belfast: Arts Council of Northern Ireland

Advertising Association (1995) *Advertising Statistics Yearbook 1995.* London: Advertising Association

Advisory Committee on Film Finance (1996) *Report to the Secretary of State for National Heritage.* London: HMSO

171

AGB Television Services (1994) *Trends in Television.* London: AGB Television Services

AIRC (1994) *Radio Advertising Facts and Figures 1993.* London: Association of Independent Radio Companies

APT (1994) *Annual Report 1993–4.* London: United Kingdom Association of Preservation Trusts

BADA (1995) *Membership Survey 1993/94 and 1994/95.* London: British Art Dealers' Association

BAFA (1995) *Arts Festivals 1994: audiences, attitudes and sponsorship.* London: British Arts Festivals Association

Bates and Wacker SC (1993) *Community Support for Culture. A study carried out for the Commission of the EC (DGX).* Brussels (mimeo)

BBC (1992) *Extending Choice.* London: British Boadcasting Corporation

BBC (1994) *Annual Report and Accounts 1993/94.* London: British Broadcasting Corporation

BFI (1994a) *Annual Report 1993/94.* London: British Film Institute

BFI (1994b) *Film and Television Handbook 1995.* London: British Film Institute

Blanc Media (1993) *Mapping the Moving Image Industry in Liverpool,* a report for the Moving Image Development Agency (mimeo)

BML (1994) *Book Facts 1994.* London: Book Marketing Limited

BML (1995) *Books and the Consumer 1994 Survey.* London: Book Marketing Limited

British Invisibles (1994) *Overseas Earnings of the Music Industry 1993.* London: British Invisibles

British Library (1994) *Annual Report 1993/94.* London: British Library

BPI (1994) *BPI Statistical Handbook, 1994.* London: British Phonographic Industry Limited

BTA (September 1995) *Festival of Arts and Culture News,* issue 8. London: British Tourist Authority (mimeo)

BTA/ETB (1991, 1994b and 1995a) *Sightseeing in the UK. A survey of the usage and capacity of the United Kingdom's attractions for visitors.* London: BTA/ETB Research Services

BTA/ETB (1993, 1994a and 1995b) *English Heritage Monitor.* London: BTA/ETB Research Services

BTA/ETB (1994c) *Visits to Tourist Attractions 1993.* London: BTA/ETB Research Services

BVA (1995) *Yearbook 1995: a year in video.* London: British Video Association

CAA (1994) *Cinema and Video Industry Audience Research,* no 12. Cinema Advertising Association (mimeo)

CAF (1993) *Directory of Grant Giving Trusts 1993.* London: Charities Aid Foundation

Cameron, S (1991) "Review of literature and research on the socio-economic effects of the arts". In *The Socio-Economic Effects of the Arts. National Arts and Media Strategy Discussion Document 4*, pp17ff. London: Arts Council of Great Britain

CC (1986 and 1994) *Annual Report.* London: Crafts Council

CC (1995) *Why do the Crafts Matter?* London: Crafts Council

Central Office of Information (1995) *Britain 1996: an official handbook.* London: HMSO

CIPFA (1994) *Leisure and Recreation Statistics, 1993/94 Estimates.* London: Chartered Institute of Public Finance and Accountancy

CIPFA (1994 and 1995) *Planning and Development Statistics.* London: Chartered Institute of Public Finance and Accountancy

Corporation of London (1994) *Working for London. Annual review 1993/94.* London

Crafts Occupational Standards Board (1993) *Occupational & Functional Mapping Report.* (mimeo)

CSO (1994) *Business Monitor SDA25, Distributive and Service Trades 1993: Retailing.* London: HMSO

*Cultural Trends 20* (1994) London: Policy Studies Institute

*Cultural Trends 22* (1995) London: Policy Studies Institute

*Cultural Trends 25* (forthcoming, 1997) London: Policy Studies Institute

*Cultural Trends 26* (forthcoming, 1997) London: Policy Studies Institute

Davies, S (1994) *By Popular Demand. A strategic analysis of the market potential for museums and art galleries in the UK.* London: Museums & Galleries Commission

DNH (1994 and1995) *Annual Report.* London: HMSO

DNH (1995) *Note: Museums and galleries in the UK.* London: Department of National Heritage (mimeo)

DNH (1996) *People Taking Part.* London: Department of National Heritage

DNH/WO (1996) *Protecting Our Heritage: A Consultation Document on the Built Heritage of England and Wales.* London/Cardiff: Department of National Heritage/Welsh Office

Doulton, A M (1994) *The Arts Funding Guide.* London: Directory of Social Change

DTI (1994) *Final Report on the Fine Art and Antiques Trade* prepared for the Business and Consumer Services Section by Butler Research. London: Department of Trade and Industry (mimeo)

East Midlands Arts (1994) *Annual Report 1993/94.* Loughborough: East Midlands Arts

Eastern Arts (1994) *Report and Accounts 1993/94.* Cambridge: Eastern Arts

EH (1994) *Annual Report and Accounts 1993/94.* London: English Heritage

*Family Spending: A report on the 1993 Family Expenditure Survey.* London: HMSO

Feist, A and G Dix (1994) *A Survey of Local Authority Expenditure on the Arts in England.* London: Arts Council of Great Britain

Fitzherbert, L, C Giussani and H Hurd (1996) The National Lottery Yearbook. London: Directory of Social Change

Garnham, N (1987) "Concepts of Culture: Public Policy and the Cultural Industries", *Cultural Studies*, 1

*General Household Survey 1993*: London: HMSO

Government Statistical Service (September 1994) *Labour Force Survey Quarterly Bulletin No 9.* London: Government Statistical Service

Gunter, B, J Sancho-Aldridge and P Winstone (1994) *Television: the public's view, 1993.* London: Independent Television Commission

Heaton, D (1992) *Museums Amongst Friends. The wider museum community* London: HMSO

Hewison, R (1987) *The Heritage Industry. Britain in a climate of decline.* London: Methuen

HHA (1994) *Annual Report 1993/94.* London: Historic Houses Association

HM Treasury (1995) *A Framework for the Evaluation of Regional Projects and Programmes.* London: HM Treasury

Home Office Voluntary Services Unit, *List of Voluntary Organisations in Receipt of Central Government Funding, 1993/94.* London (mimeo)

House of Commons Employment Committee (1994) *Employment in the British Film Industry, Minutes of Evidence.* London: HMSO

House of Commons Select Committee on National Heritage (1994) *Our Heritage, Preserving it, Prospering from it.* London: HMSO

Norman Hudson and Company (1993) *Hudson's Historic House and Garden Directory.* Banbury: Norman Hudson and Company

Hughes, G (1989) "Measuring the Economic Value of the Arts", *Policy Studies*, vol 9, no 3

Hutchison, R and A Feist (1991) *Amateur Arts in the UK.* London: Policy Studies Institute

Inland Revenue (various years) *Inland Revenue Statistics.* London: HMSO

ITC (1994) *Report and Accounts 1993.* London: Independent Television Commission

Jackson, C, S Honey, J Hillage and J Stock (1994) *Careers and Training in Dance and Drama.* Brighton: Institute of Manpower Studies

Kellaway, A (1996) *Arts Attendances in Wales. Main trends and conclusions 1993–5* Cardiff: Arts Council of Wales

Knott, CA (1994) *Crafts in the 1990s: A summary of the independent socio-economic study of crafts people in England, Scotland and Wales.* London: Crafts Council

KPMG Management Consulting (1992) *Evaluation Review of British Screen Finance Limited for the Department of Trade and Industry* (mimeo)

LAB (1994) *Annual Report 1993/94.* London: London Arts Board

LAB (1996) *The Arts and Cultural Industries in the London Economy,* prepared by the Greater London Group, London School of Economics. London: London Arts Board

Lauf, C (November–December 1990) "Snakes and Ladders. The archive of Dr Willi Bongard", *Artscribe.*

Leat, D (1992) *Trusts in Transition: policy and practice of grant giving trusts.* London: Joseph Rowntree Foundation

LISU (1995) *Annual Library Statistics, 1995.* Loughborough: Loughborough University, Library and Information Statistics Unit

London First Centre (1995) *Situation Report on the Fine Art and Antiques Sector,* prepared by Butlar Research. London (mimeo)

Marsh, A and J White (1995) *Local Authority Expenditure on the Arts in England 1993/94.* London: Arts Council of England

Martin, M (1994) *The Use of Volunteers by Arts Organisations.* A report from Martin Hamblin Research. London: Arts Council of England

MDA (1996) *Report on the DOMUS Survey for the MGC.* (mimeo)

MGC (1994) *Annual Report.* London: Museums & Galleries Commission

MGC (1995) *Registration Guidelines.* London: Museums & Galleries Commission

Monopolies and Mergers Commission (1994) *The Supply of Recorded Music: a report on the supply in the UK of pre-recorded compact discs, vinyl discs and tapes containing music.* London: HMSO

Music Publishers' Association Limited (1993) *Annual Report and Accounts 1993.* London

Myerscough, J, et al (1988) *The Economic Importance of the Arts in Britain.* London: Policy Studies Institute

Myerscough, J (1996) *The Arts and the Northern Ireland Economy.* Belfast: Northern Ireland Economic Council

NACF (1995) *Annual Report and Accounts 1994/95.* London: National Arts Collections Fund

NAO (1992) *Protecting and Managing England's Heritage Property.* London: HMSO

National Heritage Committee (March 1995) *The British Film Industry.* Second report, vol 1. London: HMSO

National Heritage Committee (1996) *Funding of the Performing and Visual Arts, First Report (1995–96 session).* London: HMSO

National Library of Scotland (1994) *Annual Report 1993/94.* Edinburgh: National Library of Scotland

National Library of Wales (1994) *Annual Report 1993/94.* Aberystwyth: National Library of Wales

NCA (1995) *Facts about the Arts.* London: National Campaign for the Arts

NFER (1996) *Discretionary Awards in Dance & Drama. A Survey of Local Authorities.* Slough: National Foundation for Educational Research

NHMF (1994) *Report 1993/94.* London: National Heritage Memorial Fund

North West Arts (1994) *Annual Report and Accounts 1993/94.* Manchester: North West Arts

Northern Arts (1994) *Annual Review 1993/94.* Newcastle upon Tyne: Northern Arts

Northern Ireland Office Department of Finance and Personnel/HM Treasury (1994) *Northern Ireland Expenditure Plans and Priorities. The government's expenditure plans 1995–6 to 1997–8.* Belfast: HMSO

NT (1994) *1993/94 Annual Report and Accounts.* London: National Trust

O'Brien, J and A Feist (1995) *Employment in the Arts and Cultural Industries: an analysis of the 1991 census.* London: Arts Council of England

O'Brien, J and A Feist (1996) *Local Authority Expenditure on the Arts in England, 1995/6.* London: Arts Council of England

OPCS (1993) *Day Visits in Great Britain 1991/2, A Survey carried out on behalf of the Department of National Heritage.* London: HMSO

OPCS (1994) *1991 Census.* London: HMSO

PA (1994) *Publishers Association Year Book.* London: Publishers Association

Peacock, A T (1976) "Welfare economics and public subsidies to the arts". In *The Economics of the Arts*, ed M Blaug. London: Martin Robertson

Peaker, A and J Vincent (1993) *Arts Activities in Prisons 1991–3. A directory.* Loughborough: Unit for the Arts and Offenders, Loughborough University

Pearce, G, L Hens and B Hennessy (1990) *The Conservation Areas of England.* London: English Heritage

PLR (1995) *Annual Report 1993/94.* Stockton-on-Tees: Registrar of Public Lending Right

Port Authority of New York and New Jersey (1993) *The Arts as an Industry: their economic impact to the New York-New Jersey Metropolitan Region.* New York: Port Authority of New York and New Jersey

Port Authority of New York and New Jersey (1994) *Destination New York-New Jersey: Tourism and Travel to the Metropolitan Region.* New York: Port Authority of New York and New Jersey

PRS (1994) *PRS Yearbook 1994/95.* London: Performing Rights Society

RICS, EH and Investment Property Databank (1995) *The Investment performance of listed buildings – 1994 update.* London: Royal Institution of Chartered Surveyors

Rolfe, H. (1992) *Arts Festivals in Britain.* London: Policy Studies Institute

Royal Botanic Gardens, Kew (1995) *Accounts 1994–5.* London: HMSO

Runyard, S (undated) *Museums and Tourism, Mutual Benefit. A guide to closer cooperation between museums, galleries and the tourist industry.* London: Museums & Galleries Commission with the cooperation of the English Tourist Board

SAC (1994) *Annual Report and Accounts 1993/94.* Edinburgh: Scottish Arts Council

SAC (1995) *A Socio-Economic Study of Artists in Scotland,* prepared by the Departments of Sociology and Social and Economic Research, University of Glasgow. Edinburgh: Scottish Arts Council

Scanlon, K, A Edge and T Willmott, *The Listing of Buildings: the effect on value* (1994). Report undertaken by the Property Research Unit, University of Cambridge on behalf of English Heritage, the Department of National Heritage and the Royal Institution of Chartered Surveyors. London: Royal Institution of Chartered Surveyors

Scott, M, M Klemm and N Wilson (1993) *Museums Sector Workforce Survey: an analysis of the workforce in the museum, gallery and heritage sector in the United Kingdom,* prepared by the Management Centre, Bradford University. Bradford: Museum Training Institute

Scottish Office (1995) *Serving Scotland's Needs: the government's expenditure plans 1995–96 to 1997–98.* Edinburgh: HMSO

Scottish Office (1996) *Scottish Local Government Financial Statistics 1993/94.* Edinburgh: HMSO

Scottish Tourist Board (1992) *Edinburgh Festivals Study 1990/91.* Edinburgh: Scottish Tourist Board

Selwood, S (1995) *The Benefits of Public Art. The polemics of permanent art in public places.* London: Policy Studies Institute

SLAD (1994) *Annual Membership Survey 1993.* London: Society of London Art Dealers

*Social Trends 24* (1994). London: HMSO

*Social Trends 25* (1995). London: HMSO

*Social Security Statistics 1995* (1996) London: Department of Social Security

South East Arts (1994) *Annual Report & Accounts 1993/94.* Tunbridge Wells: South East Arts

South West Arts (1994) *Annual Report & Accounts 1993/94.* Exeter: South West Arts

Southern Arts (1994) *Annual Report & Accounts 1993/94.* Winchester: Southern Arts

S4C (1995) *Annual Report and Accounts 1994.* Cardiff: S4C

Towse, R (1991) *The Social and Economic Characteristics of Artists in Devon.* Exeter: South West Arts (mimeo)

Towse, R (1993) *Singers in the Marketplace. The economics of the singing profession.* Oxford: Clarendon Press

Towse, R (1996) *The Economics of Artists' Labour Markets.* London: Arts Council of England

*The Training Directory 1994* (1994) London: Kogan Page

van Puffelen, F (1996) "Uses and abuses of impact studies in the arts", *Cultural Policy,* no 2

Welsh Office (1994 and 1995) *The Departmental Reports: the government's expenditure plans.* London: HMSO

West Midlands Arts (1994) *Annual Report 1993/94.* Birmingham: West Midlands Arts

Whitechapel Art Gallery (1994) *Annual Report 1993/94.* London: Whitechapel Art Gallery

Williams, R (1988) *Keywords. A vocabulary of culture and society.* London: Fontana Press

Wise, T and S Wise (1994) *A Guide to Military Museums and Other Places of Military Interest.* London: Terence Wise

Wright, P (1985) *On Living in the Old Country: the national past in contemporary Britain.* London: Verso

Yorkshire & Humberside Arts (1994) *Annual Report 1993/94.* Dewsbury: Yorkshire & Humberside Arts

# Appendix: survey methodology

The survey was divided into two separate parts, one for arts organisations and one for the built heritage. The survey of arts organisations (companies, groups and individuals, collectively termed "units") covered those units which received a grant for a cultural activity in 1993/94. As a first step, all sources of funding for arts units from government (supranational, central and local), businesses and trusts and foundations were identified. Data were collected from these sources on the level of support made, along with a schedule of all grants made and their recipients.

The survey of built heritage units was constructed differently, because built heritage organisations are usually concerned with long-term projects, financed over a number of years by loans and revolving funds rather than annual or multi-annual revenue grants. Moreover, many of the units in receipt of grants for the built heritage are not dedicated heritage organisations – such as individuals, commercial operations and churches which own, or are based in, historic properties, but the main activities of which lie outside the heritage sector. Lastly, many historic properties are directly managed by such bodies as English Heritage and the National Trusts and do not therefore hold disaggregated financial information on their own activities.

## Sampling frames

A sampling frame of cultural sector units was constructed from the schedules of grant recipients provided by funding bodies (not including the heritage bodies which contributed to the overall total funding identified, see below). These funding bodies were:

**Supra-national**
European Commission
Council of Europe
**Central government**
Department of National Heritage
Scottish, Welsh and Northern Ireland Offices
Ministry of Agriculture, Fisheries and Food
Ministry of Defence
Department for Education
Department of Employment
Department of the Environment
Foreign and Commonwealth Office
Home Office (including the Prison and Probation Service and Central Drugs Unit)
Department of Trade and Industry (DTI)
HM Treasury
Department of Health
Department of Transport
Regional government offices
**Local government and regional bodies**
Local authorities in England, Scotland, Wales and Northern Ireland
Local Enterprise Companies
Training and Enterprise Councils
City Challenge Partnerships
Urban Development Corporations
**Arts funding bodies**
Arts Councils of Great Britain, Wales, Scotland and Northern Ireland
Museums & Galleries Commission
National Heritage Memorial Fund
Crafts Council
British Film Institute
Museums and Galleries Commission
Regional arts boards of England
Welsh arts associations
Scottish, Wales and Northern Ireland Film Councils
Area museum councils
**Other organisations**
Association for Business Sponsorship of the Arts
Trusts and foundations (as listed by the Charities Aid Foundation)

It should be noted that some of the above named organisations, as well as apportioning funds or giving grants, also produce or distribute cultural provision in their own right. For example, while the BFI redistributes DNH money, a significant part of its expenditure goes on its own operations. However, for the purposes of this study, organisations responsible for the redistribution of significant amounts of funding were treated as funding bodies rather than receiving or operating units.

A database was compiled listing all identifiable units in receipt of grants in 1993/94. Against these were listed the grants received, categorised by the art form, activity or area of the cultural sector for which they were designated. This process identified approximately 7,500 units in receipt of grants worth just under £600m. However, a proportion of recipients were not arts organisations: many grants went to educational establishments, such as universities, colleges and schools, to local authorities, and to local and community organisations catering for young people, the elderly and other social groups. It would be difficult, if not impossible, to disaggregate the financial information with respect to arts activities from that which pertains to the other operations of such bodies. After excluding organisations not dedicated to the arts, a total of some 5,000 units remained appropriate for survey.

Table A.1 summarises the main characteristics of the sampling frame used for arts organisations, according to the grants distributed in 1993/94. The grants were also categorised by size, and over three-quarters of grants made were worth less than £10,000 each. Only 5 per cent of grants were worth £100,000 or more each. These grants, however, accounted for 90 per cent of the value of total grant-aid made available in 1993/94.

Arts units to be surveyed were sampled from the database. The sampling aimed to include the majority of those receiving larger grants, while random sampling was applied to the large number of units receiv-

*Table A.1 Grants distributed, by category, 1993/94*

|  | Grants | | Value | |
|  | Number | Percentage | £m | Percentage |
|---|---|---|---|---|
| Performing arts | 3,019 | 31 | 163.6 | 24 |
| Combined arts | 1,784 | 19 | 35.1 | 5 |
| Museums and galleries, visual arts and crafts | 2,741 | 28 | 288.8 | 43 |
| The media | 1,327 | 14 | 161.3 | 24 |
| Built heritage (a) | 73 | 1 | 19.7 | 3 |
| Services, training, etc | 405 | 4 | 1.6 | * |
| Other/unclassified | 271 | 3 | 1.4 | * |
| Total | 9,620 | 100 | 671.5 | 100 |

(a) These mainly represent grants given to the built heritage by arts organisations.

ing smaller grants. To do this, units were banded into groups according to the amount of grant received. Table A.2 details the sampling ratios and response rates. Overall, just under 350 responses were received, a response rate of 45 per cent.

*Table A.2 Sampling ratios and response rates*

| Level of grants identified | Sampling ratio | Response rate Numbers | Percentage |
|---|---|---|---|
| National museums and galleries | 1:1 | 22 | 73 |
| £250,000 and over | 1:1 | 69 | 75 |
| £100,000 to £249,999 | 1:2 | 48 | 61 |
| £50,000 to £99,000 | 1:2 | 60 | 49 |
| £10,000 to £49,999 | 1:5 | 80 | 38 |
| Less than £10,000 | 1:15 | 63 | 19 |
| Total (all) | – | 342 | 45 |

The built heritage units to be surveyed were selected from listings of building and church preservation trusts, which are identifiably dedicated to the built heritage. These listings were obtained from the Association of Preservation Trusts and all recorded bodies were sampled. Just over 100 responses were received, a response rate of 54 per cent. Table A.3 summarises the response rates to the built heritage survey.

*Table A.3 Survey of preservation trusts: response rates*

| | Sample number | Valid responses | Percentage response rate |
|---|---|---|---|
| County Historic Church trusts | 40 | 20 | 50 |
| Building preservation trusts (a) | 153 | 84 | 55 |
| Total (all) | 193 | 104 | 54 |

(a) A total of 173 trusts were initially sampled, but of these 20 had not been in operation in the year in question.

# Data collection

Respondents to the survey were asked to provide copies of their audited annual accounts for the period 1993/94. This had a number of advantages:

- it required less effort on the part of respondents than the completion of a questionnaire and ensured a satisfactory response rate;
- it allowed the data to be categorised into a uniform format by

researchers at PSI, minimising the scope for misunderstanding and mis-categorisation of data by respondents;
- it ensured that the data all referred to the same period.

Data received were transcribed by PSI researchers onto a standard proforma which recorded:

- geographical location, by standard regions;
- area of the cultural sector mainly operated in;
- earned income, by source, including
  - admissions charges
  - merchandise revenue
  - interest and dividends;
- unearned income by source, including
  - grants, by funding body
  - sponsorship, memberships and donations
  - investment and other income;
- expenditure, including
  - payroll and employee costs
  - acquisitions and direct costs of activities
  - administration and overhead costs
  - capital expenditure;
- for heritage units only
  - assets (tangible/physical and intangible/monetary)
  - liabilities (loans from public and private sources);
- Average number of employees

It was also intended to collect data on numbers of volunteers and total hours worked by volunteers, and on numbers of attendances and visits, but this sort of information was rarely available from annual reports and accounts.

Units receiving smaller grants (less than £50,000) were sent a short questionnaire as an alternative to providing annual accounts, as initial responses from smaller organisations showed that their accounts were sometimes not detailed enough for the purposes of the survey. This questionnaire replicated the proforma, but in abbreviated form to encourage response. Of all respondents in this category, 57 per cent responded through the questionnaire (representing 20 per cent of all responses).

## Data analysis

Data from reports and questionnaires were transcribed onto a standard proforma and punched for computer analysis. Analysis was done using a statistical computer package, SPSS.

The purpose of the survey was to be able to make estimates about the characteristics, not only of the organisations and individuals actually surveyed, but also of the whole population (ie all recipients of support). However, making estimates about a population on the basis of a sample necessarily involves a degree of imprecision. The proportion calculated from a survey relates to the proportion applicable to the population, but the population proportion might be larger or smaller by a certain amount. The range into which the population proportion is likely to fall can be calculated by reference to a "confidence interval". This makes it possible to give the upper and lower limits within which a population proportion can be expected to fall, given a calculated sample proportion. In general, the aim is to be able to say that one is 95 per cent confident that an actual figure lies within a certain interval.

Once the confidence level has been chosen, the width of the confidence interval is determined by two factors – the size of the sample in question, and the proportion of the sample estimated as having a particular attribute. The relatively small size of the sample for any one area of activity in this survey meant that, in most cases, each activity was analysed as a whole. However, where sufficient responses had been achieved, subgroups of an area of activity, or sub-areas of activity could be analysed. In general, a minimum of 50 cases had to be present for this to be possible.

Tables A.4 to A.7 show the confidence intervals, assuming a 95 per cent confidence, for different proportions, given the sample numbers for each area of activity analysed in Chapters 5, 6, 7 and 9. It shows:

- the number of units in each sample (at the head of each column);
- on the lefthand side of each table, a range of proportions, grouped in pairs (the same confidence interval applies to, for example, an estimated proportion of 30 per cent as to an estimated proportion of 70 per cent);
- the span of the confidence interval for the given sample size and

*Table A.4 Confidence intervals for the performing arts*

| Proportions | All performing arts (sample of 155) | Small organisations (sample of 49) | Medium organisations (sample of 57) | Large organisations (sample of 49) |
|---|---|---|---|---|
| 10/90 | 4.7 | 8.4 | 7.8 | 8.3 |
| 20/80 | 6.3 | 11.2 | 10.4 | 11.1 |
| 30/70 | 7.2 | 12.8 | 11.9 | 12.7 |
| 40/60 | 7.7 | 13.7 | 12.7 | 13.6 |
| 50/50 | 7.9 | 14.0 | 13.0 | 13.9 |

proportion (such that the lower limit is the estimated proportion minus the figure quoted and the upper limit is the estimated proportion plus the figure quoted).

Where two proportions are being compared, it can only be stated with confidence that they are different if the two confidence intervals do not overlap.

*Table A.5 Confidence intervals for combined arts*

| Proportions | All combined arts (sample of 96) | Arts festivals (sample of 80 ) |
|---|---|---|
| 10/90 | 6.0 | 6.6 |
| 20/80 | 8.0 | 8.8 |
| 30/70 | 9.2 | 10.0 |
| 40/60 | 9.8 | 10.7 |
| 50/50 | 10.0 | 11.0 |

*Table A.6 Confidence intervals for museums and galleries, visual arts, etc*

| Proportions | All museums and galleries, etc (sample of 72) | Museums and galleries only (sample of 52) |
|---|---|---|
| 10/90 | 6.9 | 8.2 |
| 20/80 | 9.2 | 10.9 |
| 30/70 | 10.6 | 12.5 |
| 40/60 | 11.3 | 13.3 |
| 50/50 | 11.5 | 13.6 |

*Table A.7 Confidence intervals for the built heritage*

| Proportions | All preservation trusts (sample of 104) | Building trusts only (sample of 83) |
|---|---|---|
| 10/90 | 5.8 | 6.5 |
| 20/80 | 7.7 | 8.6 |
| 30/70 | 8.8 | 9.9 |
| 40/60 | 9.4 | 10.5 |
| 50/50 | 9.6 | 10.8 |